The Future of Baptist Higher Education

The Future of Baptist Higher Education

Donald D. Schmeltekopf
and
Dianna M. Vitanza
Editors

Baylor University Press
Waco, Texas USA

Cover Design by Bob Bubnis

Chapters 5 and 12 are revised versions of Hester Lectures given by the authors at the annual meeting of the Association of Southern Baptist Colleges and Schools, June 2004. Permission to use the revised lectures has been granted by both ASBCS and the authors.

Library of Congress Cataloging-in-Publication Data

The future of Baptist higher education / edited by Donald D. Schmeltekopf and Dianna M. Vitanza.

p. cm.

Includes bibliographical references and index.

ISBN-13: 978-1-932792-27-0 (pbk. : alk. paper)

1. Baptist universities and colleges--United States. I. Schmeltekopf, Donald D. II. Vitanza, Dianna M.

LC562.F87 2006
378'.071673--dc22

2006021581

Printed in the United States of America on acid-free paper with a minimum of 30% pcw recycled content.

In memory of the founders of Baptist colleges and universities across America

Contents

Preface

In April 2003, the Council of Deans of Baylor University sponsored a colloquy on the subject "The Baptist and Christian Character of Baylor," the papers for which were made into a book by the same title. Both the colloquy and the book received favorable reviews, not only at Baylor but widely across the Christian higher education community. The colloquy prompted another question, however, which had to do with the denominational ties of Baptist colleges and universities in this country, but especially in the South. Baylor President—now Chancellor—Robert B. Sloan Jr. asked one of the coeditors of this book, Donald Schmeltekopf, to organize a conference on the scale of the earlier colloquy, only to make it a national meeting on the theme, "The Future of Baptist Higher Education." Our first act was to appoint a planning committee, of which the other coeditor, Dianna Vitanza, was a member. It was agreed from the start that the conference proceedings would be published, and that the two of us would be the coeditors, as we were for the book that came out of the earlier colloquy in 2003.

There are at least four subtexts driving the content of this book and the conference that preceded it on April 18–19, 2005. Perhaps the most visible is the denominational conflict that has afflicted Baptists, especially those connected with the Southern Baptist Convention, over the past twenty-five years or so. Another is the widespread secularization of higher education in America—the ideological roots of which go back to the Enlightenment—which has radically altered the intellectual and moral culture of our nation's campuses especially since the 1960s, including our church-related colleges and universities. A third is the dominance of the market-driven tendencies in American higher education today, including in our religious schools. The idea is to give students what they want "now"—preparation for jobs and careers—

which often means an abandonment of the long-term benefits of a liberal arts curriculum or of the more mission-driven aspects of a Christian institution.

A fourth subtext of this book, and the one most vigorously and most often argued, has to do with the meaning of Christian higher education, but more specifically, the meaning of Baptist higher education. Virtually every chapter addresses this issue in one fashion or another, beginning with the coeditors' introduction. Because the question of meaning—purpose—is so important in this context, the conference planning committee determined from the very start of its deliberations to recruit as speakers, and later writers, individuals not only with proven insight and credibility, but also of varying points of view. This variety is not in the service of some secular principle of diversity, but is an attempt to display how certain promising views might be complementary to each other rather than necessarily antagonistic. In the end, the coeditors believe that the meaning of Baptist and Christian higher education, as with the Christian life itself, is far more complex than any one imperial interpretation.

The audience for this book includes all those who are interested in and care about Christian higher education in its various denominational expressions, in particular the Baptist one. At the same time, we believe it is helpful to see this book as a case study of denominationally connected higher education. Because of Baptist history and ecclesiology there are issues addressed in this book that are distinct to a congregational form of church polity, but most of the chapters are relevant to any denomination today struggling to define its relationship to its educational institutions, from Roman Catholic to Lutheran to Methodist.

The editors wish to thank all who contributed to this volume. We also wish to thank Robert Sloan for the idea that led to the conference and the members of the planning committee who made it and this book possible. And we wish to thank Baylor University Press and, in particular, its editor, Carey Newman, for their willingness to undertake this project.

Donald D. Schmeltekopf
Provost Emeritus and The Hazel and Harry Chavanne
Professor of Christian Ethics in Business

Dianna M. Vitanza
Associate Professor of English

July 2005
Baylor University
Waco, Texas

Introduction

Chapter One

Baptist Identity and Christian Higher Education

Donald D. Schmeltekopf
Dianna M. Vitanza

I

The first Baptist institution of higher education established in America was Rhode Island College, founded in 1764. Rhode Island was a logical place to locate the institution, for in the mid-eighteenth century this American colony had more Baptists than any other, largely because the tradition of religious liberty advanced by Roger Williams was attractive to Baptists and because they were not particularly welcomed in the other New England colonies. At this early date Baptists were also not yet that numerous in the middle and southern colonies. While Baptists in general were ambivalent about the need for education, even for their clergy, they nevertheless wanted their *own* institution rather than relying on Harvard. Experience had taught them that "you could send a Baptist to Harvard but you could not get one out."[1] In 1804, Rhode Island College became known as Brown University, named after a prominent family in Providence.

Even though the number of Baptists in Rhode Island was diminishing and the number of Baptists in the middle colonies was growing rapidly, Brown remained the only Baptist institution of higher education in America until 1819, when the increase of Baptists in the middle colonies led to an ambitious effort to create a Baptist school in Washington, D.C., called Columbian College. Luther Rice was one of the major movers behind the plan for the institution, which proposed a combination of classical education, legal and medical courses, and advanced work in theological studies. Property was purchased, a large building constructed, a president and a faculty hired, and students recruited, but the school soon had serious financial difficulties, and, in spite of his best efforts, Rice was unable to save the institution for Baptists. The federal government rescued the school from collapse, granting its founding charter in 1821, and in 1904, by an Act of Congress, Columbian became George Washington University, severing all ties with Baptists. Both before and after the fading of Columbian College, Brown remained of enormous influence in training Baptist leaders from both the North and the South.[2] For example, southern educational leaders such as John A. Broadus, James Huckins, William B. Johnson, Jonathan Maxcy, and J. B. White all had the benefit of a Brown education.

In the South the earliest schools operated by Baptists were academies, usually small schools designed to give children the basics of grammar, arithmetic, literature, and the Bible. Academies flourished throughout the South, numbering in the hundreds, from about 1800 until the beginning of the public high school movement a century later. The movement to establish institutions of higher education, inspired in part by a desire for an educated clergy, began in 1825 with the founding of Furman University, named after Richard Furman, a distinguished pastor and Baptist leader in South Carolina. Known initially as the Furman Academy and Theological Institution at Edgefield, South Carolina, it was moved to Greenville in 1851, its permanent location, after interim moves to High Hills of the Santee and Winnsboro. In 1859 the Southern Baptist Theological Seminary opened on the Furman campus, but relocated to Louisville, Kentucky, in 1877.

During the nineteenth century, over thirty Baptist colleges and universities were founded in the southern and border states under the auspices of state Baptist organizations and with the encouragement and support of local communities. The most notable of these today include Union University, established in Jackson, Tennessee, chartered originally as Jackson Male Academy in 1825; Georgetown College, founded in 1829 by the Kentucky Baptist Education Society in Georgetown, Kentucky; the University of Richmond, formerly the Virginia Baptist Seminary and later Richmond College, established in 1832 by the Virginia Baptist Education Society in Richmond, Virginia; Mercer University, formerly Mercer Institute, founded in 1833 by Georgia Baptists at Penfield, Georgia, and later relocated to Macon; Wake Forest University, chartered also in 1833 by North Carolina Baptists, established first as Wake Forest Institute and then as Wake Forest College in the town of Wake Forest, North Carolina, and after 1956 relocated to Winston-Salem, North Carolina; Judson College, an all-female institution, founded in 1838 as Judson Female Institute in Marion, Alabama; Samford University, established in 1841 initially as a male college, also in Marion, and in 1877 relocated to Howard College in Birmingham, Alabama; Baylor University, established in 1845 by Texas Baptists at Independence, Texas, and later divided and relocated as Baylor University in Waco, Texas, and Mary Hardin-Baylor in Belton, Texas; William Jewell College, chartered by Missouri Baptists in Liberty, Missouri, in 1849; Mississippi College, founded in 1826 by local citizens in the area of Clinton, Mississippi, then transferred to the Presbyterians, and then given over to Mississippi Baptists in 1850; Carson-Newman College, established in 1851 in Jefferson City, Tennessee; Stetson University, chartered as DeLand Academy by Florida Baptists in 1883 in the community of DeLand, Florida; and Ouachita Baptist University, established first as Ouachita College in 1886 by Arkansas Baptists in Arkadelphia, Arkansas.

Other regional Baptist colleges chartered in the South or border states in the nineteenth century include: Chowan College (1848), Mars Hill College (1856), Campbell University (1887), Meredith College (1891), and Wingate University (1897), all in North Carolina; Hannibal-LaGrange College (1858) and Southwest Missouri Baptist University (1878) in Missouri; Averett College (1859) and Virginia Intermont College (1884) in Virginia; Blue Mountain College (1873) in Mississippi; Shorter College (1877) in Georgia; Cumberland College (1888) in Kentucky; Howard Payne University (1890), Hardin-Simmons University (1891), and Dallas Baptist University, first established as Decatur Baptist College (1898), in Texas; and North Greenville College (1892) in South Carolina. Approximately twenty additional Baptist colleges and universities were chartered in this same region of the country in the twentieth century.[3]

In addition to these colleges and universities in the South, Baptist institutions of higher education were also founded in the North and the Midwest. However, these have largely lost their association with their Baptist origins. The first Baptist college to receive a charter in the nineteenth century was Colby College (1813) in Waterville, Maine. Because there were few Baptists in Maine at this time, most of the support for Colby came from local business leaders who believed that the college would serve the public good. The first president of Colby, Jeremiah Chaplin, came to the post from being the pastor of the Baptist church in Danvers, Massachusetts. His task was to build a Baptist "literary and theological institution"[4] on the banks of the Kennebec River. His greatest challenge, however, was gaining the support of Baptists. "About the only Baptist support Chaplin could count on," according to David B. Potts, "was that of a small body of laymen and ministers who favored ministerial education."[5]

Chaplin was also influential in the founding of another Baptist school, Colgate University, in 1819 in Hamilton, New York. Chaplin had written a widely circulated letter on behalf of the Boston Baptist Association in 1816 urging the establishment of several regional Baptist seminaries. Hamilton was a Baptist stronghold, so the initiative took hold there. Baptists in Hamilton met and decided "to found an institution devoted exclusively to ministerial training,"[6] which became Colgate. The Baptist Education Society of the State of New York, organized in 1819, was given control of Colgate and thereby was able "to provide the Baptists of New York and neighboring states with their first formal institution for training ministers."[7]

Because Baptists in the North, Midwest, and West tended to be organized as societies rather than as associations characteristic of Baptists in the South, Baptist connections with the establishment of colleges and universities in these regions were generally at the local level. Such small groups of Baptists were instrumental in the founding of the following schools: in Ohio, Denison University (1831) in Granville; in Michigan, Kalamazoo College (1833) in Kalamazoo and Hillsdale College (1844, founded by Free Will Baptists) in Hillsdale; in Indiana, Franklin College (1834) in Franklin; in Pennsylvania, Bucknell University (1846) in Lewisburg and Temple University (1888) in Philadelphia; in New York, the University of Rochester (1850) in Rochester and Vassar College (1861) in Poughkeepsie; in Maine, Bates College (1855) in Lewiston; in Oregon, Linfield College (1858) in McMinnville; in West Virginia, Alderson Broaddus College (1871) in Philippi; and in South Dakota, the University of Sioux Falls (1883) in Sioux Falls.[8]

The prestige of Baptist higher education was substantially enhanced by the establishment of the University of Chicago in 1891. Not only was this new institution located in an urban area in one of the nation's leading cities, its mission was to provide needed graduate education in addition to an excellent undergraduate program. Furthermore, the already existing Baptist seminary in Chicago was annexed as the divinity school to offer theological education as well. The nation's wealthiest Baptist, John D. Rockefeller, was recruited to be the principal underwriter of the university, giving $20 million in the first twelve years. Control of the university was in the hands of Baptists as evidenced by the fact that the founding documents required that the president be a Baptist and that two-thirds of the board be Baptists. However, the education provided by the new university was to be nondenominational. As William Rainey Harper, the first president of Chicago, stated, ". . . it is clear, that in all departments, save the theological, there can be no such thing as denominational spirit or instruction. . . . [B]y the grace of God [we] shall be Christian in tone, in influence and in work."[9]

A final category of Baptist schools founded in the nineteenth century was established to provide education for members of ethnic communities. One of the oldest of these is Ottawa University in Ottawa, Kansas, established in 1865 by the American Baptist Churches USA to serve Native Americans in the area. American Baptists also founded, in 1865, Virginia Union University in Richmond, Virginia. Virginia Union was one of many schools established after the Civil War intended to serve the educational needs of the freed black slaves and their progeny. Other Baptist schools in this category include Shaw University (1865) in Raleigh, North Carolina; Morehouse College (1867) and Spelman College (1881), both in Atlanta, Georgia; Benedict College (1870) in Columbia, South Carolina; and Florida Memorial College (1879) in Miami, Florida. In addition, a Swedish Baptist college, Bethel, was established in 1871 in Saint Paul, Minnesota.

This brief survey of the origins of Baptist higher education in America reveals three important points. First, beginning in 1764 with Rhode Island College, or Brown University, and extending through the nineteenth century, over fifty Baptist colleges and universities were established throughout the United States, including some west of the Mississippi River. Others were founded but did not survive, primarily owing either to financial difficulties, the cataclysmic effects of the Civil War, or both.

Second, the pattern of development of Baptist schools tended to be different in the North, Midwest, and West compared to the South. While the role of local constituencies was important everywhere, such groups or individuals, often wealthy, were clearly more determinative for institutional founding and development in the North, Midwest, and West than in the South. Vassar College serves as an example. Under the influence of Milo Jewett, organizer of Judson Female Institute, now Judson College, in Marion, Alabama, Matthew Vassar, from a wealthy brewery family in Poughkeepsie, determined to build a first-class college for women in New York State. Vassar intended that the college would be Baptist "but . . . not . . . denominational in its . . . management,"[10] and he contributed over seven hundred thousand dollars to help the school get off the ground. By contrast, Baptist colleges in the South tended to be founded under the auspices of a Baptist association or state convention rather than through the efforts of individuals. Wake Forest University serves as an example. In 1832 the Baptist State Convention of North Carolina purchased land in Wake County and in 1833 appointed a board of forty trustees for the development of a specifically Baptist institution. The board named the first president, Samuel Wait, and provided for the means "to raise money to equip the school properly."[11]

The third point to be drawn from a review of the origins of Baptist higher education is that in the South the bonds or connections with the Baptist denomination played a much more important role in the founding of institutions and remain much stronger today than is the case in the North, Midwest, and West. Excluding those institutions with an ethnic identity, the self-reported information in the *2004 Higher Education Directory* for the colleges and universities with Baptist beginnings surveyed here reveals that in the South about 84 percent have maintained ties with Baptists and only 16 percent (in actual numbers, five) of the colleges and universities have severed this relationship. Almost the opposite is true in the North, Midwest, and West, where 75 percent of the institutions have severed their ties with Baptists. Several factors account for this dramatic difference, one of which is the strong sense of connection between the Baptist organizations and their educational institutions advocated in the early 1800s by influential Baptists in the South, such as Richard Furman, for many years the pastor of the First Baptist Church of Charleston, South Carolina. As state conventions were established in the South, they came to sponsor Baptist colleges, providing both funds and a measure of control through the appointment of trustees. On the other hand, as Leon McBeth writes, "Colleges among Northern Baptists . . . tended to be sponsored by independent educational societies [and individuals] not organically connected to the denomination."[12]

In addition, regional bonds of a sociopolitical type came actively into play in the South to help forge strong connections among Baptist institutions. The formation of the Southern Baptist Convention (SBC) in 1845, though it was in response to the issue of slavery, encouraged cooperation among and within Baptist institutions. According to William Brackney, the SBC was "the first comprehensive Baptist organization." Brackney argues that, beyond the issue of slavery, "As a region, the South had peculiar social needs and expectations. Southerners in general preferred more centralized organizational styles that promoted a variety of programs . . .,"[13] including not only missions but also education. One important consequence that emerged out of this ethos in the South was the pattern of control of Baptist schools by associations or conventions, specifically through the power of appointment of institutional trustees.

Finally, a word needs to be said about the purpose of Baptist institutions of higher education and the level of support among Baptists in the nineteenth century, especially in the South, that is perhaps not apparent in a simple historical survey. The first Baptist college in the South, Furman, was established by the Baptist State Convention of South Carolina for the purpose of promoting "religious education," the "education of indigent, pious young men, designed for the gospel ministry."[14] Many other early Baptist schools were organized with this same motive in mind. Along with this purpose, however, there was another: the dissemination of "useful knowledge." Baptists wanted to raise the educational level of the citizens of the various states. As America expanded westward, the higher education movement spread with it, and Baptists were as active as any denomination in building colleges along the way. In fact, in the later decades of the nineteenth century, Baptists, according to James T. Burtchaell, "had more students enrolled in their seminaries than either of the two 'educated' denominations [Congregationalists and Presbyterians] had in theirs, and more—many more—in their colleges and academies than the Congregationalists, Presbyterians, and Methodists."[15]

Baptists, however, were nevertheless definitely of a mixed mind about education. They saw ample evidence of people who, in their judgment, were educated but spiritually indifferent and unaffected. The clergy of the Church of England and its Episcopal descendants in America were considered a prime example. How could they not understand, in all their purported education, that the only true basis for church membership is in the baptism of the regenerate individual, a Spirit-caused confession of faith freely and knowingly given before the congregation? The problem with human learning is, as some Baptists expressed it, "There ain't no Holy Ghost in it."[16] This linguistically crude formulation should not disguise a persistent and important question for Baptists—indeed, for all of Christian higher education—and one that remains to this day: does human learning enrich or tend to drive out genuine faith? This is very much the underlying question that informs this book and the conference that occasioned it.

Perhaps Baptists face a particularly difficult task in addressing this issue because they are not a monolithic church but a denomination of independent congregations. Furthermore, beginning in the eighteenth century, Baptists in America were divided into a bewildering variety of expressions: General, Particular, Regular, Separate, Free Will, Six-Principle, Landmark, Liberty, Primitive, Progressive, Reformed, Seventh Day, Missionary, Two Seed in the Spirit, and others. The Baptist gift for schism continues today, under the labels of Southern Baptist, American Baptist, Baptist General Conference, General Association of Regular Baptist Churches, National Baptist, and Cooperative Baptist Fellowship. In addition, there are various modes in Baptist life: moderate, mainstream, conservative, fundamentalist, charismatic, nonaligned, seeker, and traditional. Thus, when we pose the question about the future of Baptist higher education, it seems altogether appropriate, given the plethora of Baptist expressions and experiences, both historically and today, to ask first: what is a Baptist? In other words, while the title of this book, *The Future of Baptist Higher Education*, might appear to assume a common understanding of the meaning of the word "Baptist," we believe that assumption is not justified, that there is, in fact, not an informed and shared consensus today about what it means to be a Baptist. Some clarification of this matter is essential if we are to achieve any consensus in our thinking about Baptist higher education.

II

The issue of Baptist identity is not new, of course.[17] At several points in their history, beginning in England in the seventeenth century, Baptists have felt the need, usually because of theological controversies in their midst, to affirm in clear and unmistakable terms who they are as Christians. The earliest confessions of faith—for example, A Short Confession in Twenty Articles, 1609, by John Smyth, and The London Confession of 1644—occurred within the context of disputes between the General and the Particular Baptists over the atonement, whether it was unlimited—"General"—in the Arminian tradition, or limited—"Particular"—in the Calvinist tradition.[18]

In America, the earliest important statement of faith was the Philadelphia Confession of 1742, promulgated by the Philadelphia Association, the first Baptist association in America. This confession came to be the model of subsequent Baptist confessions of faith in this country. The Philadelphia Confession affirmed the "Holy Scriptures" as ". . . given by the inspiration of God, to be the rule of faith and life." It affirmed God as Holy Trinity in "the Father, the Word (or Son), and Holy Spirit." It acknowledged the creation by God of all things, "visible or invisible," as well as Divine Providence. It declared that humans are made "after the image of God" and possess "natural liberty" but that "Man, by his fall into a state of sin, hath wholly lost all ability of will to any spiritual good accompanying salvation." The Philadelphia Confession also dealt with doctrinal disputes, such as issues surrounding atonement ("Once saved, always saved?" "Are infants who die of the elect?"), "religious worship," and the keeping of the Sabbath holy as "unto the Lord."[19] According to McBeth, the Philadelphia Confession "fixed for generations the doctrinal character of Baptists in this country . . .,"[20] including in the South.

The next major confessional statement by Baptists in America was the New Hampshire Confession of 1833. The background for this statement of faith was the growing sense among New Hampshire Baptists that there was a softening of the theological position "of Calvinistic Baptists in the New Hampshire area . . . by the rise of the Free Will Baptists." Many in New England, especially among the growing middle class, were far more comfortable with the message of free will and general atonement than the "rigid theological system of some Calvinistic Baptists." Thus, the Baptist Convention of New Hampshire determined that a restatement of the faith was needed, one that would reaffirm its Calvinistic teachings but "in very moderate tones."[21] For example, while article four of the Confession states that "salvation of sinners is wholly of grace," article six declares that "the blessings of salvation are made free to all by the Gospel . . . and that nothing prevents the salvation of the greatest sinner on earth except his own voluntary refusal to submit to the

Lord Jesus Christ." Article eight reads, "That election is the gracious purpose of God, according to which He regenerates, sanctifies, and saves sinners; that being perfectly consistent with the free agency of man."[22] Though written to address theological issues present in the Northeast, the New Hampshire Confession was eventually to have significant influence in the South.

Questions of Baptist identity entered another critical phase in the early 1900s with the attacks of J. Frank Norris of Fort Worth, the outspoken leader of the Fundamentalist movement in the South. Norris developed strongly conservative views while a student at Baylor University and at Southern Baptist Theological Seminary in Louisville. After he became a pastor, he soon launched crusades against gambling and drinking, along with the teaching of evolution in Baptist colleges and progressive views of Scripture in Baptist seminaries. Norris was a biblical literalist of the most rigid kind. Because his repeated attacks on the SBC drew wide attention, the convention voted in 1924 to issue a doctrinal statement of belief. The statement came to be known as the Baptist Faith and Message of 1925, formulated by a committee chaired by E. Y. Mullins, president of Southern Baptist Seminary and a renowned Baptist statesman. This 1925 statement of Baptist belief was based substantially on the New Hampshire Confession of 1833.[23] In 1963, a second Baptist Faith and Message was adopted by the SBC, this time to deal with the controversy surrounding an issue from the left, the publication of Ralph H. Elliott's book *The Message of Genesis*, in which he gave a theological interpretation of Genesis in contrast to a literal historical reading.

Through a review of these and other confessions of faith, as well as additional sources of Baptist life, what do we learn about Baptist identity? What do we learn about the content of the faith as confessed by Baptists? First, we must address the issue of authority. That is, what is the one true foundation for defining the beliefs held by Baptists? Throughout their history, Baptists have uniformly given one consistent answer: Scripture. The underlying authority for what Baptists confess about the Christian faith is not to be found in the church, apostolic succession, or tradition, but in the Bible: the Old and New Testaments. The Bible is seen in all Baptist statements of faith as the "truth and final authority" for Christian faith and practice. Yes, Baptists have disagreed over the problem of *interpretation* of the Bible, especially as it relates to the question of the "infallibility" of Scripture, but they nevertheless all go back to the Bible as the starting point for understanding the Christian faith. Because of this strong emphasis on the authority of Scripture, some have accused Baptists of "bibliolatry," of worshiping the Bible instead of the One Triune God. Primarily to check this potential heresy in Baptist life, the Baptist Faith and Message of 1963 declared, "The criterion by which the Bible is to be interpreted is Jesus Christ."

On the basis of Scripture, then, the Baptists have from time to time spelled out for the world and for themselves the content of their beliefs. These may be conveniently summarized in the following way, organized substantially around the doctrines outlined by McBeth in *The Baptist Heritage.*[24]

(1) The Holy Trinity.[25] Clearly the central affirmation of Baptist confessions is the belief in one God, who is revealed as Father, Son, and Holy Spirit. Baptist statements about God generally agree with those of all orthodox Christians. God is the creator of the world and all creatures therein, including humans, whom he made in his own image. Christ is the eternal Son of God and is both fully human and fully divine. His death on the cross "made provision for the redemption of men from sin." He was raised from the dead, ascended into heaven, and is now exalted with the Father. The Holy Spirit, "proceeding from the Father and the Son,"[26] is the presence of the Triune God in the world, who convicts of sin, effects regeneration, comforts believers, grants spiritual gifts, and "enlightens and empowers the believer and the church in worship, evangelism, and service."[27]

(2) Human beings. Baptists affirm, with Christians everywhere, that all human beings are created in God's image and thus are made for communion with him and with one another. In the beginning humans were in "a state of holiness,"[28] innocent of sin, and "left to the liberty of their own will."[29] However, "[b]y his free choice man sinned against God and brought sin into the human race." All human beings are now "inclined toward sin, and as soon as they are capable of moral action become transgressors and are under condemnation." Only by God's grace can humans be brought back into proper fellowship with God and with one another. Moreover, "[t]he sacredness of human personality is evident in that God created [human beings] in His own image, and in that Christ died for [them]; therefore every [human being] possesses dignity and is worthy of respect and Christian love."[30]

(3) Atonement. Baptists believe that salvation is an act of God's grace that involves the regeneration, or rebirth, of the sinner, who, through God's grace, is set apart for God's service. While Baptists generally hold common views on salvation and sanctification, other aspects of the doctrine of atonement have long divided Baptists. Did Jesus die for all, and will whoever believes in him be saved? Or, is salvation possible *only* through God's initiative ("before the foundation of the world"—Eph. 1:4), hence must the believer be of the elect? The first view historically implied that the saved can "fall from grace," while the second held that an individual "can neither totally nor finally fall from the state of grace."[31]

(4) The church. Baptists have consistently agreed that the church "is a company of Baptized believers, that it must observe the gospel ordinances, preach the gospel, and discipline its members." Infants cannot become mem-

bers of the church, nor should they receive baptism. Baptists have acknowledged a distinction between the universal church, the Body of Christ of all the ages, and the local congregation made up of "visible saints."[32] While Baptists disagree on how churches should relate to one another, they agree that the local congregation "is an autonomous body, operating through democratic processes under the Lordship of Jesus Christ."[33]

(5) The ministry. The ministry of local Baptist churches has been seen under the order of two offices: pastors and the deacons (elders). The responsibilities of pastors have included preaching, teaching, administering the ordinances, and providing leadership in worship, witness, and church discipline. Deacons take care of the sick and needy in the congregation, as well as assist in church discipline and leadership.

(6) Baptism. All Baptist confessions deal with baptism, which is taken to mean "the immersion of a believer in the name of the Father, the Son, and the Holy Spirit." Furthermore, baptism is seen as "an act of obedience symbolizing the believer's faith in a crucified, buried, and risen Savior, the believer's death to sin, the burial of the old life, and the resurrection to walk in newness of life in Christ Jesus."[34]

(7) Communion. Baptists everywhere see the Lord's Supper—the taking of the bread and the fruit of the vine—as a "perpetual remembrance" recalling the death of Christ, as well as the confirmation of the faith of the believers, the promise of the believers' obedience to Christ, and the "bond and pledge of their communion with Him and with each other."[35] The frequency of communion varies by local congregation, although in early Baptist services it was held almost every Sunday. The main dispute surrounding the ordinance has been the issue of "closed communion," limiting participation only to believers baptized by immersion, or "open communion," permitting participation to all professing Christians, regardless of mode of baptism.

(8) Religious liberty. From the very beginning, Baptists have affirmed religious liberty and separation of church and state. This position was grounded not only in the political environment of the early Baptists, but also in their reading of Scripture and their understanding of the Christian experience itself—"the Freeness of Salvation" and its correlate, believer's baptism. The "blessings of salvation are made free to all by the gospel . . . and . . . nothing prevents the salvation of the greatest sinner on earth except his own voluntary refusal. . . ."[36] The precondition of this accountability of each individual before God is the uncoerced conscience. The gospel of Christ cannot be imposed upon anyone, whether by church or state. Therefore, "[a] free church in a free state is the Christian ideal, and this implies the right of free and unhindered access to God on the part of all [persons] and the right to

form and propagate opinions in the sphere of religion without interference by the civil power."[37]

(9) The social order. Civil authority is ordained by God to serve the commonweal, "and to this end hath armed . . . [rulers] with the power of the sword, for defense and encouragement of them that do good, and for the punishment of evil doers."[38] Every Christian should provide for those in need, and "should seek to bring industry, government, and society as a whole under the sway of the principles of righteousness." In the pursuit of these ends, Christians should be prepared to work with others of good will, never compromising their loyalty to Christ.[39]

(10) Kingdom of God. Baptists are alike with other Christians in affirming God's "general sovereignty over the universe and His particular kingship over men who willfully acknowledge Him as King." Moreover, "[t]he full consummation of the kingdom awaits the return of Jesus Christ and the end of this age."[40]

This list is not, of course, a complete set of doctrines that Baptists have affirmed. For example, the Philadelphia Confession of 1742 contains thirty-four "chapters" or doctrinal teachings. In addition to these ten, other affirmations included in the Confession concern the law of God, religious worship and the Sabbath day, lawful oaths and vows, marriage, communion of saints, and the Last Judgment. Moreover, it is important to note, as does the 1925 Baptist Faith and Message, that Baptist confessions reflect a "consensus of opinion of some Baptist body," and are not intended in any way to override the saving gospel of Jesus Christ or the teachings of the Old and New Testaments. In fact, "any group of Baptists, large or small, have [*sic*] the inherent right to draw up for themselves and publish to the world a confession of their faith whenever they may think it advisable to do so," as long as such statements are "drawn from Scriptures, and are not . . . used to hamper freedom of thought or investigation in other realms of life."[41]

At the same time, even though Baptists maintain the right to draw up statements of faith, their confessions are not generally statements about "Baptist distinctives," but rather about the essentials of Christian belief. As Leon McBeth has written, "Patiently refuting false charges, Baptists often used confessions not to proclaim 'Baptist distinctives' but instead to show how similar Baptists were to other orthodox Christians."[42] Thus, what these various confessions make clear about Baptist identity is that Baptists are first and foremost *orthodox Christians*. That is, Baptists join with other true believers across the world and across the ages in worshiping and serving the one God, revealed as Father, Son, and Holy Spirit. Baptists share with other Christians the belief in God the Father as creator, God the Son as redeemer, and God the Holy Spirit as preserver. Baptists share with other Christians the belief that all human beings are created in God's image, that all human beings are sinners and in need of forgiveness and the saving grace of the gospel of Christ, that true believers find fellowship and instruction in the gathered church, that Scripture is authoritative for faith and practice, and that God's sovereignty is over all things.

The major Baptist distinctive—though it is not, in fact, unique to Baptists—is believer's baptism. Baptists hold, in contrast to many Christian traditions, that genuine faith requires a personal, individual, and voluntary commitment. Thus, one cannot be born into the Christian faith. To become a Christian requires a second birth that the individual freely embraces. Therefore, Baptists have consistently rejected any kind of human interference between the individual and God, even parental interference such as that involved in infant baptism, and "every form of religion by proxy." As Mullins asserts, "Religion is a personal matter between the soul and God."[43] The insistence of Baptists on this point arises out of their understanding of the salvation experience as described in Scripture, and from this principle of the voluntary response of the believer to God flow all the other Baptist "distinctives," including the priesthood of all believers, democracy in the local congregation, and separation of church and state. Being made in God's image, we humans have the capacity for God, and he in turn can communicate with us, which he has done preeminently in Christ.[44]

III

What, then, does this summary of Baptist belief—the content of the faith as confessed by Baptists—have to do with higher education? When we modify the term "higher education" by the word "Baptist," what difference does it make? Does the longstanding suspicion on the part of some Baptists that human learning tends to drive out genuine faith have an element of truth? Or is there available to Baptists a "philosophy of higher education" that arises out of their own tradition? Is there a view of Baptist higher education that is informed by the essential elements of Baptist belief but that still provides an intellectually persuasive account of the world about us and of the role of humanity in that world, one that speaks with genuine relevance to the culture in which we live today?

Ironically, one of the main obstacles to a Baptist "philosophy of higher education" is the dominance in our contemporary culture of a value that is also inherent in the Baptist ethos itself, the value of individualism. In contemporary society most people chart their lives not primarily in relation to communal bonds or for the common good, but to serve the interests—both utilitarian and emotive—of the private self. With respect to Baptist belief, the importance of the individual responsibility to acknowledge and develop one's own personal relationship with God sometimes gets translated into a highly personalized version of the Christian faith. Since Baptists are not creedal and since religion is a personal matter, this thinking goes, individual Baptists should have wide latitude to believe what they choose to believe. Added to this obstacle is another, the secularization of contemporary culture, one aspect of which is the fragmentation of human experience. This secularization and fragmentation mean that religion and various elements of life—including education—are too often manifestly independent of each other. And for Baptists, these two dominant and related themes of contemporary culture, individualism and secularism, have tended to produce a conception of Christian higher education that, on the one hand, separates human learning from genuine faith, and, on the other hand, limits the religious aspect of this educational task to the development of moral character and godly piety. Such a view usually gets expressed in Baptist circles, as well as in others, as a "college education in a Christian environment."

This view conspicuously ignores any intellectual engagement with the defining beliefs of our Baptist identity reflected through almost four centuries of Baptist confessions of faith. While it is true that religion is a personal matter, it is also true that Baptists have always shared a more or less common core of beliefs, a "consensus of opinion" about the truths of the faith drawn from Scripture. When Baptist identity is seen in this light, it is clear that we can offer a philosophy of Baptist higher education that is far richer and substantially more significant intellectually than one that promotes merely education in a Christian environment. With Anselm we can declare, "I believe in order to understand," and we can ground a Baptist philosophy of higher education in the foundational belief that the truths of the Christian faith have the capacity to clarify reality.

Both secular learning and Christian learning embody genuine aspects of knowledge. Secular learning, however, excludes any consideration of God in the world whereas the subject matter of Christian higher education, elegantly described by John Henry Newman, is threefold: God, nature, and human beings. The first of these areas of knowledge, the knowledge of God as "Holy Trinity," should be an important element within the curriculum of every Baptist institution of higher education. This is not a matter of catechesis. It is rather an opening of the intellect through courses in biblical, religious, philosophical, and other relevant studies to the activity of God, in creation, redemption, and preservation on the one hand, and to the relational character of God on the other.

The implications of this knowledge of God are numerous for our proper understanding of the other two areas of learning: nature and human beings.

For example, with regard to the latter, one of the core beliefs of Baptists and Christians everywhere is that God made human beings in his own image. Our knowledge of God—grounded in Scripture—reveals that God is personal and relational. Because we are made in the image of God, we not only have the capacity for fellowship with God, but we are also, by our very nature, relational beings. This truth about ourselves is fundamental to understanding who we are as humans. In addition, the *imago dei* view of human nature provides a lasting foundation for our moral understanding of others. Christ died for all people, and all people, regardless of circumstances or station in life, are made in the image of God. Thus, all people are to be treated with respect and compassion. This knowledge about the nature of human beings is immensely relevant to the enterprise of Christian higher education. It implies that Baptist colleges and universities, both in our academic programs and campus life, should seek ways to nurture mutual respect among students, faculty, and administration and also within communities beyond the campus and to encourage the formation of communal bonds. In addition, this knowledge of human beings frames our moral understanding of all the professions as being primarily informed by the call to service on behalf of others.

At the same time, our understanding of human beings also includes an acknowledgment, as our defining beliefs remind us, that all human beings are sinners. All are "inclined toward sin, and as soon as they are capable of moral action become transgressors." The ramifications of this understanding of the human self for Christian higher education are virtually too numerous to count. For example, the study of political science at a Baptist institution can consider the fact that the tradition of constitutional government with its system of checks and balances and the notion of "a government of laws, not of men" are based on the belief that no one can be trusted with too much power, since all are sinners. Similarly, disciplines that prepare students for the "helping professions," such as psychology or social work, can consider the effect of sin and guilt on human beings and their behavior. Thus, while students must be prepared to use traditional therapy effectively to treat psychological disorders, they can also be prepared to understand that the confession of sin before God and others is a proper response to spiritual and moral brokenness, to the restoration of internal peace and communal bonds.

The doctrine of *imago dei* also instructs us about the relative value of human life in contrast to all other forms of life, both sentient and nonsentient, and encourages the proper understanding of and an appropriate human relationship with the third area of learning: nature. Only humans are made in God's image, and this fact separates human beings from animal or vegetative life. However, our "dominion over the fish of the sea, and over the birds of the air, and over the cattle, and over all the earth" is to be understood as our God-given obligation of stewardship, not the power to abuse and use improperly. At a Baptist institution of higher learning this understanding of the proper relationship of human beings to the natural world should influence the way in which we approach the study of the sciences and the environment.

As these and other considerations suggest, the basic relevance for higher education of the defining beliefs of Baptists, as orthodox Christians, is that they form a *Weltanschauung*, a comprehensive worldview, grounded in a trustworthy and accepted set of teachings about God, the universe, humans, the social order, history, the church, salvation, the kingdom of God, and the like, teachings that serve as lenses through which we see all things. One can arrive at similar or competing positions from other perspectives, to be sure, and in this respect Baptist higher education is a contested form of learning.[45] It is not, after all, the only epistemological narrative available. But it is the narrative, formed out of the biblical witness, that has been affirmed by Baptists and other orthodox Christians for centuries. And it is a coherent narrative.

The coherence of the Christian narrative provides for an additional and central consideration for our understanding of Baptist higher education: the connectedness of knowledge. The connectedness of knowledge within a Baptist college or university depends on the presence and interrelationship of all the major areas of learning, God, nature, and human beings. If the first is not present, in particular the acknowledgment and exploration of the One Triune God, the whole structure of knowledge is incomplete and impaired. Of course, this is surely a contested vision of knowledge and truth. But so are all other visions. As Stephen Evans points out, we in the academy can no longer pretend that the university is a place where only objective reason is exhibited. Regardless of who we are, our "basic values and convictions . . . shape the way we function as scholars," although this will be less the case in some areas of inquiry than others. This statement does not mean that the quest for truth is reduced to political or ideological agendas. Rather, Evans declares, "we must reconceive the quest for truth as a pluralistic conversation, where no party to the conversation can claim to represent 'pure reason.'"[46]

Within this context we offer a final component of Baptist higher education born out of Baptist identity, the affirmation of religious liberty and its relationship to academic freedom. The central distinctive of Baptists within the orthodox Christian community is and has been its belief that genuine faith requires a personal and voluntary commitment. One of the conditions for this expression of faith is that it must be uncoerced; it is a willful and personal response to God's grace. From this implicit freedom of the individual before God, Baptists have professed that "God alone is the Lord of the conscience." This freedom before God implies the freedom of Baptists to express responsible dissent within the church body, not as a means of dividing the congregation, but as an attempt to strengthen the community. Accordingly, Baptist colleges and universities must affirm the secular counterpart to the Baptist notion of responsible dissent—namely, academic freedom within the community of mutually accountable scholars. Thus, the Baptist affirmation of academic freedom is not a concession to a secular academy but a reflection of our own theological convictions as Baptists.

While the foregoing attempt to outline some basic elements of a Baptist philosophy of higher education is incomplete, our purpose here is a modest one: to be suggestive of what the content of Baptist identity might mean within the context of higher education. At a minimum, we hope we have offered conceptual avenues by which we can understand why human learning need not drive out faith, as well as embrace Anselm's claim that true belief clarifies reality. Moreover, as the various essays in this book demonstrate, a vital philosophy of Baptist higher education needs to incorporate *both* faithful learning and godly piety, knowledge and character. And such a mission requires that we continue to nourish our relationship to Baptist churches and bodies, as well as the larger Christian community.

IV

As this introduction has demonstrated, the history of higher education in America records a continuous decline in the number and influence of educational institutions that identify themselves as Baptist and Christian. The causes for this phenomenon of secularization are as varied as the institutions that have experienced it—Harvard, Yale, Brown, the University of Chicago, and some would include Furman and Wake Forest. Against the background of this history of secularization, the essays in this collection explore many of the critical issues facing Baptist institutions of higher education today.

Baptist colleges and universities, if they are to survive as religiously affiliated institutions, must have a strong sense of identity and a commitment to their missions. Establishing such an identity and mission is made more difficult in Baptist life by the fragmented nature of the denomination. The divisions among moderate, conservative, and fundamentalist Baptist bodies with decidedly different views on theological, biblical, and social issues complicate not only the question of Baptist identity but also the question of sustained support for educational institutions.

The essays in part 1 offer four models for Baptist higher education that can help Baptist colleges and universities develop a stronger and more authentically Baptist religious identity. David Gushee focuses on "the conversation about Christian higher education that has been occurring outside the Baptist world" and undertakes the enormous task of proposing a "normative intellectual vision and theological identity of Baptist universities." William Hull and

Bill Leonard both look to Baptist denominational history for the resources that can guide the future of Baptist higher education. Hull argues that the future of Baptist colleges and universities "must be grounded in a shared vision of what it means to be Baptist that is embraced both by our schools and by a critical mass of our churches." Similarly, Leonard argues that in the past, controversies among Baptists in the South were moderated by the "cultural hegemony that Baptists maintained inside southern culture," a hegemony grounded in a consensus regarding what it meant to be a Baptist. Although this early consensus has been lost, Leonard suggests that the ideals held by early Baptists can help to reestablish a distinctive identity for Baptist colleges and universities today. And in the final essay of this section David Dockery argues that Baptist identity can be enriched through more intentional efforts to "carry on the great Christian intellectual tradition, and to develop a theology of Baptist higher education."

Related to the issue of religious identity facing Baptist institutions is the problem of responding to the continuing pressures to abandon core religious principles in an effort to strengthen academic reputation and to compete with publicly supported institutions for the best students and faculty. The essays in part 2 address these issues. Richard Franklin examines the generation of students called Millennials, the cohort of students born between 1982 and 2002 who will fill our institutions until 2024, and argues that if our Baptist colleges and universities are going to be successful in attracting these students and meeting their needs, we have much work to do. In the second essay Larry Lyon examines relevant data about sixteen national universities that maintain a serious religious identification to "assess empirically" if it is possible for a university to achieve a strong academic reputation while maintaining its religious identity.

If Baptist colleges and universities are successful in developing a strong religious identity, in maintaining a strong academic reputation, and in attracting well-qualified faculty and students, they still must confront the problem of how best to maintain the financial and spiritual support of their sponsoring bodies, of Baptist churches, and of an increasingly diverse and needy population. Thus, the essays in part 3 focus on the relationships between Baptist institutions of higher education and those external constituencies on which the institutions depend. James C. Denison examines the question of whether or not Christian education is a "justifiable mission" of the church or "peripheral to the mission of the church." Albert Reyes surveys the current diverse population of potential students and asks if Baptist colleges and universities will be accountable to "provide Christian higher education to the next generation of Baptists" and wonders whether or not this educational experience will be readily "available and accessible to our sons and daughters thirty-five years from now."

Similarly, Denton Lotz explores the effect that the events of September 11, 2001, have had and will continue to have on our students in the twenty-first century and raises the question of whether or not religious institutions can help students to prepare to live in a post-9/11 world. Daniel Vestal and R. Kirby Godsey both address the question of accountability of Baptist institutions of higher education to their sponsoring bodies "within the context of a changed and changing denominational reality," but they suggest quite different models for what they believe the relationship of accountability ought to be. Thomas Corts, in the final essay of part 3, explores the dilemma facing Baptist institutions of higher education that see themselves as "in the world, but not of this world" but that also recognize that if they are to survive, they must engage the secular culture that threatens their existence.

A final critical issue facing Baptist institutions of higher education today that these essays address is the challenge of charting a course into the future that will ensure their survival as strong academic and religious institutions. Both of the essays in part 4 by Martin Marty and Curtis Freeman provide synthetic reflections about the future of Baptist higher education. Marty and Freeman each argue against the assumption underlying many of the essays in the collection that secularization represents a threat to religion, and they propose alternative visions for the future of Baptist higher education.

Though the following essays point out serious and persistent problems facing Baptist colleges and universities, they also offer hope that these problems can be addressed, and that with hard work and a sense of mission we can be optimistic about the future of Baptist institutions of higher learning.

Part One

Four Models for Baptist Higher Education

Chapter Two

Integrating Faith and Learning in an Ecumenical Context

David P. Gushee

Introduction

The ultimate task of this essay is to make a proposal concerning the normative intellectual vision and theological identity of Baptist universities.[1] My particular assignment has been to focus on the conversation about Christian higher education that has been occurring outside the Baptist world. Even with this limitation, my task remains daunting. But it is what I have been asked to do, and since fools go where angels fear to tread, here is how I will proceed.

First, I offer a brief assessment of what has happened to the identity and vision of most Christian colleges and universities in America, and what this has left us in terms of the landscape of church-related higher education today. While this is familiar ground for those who have read much in the burgeoning literature of Christian higher education, it is increasingly contested ground, and I need to offer my own reading of the evidence.

Second, I review and evaluate what I classify as four key types of responses in the world of Christian higher education to the question that is the focus of this paper. We are asking here about the purpose, vision, and identity of Baptist higher education that seeks to be seriously Christian, but many are already asking about such matters in the world of Catholic and Protestant, evangelical and mainline, denominational and "church-related" higher education. By proposing a simple taxonomy of the most significant current models related to the identity and vision of the Christian university, it should be possible to gain greater clarity about the options facing Baptist universities. At each step I briefly comment on ways in which my own Union University has discussed, affirmed, qualified, and/or employed each model.

In the final section of the paper, I offer my own proposal concerning the normative theological identity and intellectual vision of Christian (especially Baptist) colleges and universities.

The Soul of the American University

The baseline from which all discussions of Christian higher education must begin is this: with few exceptions, institutions of higher education in America began as explicitly Christian endeavors, and yet over time their religious identities and vision have consistently changed in a manner that can best be described as a weakening or erosion. Five significant studies have all traced the same phenomenon. George Marsden describes the religious roots of America's most influential universities, such as Harvard, Yale, Columbia, Stanford, Chicago, Duke, and Vanderbilt, and their consequent abandonment of religious identity. Philip Gleason examines Catholic higher education in America from its origins in the nineteenth century through its radical transformation and widespread loss of Catholic distinctiveness in the 1960s and thereafter. Douglas Sloan reflects on the liberal Protestant experience in higher education in the twentieth century and how most mainline Protestant schools ultimately failed to find a compelling way to reunite faith and knowledge after it had been sundered, eventually leaving them as vaguely Christian or post-Christian schools. James Burtchaell's magisterial though deeply pessimistic book examines key colleges and universities associated with numerous denominations, finding that almost all of them have disengaged from the churches that founded them as well as the religious vision on which they were based. Robert Benne summarizes these and other studies, examines the underlying factors contributing to the secularization of Christian colleges, proposes a typology of church-related colleges, and examines six schools that he thinks exemplify successful "quality with soul."[2]

With inevitable variations in detail, all tell the same basic story related to what has happened to Christian universities: secularization and disengagement from their Christian churches and/or founding identity.

Marsden's study of the elite American universities establishes that most such schools reflected in their founding and for many years thereafter the culturally established Protestant Christianity that dominated our national life well into the twentieth century. Explicit affirmations of Christian faith and coercive expectations of Christian practice were long required at such elite schools as Harvard, Princeton, Yale, Stanford, and Chicago. As late as 1870, most of these schools were quite explicitly biblical, pietistic, and evangelical. By 1920 they were still explicitly Christian, though they had backed away from what might be recognized today as conservative Christianity. By

1970 most had abandoned the remaining traces of their earlier evangelical, and later liberal, Christian identity to arrive at a position that Marsden calls "established nonbelief." Today traditional Christian views are among the least welcome perspectives to be found in the modern university, though the ice may be cracking somewhat under the impact of a postmodernism that increasingly welcomes a smorgasbord of perspectives. The trajectory Marsden traces can be summarized as evangelical Christian, to liberal Christian, to secular. The pace of this trajectory has varied from school to school, as has the pervasiveness and uniformity of any particular identity at any particular stage of the process. Despite recent objections that this depiction of reality is too pessimistic because it fails to notice the fragments of religiosity that still survive in church-related colleges and even in secular universities, I remain convinced both from research and experience that it is essentially correct.[3]

Why did this happen? The first reason is clearly the overall secularization of Western culture. Historic biblical faith faded gradually in the Western world, a decline that can be traced at least to the Enlightenment if not to the Renaissance and even, ironically, to unintended effects of the Protestant Reformation. As modern thinkers rejected the axis of authority that had been provided by the church and the Bible, rationalism and empiricism emerged as the primary means by which people who viewed themselves as intelligent and thoughtful understood and explained their world. Darwinian science in the late nineteenth century, as well as broader currents of evolutionary naturalism and historicism circulating at the same time, radically undermined historic Christian convictions and grassroots Christian confidence in the Bible and its claims. Today, neither an Enlightenment confidence in reason or science nor any other (earlier or later) alternative can command full confidence or universal assent; our intellectual environment is marked by a lack of any sure and broadly accepted foundation for knowing anything. We live among fragments—all "foundations" for knowledge have been cracked.

In one sense, then, the decline of the religious faith once so present in the American university is a symptom (and, undoubtedly, also a cause) of the overall decline of such faith in Western culture. While secularization and de-Christianization have not taken the same course or penetrated society as thoroughly in the United States as in Europe, similar dynamics can be identified. And in both cases, a substantial portion of our cultural elites, primarily located in the great public and private universities as well as at think tanks and in the top ranks of the media, have gone over to a thoroughly secular and/or post-Christian worldview. It only stands to reason that at the great universities themselves, and in the hearts of the students who matriculate there and are not strongly committed to an alternative vision, and on the campuses of the less "great" colleges and universities which look to the elite schools for their models of success and status, secularization proceeds as an almost irresistible force.

General secularization trends certainly constitute one reason that so many formerly Christian colleges have lost or abandoned their Christian identity. But other factors in their own way have contributed to this phenomenon, including the rise of professional and graduate education with their externally imposed standards; the programming and ethos-shaping power of accrediting bodies; the intimidating power of government and the strings it sometimes attaches to its money; the growing influence of business and technology, and education designed to support their enterprises; the development of a faculty guild mentality; and the emergence of mass education, in which larger and larger percentages of American young people attend college as a matter of course. But Marsden identifies a more subtle dynamic that affected the elite universities covered in his study in particular. The erstwhile religiosity of these universities represented the convictions of the Protestant elites who once governed with nearly unquestioned hegemony this nation and its culture. It is easy to forget this white Anglo-Saxon Protestant cultural hegemony until one is brought up short by reading comments like this one from liberal Democratic hero and president, Franklin D. Roosevelt: "This is a Protestant country, and everyone else is here by sufferance."[4]

So, if "this is a Protestant country," its great universities would be founded as Protestant institutions. And thus it was for the earliest schools, such as Harvard, Yale, and Princeton, in a pattern that continued through the founding of even our late-born elite universities, such as Duke, Vanderbilt, and Chicago, in the late nineteenth and early twentieth centuries. Marsden is able to document that even at Harvard and Yale explicit Protestant Christianity survived far longer than one might have imagined in looking at such schools today—indeed, significant traces can still be found, especially in their divinity schools. However, the growing diversity of the American population and the gradual cultural disestablishment of Protestant evangelicalism in the late nineteenth and early twentieth centuries meant that if such schools wanted to remain broadly representative of Protestant (=American) opinion, they would have to move away from any kind of "sectarian" Protestant identity.

Schools that once required faculty to pass explicitly biblical and theological Protestant religious tests abandoned them, also along the way abandoning required Bible classes, required Sunday church attendance, required chapel, and strict student moral codes, not to mention any effort to bring Christian theological convictions to bear on the various academic disciplines taught outside of the religion department. The leaders of such schools until the 1950s usually attempted to proclaim the school's continued allegiance to broadly Christian, Protestant, Judeo-Christian, American, civic, or moral convictions or values, often by highlighting various extracurricular religious and ethical programming opportunities intending to create a certain "atmosphere" or "ethos." But it is quite easy to watch various schools' language evolve from "committed to Jesus Christ," to "committed to Christian principles," to "committed to the highest ideals of liberal learning, service, democracy, and character," to "committed to the quest for truth," to something even more nondescript than that.[5] Christian scholars are not the only ones deeply concerned about what the loss of a meaningful governing vision has meant for the identity and mission of the modern university, and they are not the only ones to note the deleterious impact this loss has had on the students the university serves. Indeed, confidence in distinctively Christian higher education is growing in the same proportion as confidence in the secular university is declining.[6]

Clearly the social revolutions of the 1960s precipitated the "official" death of explicitly Christian or even broadly moral values at many of our nation's universities, but the way had been prepared for a very long time before the events of that period drove the final nail in the coffin. The shock was especially intense at Catholic universities because their developmental path outside of establishment Protestantism had shielded them far longer from both the corrosive effects of secularization and from any necessity to try to maintain a broad cultural hegemony that they had never had. By the end of the 1970s, however, it was possible to trace similar patterns at the old elite universities, the smaller private Protestant colleges of numerous denominations, and a number of Catholic colleges and universities as well. In the majority of cases, one could see an originating religious vision gradually watered down and finally either explicitly or implicitly abandoned.[7] Burtchaell is able to identify the pattern in schools of various denominations, including, ironically, evangelical schools founded in the twentieth century with the explicit rationale of resisting the acids of modernity and secularization. "Time, like an ever-rolling stream, bears all its sons away," the old hymn says, tempting us to the relevant paraphrase: "Secularization, like an ever-rolling stream, bears all Christian colleges away."

This state of affairs leaves the contemporary landscape of American university life deeply secularized. Certainly all of the major public and most of the major private universities have embraced some form of "established nonbelief." If "religion" is taught at all, the subject is usually confined to religion departments operating on the basis of a comparative "study of religion" model. As well, a large percentage of the officially "church-related" schools have gone a long way in the same direction, though the details of the transition from explicitly and confessionally Christian to something other than that vary from school to school.[8] Meanwhile, a small percentage of the higher education landscape is occupied by explicitly and ardently Christian colleges and universities from various denominational traditions. On the Protestant side, many of these are members or affiliates with the Council for Christian Colleges and Universities (CCCU). The schools associated with the Roman Catholic tradition also range from post-Catholic to liberal Catholic to conservative Catholic, though, in a move paralleled on the Protestant side, some of the latter represent new schools founded to counter Catholic educational drift.

Robert Benne proposes that there are four types of formerly or currently church-related universities in America today.[9] Current or former Baptist universities can be found that fit each one of these four types. Those schools that have gone the furthest with secularization are categorized as *accidentally pluralist*. Such schools present themselves as secular with little or no allusion to their historic Christian heritage. No effort is made to guarantee that Christian faith has an assured place in the ongoing campus conversation or in the curriculum. Such schools are only "accidentally pluralistic" in that a monistic secular paradigm so predominates that Christian (or other religious) influences are essentially accidental. They may emerge from particularly influential students, some of whom are deeply frustrated by the secularism of their universities, or the occasional faculty member, but the promotion of Christianity is no part of the university's mission.[10]

For Benne, *intentionally pluralist* schools are not quite so thoroughly secular. They do assure Christian perspectives an ongoing voice in university life. They are a bit less quiet about their historic Christian heritage, if that is their history, while still presenting themselves primarily as secular liberal arts colleges. While the presence of explicitly Christian courses in the curriculum is usually quite small, it has not entirely disappeared. There may be an endowed professorship or annual lecture series aimed at keeping a Christian perspective in front of the community on a regular basis. However, in general, Christian faith is not privileged in any way. Some of the most creative of these schools work to ensure a similar ongoing presence for voices from other religious traditions or major ideologies and perspectives. The benefit of such a model over the accidental pluralist schools is obvious, at least from a Christian perspective. Christians at least have a space to articulate their views, and Christian students have at least some faculty members with whom to identify. The sometimes quite robust ideological and religious pluralism of such schools is an improvement over monistic secularism, but there is no intention to function as "Christian universities."

There is another possibility available to university leaders who are uneasy with a strong Christian vision and identity but for various reasons cannot quite do away with it altogether. *They can promote the university as if it were an explicitly Christian enterprise even though this is no longer actually the case.* The incentives for taking this course are sometimes quite strong. Pitching the university's supposed Christian identity and mission helps a university retain the support of some alumni, church leaders, and donors. But maintaining a university climate in which this promised Christian identity is not actually what is pursued satisfies other constituencies, such as secularized faculty and students. The problem with this strategy—pitching the institution's Christian identity while actually weakening or abandoning it—is that it is immoral. It is duplicitous. It is lying to people who deserve the truth. And ultimately, living a lie will fail anyway, because the truth will come out. Whatever we decide to do in our universities about our identity and vision, let's at least be honest.

Accidental and intentional pluralism and lying about who we are and what we believe are not options for an authentically Christian university. This leaves two other categories for Benne, which he often discusses together: the *critical-mass* and *orthodox* universities.[11] Schools in both categories employ a Christian vision as their organizing paradigm. In both, Christian faith is clearly privileged on campus, including in the classroom. In both, schools attempt to recruit at least a large percentage of students and faculty from within the Christian faith, especially the faith of the sponsoring denomination or movement. In both, several courses with explicit Christian content are required of all students; in orthodox schools, the aim is to have *all* courses influenced by a shared Christian perspective. The dominant atmosphere of such schools clearly reflects the piety of the sponsoring tradition. Chapel continues to play a major role. The sponsoring church remains warmly related to such schools and sends a significant percentage of its young people there for college, as well as providing significant financial support, and the board continues to have at least a majority of members come from the sponsoring religious tradition or movement. The difference between critical-mass schools and orthodox schools is primarily that the former do not seek 100 percent sponsoring-tradition-domination in every aspect of university life. For example, they are Baptist schools willing to hire committed Catholics, Lutherans, or Eastern Orthodox to teach, maybe even in the religion department. They may even be open to the occasional faculty member of another faith or even the secularist faith. I would classify Baylor right now as aiming to be a critical-mass university. Notre Dame seems to occupy a similar spot on the spectrum. Meanwhile, Calvin College is a quintessential orthodox school. My own Union University is best classified as an orthodox school as well.

The rest of this chapter is relevant primarily to university leaders who are committed to maintaining or developing institutions that are either orthodox or critical-mass Christian schools. Concluding that preserving or renewing this deeply and pervasively Christian identity is the central priority for the university, such leaders are naturally curious about how to get there. In the next section of this essay, I turn to what I believe to be the four major current alternatives for the governing intellectual vision and theological identity of explicitly Christian universities. If we are not willing to accept secularization and go gently into that good night, what must we do to articulate a vibrant and compelling vision of our Christian identity today? What strategies must we undertake to turn that vision into a reality?

Keeping the Faith in Christian Higher Education: Four Models

The Faith/Learning Integration and Worldview Model

The most robust and best-established vision for Christian higher education for at least the last thirty years has been the faith/learning integration model. I consider it in tandem with the related but distinguishable *worldview approach*, for they are often employed together in Christian higher education.[12] The intellectual provenance of the concept of faith/learning integration using worldview analysis can be traced to the Dutch Calvinist approach in place at Calvin College in Grand Rapids. The story of Calvin College has been told most recently in a collection of essays called *Keeping Faith*, published in 1996 on the occasion of a new president's inauguration.[13]

The Calvin College model is ultimately traceable not just to John Calvin himself but especially to the brilliant Abraham Kuyper, the late-19th-century Dutch scholar, pastor, politician, and educator who founded the Free University of Amsterdam while along the way finding time to serve as prime minister of Holland.[14] Working at a moment when the winds of secularism were blowing fiercely in Western Europe, Kuyper proposed a comprehensive Christian intellectual and social vision aimed at the reclaiming of the entirety of western culture for Christ and his kingdom. Recognizing that the social changes occurring in Holland and throughout the Western world had deep intellectual roots, Kuyper initiated a pattern of offering critical philosophical and theological analysis of modern thought and the overall modern "worldview." The way to work toward reclaiming Western culture for Christ was to challenge the ideas that were threatening to sweep away the Christian worldview and its associated culture. It was a strenuous intellectual and institutional project that largely failed to stem the tide of secularism in the Netherlands, as can be seen in that nation today. But its legacy lives on in higher education among Dutch Calvinists in North America.

The impact of the theology of John Calvin can be seen here primarily in his emphasis on the sovereignty of God, the pervasiveness of sin, and the unity of divinely revealed truth in all of its forms. The tradition articulated by Kuyper and since then by Calvin College's many thoughtful scholars has emphasized the same themes. God is sovereign, human beings can't touch anything without it being affected by our sin, and "all truth is God's truth." If those working in various academic disciplines arrive at findings that seem to contradict biblical revelation, it must be because their disciplinary paradigms contain worldview assumptions or epistemological assumptions tainted by sin, or perhaps the scholars themselves are unintentionally distorting their interpretation of the data they have gathered. The findings of the leading scholars of various fields are studied closely and taken seriously, but never accepted uncritically.

Christian scholars therefore must become skillful in interpreting the philosophical and theological presuppositions and worldviews of the various (increasingly secularized) academic disciplines. This critical task then lays the groundwork for the even more difficult work of reclaiming or redeeming each academic discipline from secularism to a coherently Christian perspective and thus, as it were, gaining victories for the sovereign God in the stubborn realm of intellectual life. This does not mean that psychology, sociology, English literature, or anthropology (etc.) are ever abandoned as disciplines, but it does mean that their work is critically assessed and interpreted, and that the finest Christian scholars offer a Christian rendering of each such discipline.

This approach is called the "integration of faith and learning" (sometimes the "integration of faith and the disciplines") because it brings faith to bear on all forms of human learning/knowing, confidently engaging the world of contemporary scholarship rather than withdrawing from it, but doing so with an agenda of claiming it for Christ's cause. Faculty members at integrationist schools are trained to approach their disciplinary subject matters via relentless critical engagement with the secularized worldviews, presuppositions, and epistemologies of their main practitioners. They are also trained to offer a cogent Christian alternative that retains what can survive of that discipline when its flawed assumptions are exposed and removed. Moreover, this constant analysis of worldview assumptions and presuppositions then generates an entire body of teaching and research offering general worldview analysis and assertions related to the essentials of a, or *the*, "Christian worldview" as well as other competing worldviews.

This integrationist or worldview perspective has unquestionably come to dominate the world of evangelical Christian higher education.[15] It is even possible to say how it happened that the Dutch Calvinist tradition came to have such wide influence. Wheaton College philosopher Arthur Holmes published *The Idea of a Christian College* in 1975, and in this book he made heavy use of "integration of faith and learning" language, which had been deeply influenced by his engagement with scholars of the Calvinist tradition.[16] Integrationism became a pivotal concept at Wheaton College under his intellectual leadership, and the influence of Wheaton as the flagship evangelical university cannot be overstated. Eventually, the Christian College Coalition (now the CCCU) adopted integrationist categories in its own discussion of the identity and mission of Christian colleges. This is now embraced as a matter of course by most of the over one hundred CCCU schools, many of which employ seminars, faculty workshops, and conferences to train their faculty in the concept and its practice.

Integration of faith and learning and worldview analysis have become key concepts at Union University under David Dockery in the last decade as we have moved aggressively into the wider CCCU orbit. It can be seen in our publications, in the president's articulation of our mission, in the development activities made available to faculty, in the criteria for faculty evaluation, and in the thought categories embraced by at least some of our students.[17] The language has to some extent also been employed in Baptist higher education circles more generally, though not always with much thoughtfulness and not without opposition.[18]

Inevitably, no popular idea goes unchallenged in academia, and integration of faith and learning via worldview analysis is no exception. Some objections are trivial and can be easily swept aside. For example, we can dismiss the objection that academic disciplines are purely objective and lack worldview presuppositions or assumptions. Surely we have progressed beyond that point in our postmodern intellectual world, with its cautious epistemological perspectivalism and its emphasis on the community contexts defining and determining what is considered to be true. We can likewise dismiss the naïve belief that well-established academic disciplines can be counted on to have trustworthy worldview foundations and that it is somehow wrong to challenge them. Such a claim would represent a faith itself rather than a defensible intellectual claim. We can dismiss the peevish rejection of the ascendant Calvinist perspective from those who simply don't like what they *think* they know about Calvinism or who tend toward jealousy of whoever happens to be on top at a given time.

It makes more sense to challenge a worldview idea on worldview grounds, and this is where the most significant objections lie. One could argue that even if God is sovereign, as Christians believe, we would be wise to be less than certain of *our limited human ability* to discover all of what the sovereign God has established as truth, or even less than certain that we understand Christian faith with full and unhindered clarity. Or one could question Calvinist anthropological pessimism, and thus have a greater confidence in the rational and empirical findings of the best practitioners of the social and natural sciences and humanities—even if they are working apart from a consciously applied Christian worldview. One could worry about the tendency in integrationist circles to dream of, and grieve over, a former Golden Age such as might have been found in thirteenth-century Paris or sixteenth-century Geneva, because nostalgia is rarely intellectually productive. Or one could be sufficiently postmodern to doubt that there can be such a thing as a "unity of all truth" in a world filled with incommensurable worldviews, perspectives, ways of knowing, narratives, communities, and life experiences. Finally, one could simply seek a stance of greater humility, tolerance for different perspectives, and epistemological modesty on the part of Christians.

For some, such as a team of Messiah College scholars in an important recent book, integrationist language lacks precisely such virtues.[19] Crystal Downing, an author in the Messiah College volume, proposes an *imbricationist* rather than integrationist model; imbrication is an architectural term meaning to overlap in multiple, interlocking, and not always neat layers.[20] The idea here is not just that Christian concepts overlap with secular ones, but that there are various overlapping Christian perspectives as well, and that to speak of integrating "faith" or "the Christian worldview" with "learning" does not accurately reflect the multiplicity and diversity of perspectives of all types as well as the various ways in which serious, faithful Christians do their scholarship—both in Christian and in secular institutional settings.

We have had similar quiet conversations on the Union campus, as some faculty members have wondered about whether integrationist language is adequate. Those who find themselves somewhat outside of the majority religious perspective in our community have perhaps inevitably asked the MacIntyrean question, "*Whose* Christian faith, *which* version of 'the' Christian worldview shall we privilege?" Behind such questions lies the fear that to embrace integration and worldview language is essentially to give a certain version of Reformed theology preeminence as the prevailing Christian vision on campus; or worse, to open the door to a kind of fundamentalism in which a single, very conservative Christian stance will come to be expected of all faculty members and indoctrinated in all students. Dockery understands these concerns and has clearly disavowed any kind of fundamentalist trajectory for Union, but still concerns remain among certain faculty members, which is perhaps inevitable in our denominational context.

A far-reaching objection articulated by the Messiah College team is the concern that worldview and integration of faith and learning privilege the disciplines of theology and especially philosophy.[21] That there are few workaday historians, biologists, and literature professors on our Christian college campuses who have the skills, training, or background to do adequate worldview analysis and full-blown faith/learning integration is not a coincidence. It can be argued that the integrationist approach asks every scholar in every discipline to function as a philosopher or theologian, and then when that proves impossible requires that each school hire more philosophers and theologians. Neither is it a coincidence, therefore, that Calvin's specialty has been the production of some of the nation's finest philosophers, such as Alvin Plantinga and Nicholas Wolterstorff. But how many such scholars can one hope to find?

Moreover, anyone with more than a passing familiarity with contemporary theology and philosophy knows that there are ways of doing work in these disciplines that differ from the worldview approach. For example, the growing emphasis on narrative in various disciplines today reminds us that one can explore texts and articulate theological claims in ways other than the doctrinal/propositional paradigm most common in worldview and faith/learning integration circles, as well as in conservative theology. Narrative theology especially is more open-ended, more willing to entertain questions and leave paradoxes unresolved, and more open to surprise and a variety of interpretations rather than a single normative "reading" or "answer." On the other hand, classic Christian theology has always found it important to emphasize that amidst a certain range of variations, subjective experiences, and open-ended questions there are certain settled doctrinal claims, often summarized as the *regula fidei* or rule of faith.[22] There is not just "faith" but *the faith* once delivered to the saints and passed on through the generations in every major branch of the Christian tradition. Here the debate in Christian higher education reflects the broader debate between theologians related to subjectivity and objectivity in the nature of (the) Christian faith.

A final, very important objection is this: the language of faith/learning integration and worldview seems to privilege the cognitive over the practical or, to borrow Dennis Hollinger's helpful categorization, to privilege the head over either the heart or the hands.[23] The idea is to develop a certain kind of worldview—that is, a way of looking at the world and thinking about it. Those are cognitive activities. Or, the idea is to integrate faith and learning—that is, to bring together in one's head the ideas communicated by the Christian faith with the ideas communicated by contemporary psychology or physics. Again, those are cognitive activities. But human beings are more than cognitive creatures. We have bodies as well as minds, emotions as well as thoughts. We pray and act, not just think and ponder. Certainly the best faith/learning integrationists understand this, usually emphasizing that ultimately integration of faith and learning must become integration of faith and *living*, and that ideas always have real-world consequences. But there are good reasons to question whether this faith/living integration "second step" is really where the energy is to be found in worldview and integrationist scholarship and teaching. Inadequacies in this area have been great enough to evoke a significant challenge from within the world of Dutch Calvinism itself.

The Education for Social Transformation Model

Former Calvin College professor Nicholas Wolterstorff, mentioned just above, played a key role in the modern articulation of the faith/learning integration model. According to James Bratt and Ronald Wells, Wolterstorff was the Calvin faculty member who resolved long-standing internal tensions in the Calvin vision with an integrationist proposal in 1975 that eventually won the day on that campus, including in its curriculum. Therefore it was actually Wolterstorff who interpreted the Kuyperian vision in a way that would allow the vision to be embraced not only at Calvin but more widely in the evangelical world.[24]

But Wolterstorff, a brilliant philosopher and prolific scholar who now teaches at Yale University, was not done. In 1982, he proposed that Christian colleges needed to shift to a new stage, moving beyond "integration of faith and learning" to "a collegiate commitment to social transformation." Working out of a "peace and justice" interpretation of Scriptures and Christian identity that reflected the convergence of his vision with the progressive evangelicalism of thinkers like Ron Sider and Jim Wallis, Wolterstorff proposed that the Christian college should become a force in society for engaging such issues as "peace and war, nationalism, poverty, urban ugliness, ecology, crime and punishment."[25] Wolterstorff has continued to work with such themes in various articles and books, including two recent books addressed to Christian schools of all types, not just colleges.[26] Eastern College sociologist and itinerant lecturer Tony Campolo has also made similar proposals in lectures related to what he calls "the radical Christian college."[27]

Bratt and Wells gently point out that Wolterstorff's proposals have made little headway at Calvin. The social vision of evangelical Christian colleges is, in general, quite conservative, as such schools are the products of various conservative Christian subcultures. The effort to employ the Christian college as a progenitor of politically and socially progressive values has had about as much success as broader efforts on the part of many, including myself, to broaden the political and social vision of evangelical Christians more generally.[28] Put directly, it is hard to get red-state, red-meat evangelicals to warm to the idea of their colleges as centers of criticism of American capitalism, consumerism, nationalism, and militarism. Evangelicals tend toward social conservatism, not progressivism and certainly not radicalism, though they do remain open to at least some aspects of the progressive vision when it is presented persuasively, on biblical grounds, by people whom they trust. Dockery has sought to define Union as a "great commandment university," focusing on love of both God and neighbor, a paradigm that has been employed in recent years to ground certain new or more visible moral commitments such as a growing emphasis on intercultural competence and racial reconciliation.[29] Still, no one would confuse Union's cultural vision with that of Tony Campolo or Jim Wallis.

The import of this proposal as it relates to Christian higher education is not, therefore, that dozens of Christian and/or Baptist colleges will soon start graduating thousands of politically progressive students. Indeed, it is far more likely that if a Christian college swung its mission in the direction of social engagement, it would articulate a socially conservative, pro-business, pro-patriotism message. This stance, for example, was an explicit part of the founding vision of Florida's Palm Beach Atlantic College in 1968. Burtchaell worries that capitulation to such political and economic conservatism is simply a variant of the corruption of the mission and identity of Christian universities, this time from the right rather than the left, and much more likely to happen among later-founded religious colleges.[30] No, given all of these factors, the cultural resistance to a progressive social transformation agenda is much too deep for it to get far with most Christian college presidents, trustees, donors, and even students, and on balance it is probably better to avoid shifting our sense of mission in this direction.

However, seeing the Christian college as an engine of progressive social transformation does point to a very different kind of vision for our universities. It is action-based rather than primarily cognitive; it is political rather than solely intellectual; and it engages culture in a very different way than the ideological combat most often treated as central in integrationist strategies. It reminds us that the Christian faith is about *orthopraxy*, not just *orthodoxy*. To be fair to Wolterstorff, his vision of social transformation emerges out of his dream that our colleges will be places of deep Christian intellectual engagement with the "major social formations" of American life. He proposes that "normative and strategic Christian reflection on our major social institutions is an obligation of the Christian community and a need of our society. . . . There is no better place to cultivate such reflection than in the Christian liberal arts college."[31] There is realism here. If the Christian college is to be an engine of any kind of positive social change, it must think its way there, not just act its way there. We cannot be all "hands" and no "head," any more than we can be all head and no hands. We will need our own internal moral, intellectual, and spiritual change before we will be interested in working for the right kinds of changes in the broader society.

Those schools already deeply committed to progressive social transformation along the lines of Wolterstorff's proposal tend to be institutions like Berea College, whose interpretation of the Christian faith has been progressive, transformationist, and praxis-oriented for decades. Schools like Berea remind us that a small number of the kind of colleges that Wolterstorff and

Campolo seem to be dreaming about already do exist. But they tend to be found in the kinds of faith traditions whose piety *organically generates* such moral commitments, rather than having such a vision imposed on them for a time by a cadre of influential faculty members or administrators. This leads to our third proposal for Christian higher education.

The Creation of a Pious Ethos Model

The idea that the central task of the Christian college is to create an ethos conducive to the development of godly piety goes back deep into the history of most such schools. In fact, it is probably not an overstatement to say that the "common sense" understanding of what Christian colleges exist to do, at least in pietistic circles, continues to land here. Baptist (and Methodist, Quaker, Anabaptist, and Pentecostal) families send their pious kids to their pious schools in the hope that when they graduate they will still be pious, not just in formal affiliation but in their hearts and in their lifestyles.

In fact, many have remarked that in traditions in which pietism and an emphasis on personal godliness run deep, the nurture of such godliness has often been seen as the primary task of the Christian university. Both Burtchaell and Benne notice this and see that it has long been characteristic of Baptist higher education, among other pietistic traditions.

In fact, Benne argues that the now-famous "two-sphere" or "add-on" vision of Christian higher education was once characteristic of Baylor, a school that he studied closely in *Quality with Soul.* The two-sphere approach basically means that classroom and chapel, or classroom and dorm room, are treated as two separate spheres, in that while what happens in the classroom at a Christian college will differ little if any from State U, student life will be pervasively and intentionally Christian as far as possible. The Christian faith is therefore an add-on to a "solid" general education taught along accepted lines in the broader culture.[32]

If this is the vision, the Christian university can hire faculty without significant concern about their religious convictions, except perhaps in the religion department. It is important that faculty and administrators set a good "Christian" (= moral) example, go to church, live a decent life, and so forth. But there exists no vision for any such project as integrating faith and learning or inculcating a Christian worldview, at least not in the classroom. However, outside of the classroom one can expect to find required chapel, revivals, mission trips, dorm Bible studies, Christian music and drama groups, and rather strict codes of personal morality. The goal is to get the student from orientation to graduation as a person who still prays, reads the Bible, goes to church, evangelizes, and refrains from immoral behavior, while also picking up as much "book learning" as possible along the way.

Many concerned Christian parents and other onlookers would be very happy if Baptist, and other Christian, universities did at least this for their sons and daughters, nieces and nephews, church members and graduates. But observers of Christian higher education now very widely recognize that at least in our time the two-spheres approach gives away the game before it really gets started. If ideas matter at all, and if any link exists between ideas and life choices, then the university that teaches, say, philosophical naturalism and materialism between eight and twelve cannot undo the damage between one and two at chapel, or over spring break on the mission trip, or in service-learning activities downtown. There may be some students who are able not to notice that their professors are actually teaching them the ingredients of a thoroughly agnostic secular life, or who are able to compartmentalize so profoundly that this has no effect on their prayer life or church attendance. But the evidence is in that at least the stronger and more attentive students all too often cannot fail to notice and cannot compartmentalize. Ideas have consequences, and piety is not enough. Unless some effort is made to bring Christian convictions to bear in the classroom itself, the Christian vision and identity of the school (and of its graduates) will not long survive amidst the swirling winds of a faith-corroding culture.

But this rejection of a merely two-spheres kind of pietism does not diminish the significance of creating a pious ethos as *one aspect* of an overall vision for Christian higher education. Benne himself consistently emphasizes that one ingredient necessary for "keeping faith" with the founding religious traditions of Christian universities is the creation of a meaningfully Christian ethos, and he commends those schools that do this. Though it is not a focus of this chapter, clearly the work of student life departments, campus ministry offices, and chapel programs are fundamentally important to maintaining the identity and vision of Christian universities. At Union, while we have rejected the two-spheres approach, it is abundantly clear that creating and maintaining a pious ethos of a Baptist and evangelical type for the university is a very high priority and a major selling point with both students and parents.

But the kind of ethos or atmosphere I am thinking about here goes beyond what student life officials can do. Our schools need not just a sweet-spirited cocurricular piety but a community of learning that is itself characterized by Christian spirituality, its practices and virtues. As Mark Schwehn has pointed out, the academic vocation requires subtle but critically important virtues, such as humility, self-sacrifice, faith, and charity, and a certain kind of community life, which he summarizes as friendship in the work of spirited intellectual inquiry.[33] Schwehn argues that such virtues are relevant to any academic community, and as such have been discussed for centuries in works as diverse as Plato and John Henry Newman.[34] They are most likely to survive today in a self-consciously Christian educational setting, though Schwehn and others are strongly advocating the renewal of such virtues in all institutions of higher learning.

Here form and function, educational content and educational delivery, are intrinsically related. The British model, for example—in which a relatively manageable number of teachers, visiting scholars, and students at various stages of their journeys gather together in residential colleges and live according to a common schedule of study, lectures, and shared conversation—is very different from the more mechanistic and assembly-line-like American schedule with which we are all so familiar. One is reminded also of the model of community life established by Dietrich Bonhoeffer when he served as leader of the Confessing Church seminary at Finkenwalde. This truly was life together, as the English edition of the book is titled. Bonhoeffer's community of seminarians lived together, practiced the spiritual disciplines on a common schedule, studied, talked, and worked, all in community, and all with the goal of developing a certain shared community life characterized by a set of common virtues, and not just acquiring a body of knowledge.[35] It seems, then, that what we need is the integration not just of faith and learning but of piety and learning, of spirituality and education, in meaningful and creatively designed forms of community. Here few American schools, including my own, have been able to make much progress in changing the educational paradigm so prevalent among us, even as we increasingly recognize the significance of the communal context of our educational enterprises.

The Transmission of an Ecclesial Tradition Model

A final approach to the intellectual vision and theological identity of the Christian university can be labeled as *the transmission of an ecclesial tradition.*[36] This is the most comprehensive vision of any yet discussed, and in some ways can be seen as synthesizing the other three approaches.

While I indicated above that the creation of a pious ethos was a goal of many who founded and have supported institutions of Christian higher education, there have always been some institutional founders and leaders whose vision has been bigger than that. These leaders, and the religious bodies they have served, have desired not just to create a pious ethos but to serve their sponsoring church bodies by participating in transmitting an entire ecclesial tradition—intellectual, theological, moral, and spiritual—from one generation to the next. This tradition-transmission process certainly includes whatever is understood to be normative piety, but it goes beyond piety to encompass the entire way of life of a particular faith community, including its intellectual tradition.

The vision of such universities is rooted in a confident and coherent sense of religious identity and an ongoing accountability relationship with their founding bodies. These are schools that are definitively and happily Catholic, Reformed, Lutheran, Anabaptist, Methodist, or whatever else. Generally speaking, the older, the sturdier, and the more comprehensive and coherent religious traditions have been the ones most likely to view their mission in this way. It has also helped in many cases when such faith traditions have been outside the dominant mainstream culture in our nation, and thus have been especially interested in preserving and transmitting what they perceive to be an endangered or marginalized way of life.

Here the case of the Catholic universities is quite relevant. Roman Catholics are heirs to a comprehensive and formerly "established" religious tradition in Europe, and yet in this country and in England they definitely saw themselves as standing outside the mainstream of society; in American life this view continued until well into the 1960s. This perception was well-founded and, unfortunately, constantly reinforced by the various forms of marginalization they experienced.

Catholic universities, then, were viewed by the church as an agency for communicating Catholic values to Catholic young people in a hostile culture. As such they were a kind of extension of the well-developed network of Catholic parochial schools as well as numerous other distinctive expressions of Catholic educational and religious life. The Catholic college, like the Catholic parochial school, needed to be a place where the distinctive Catholic way of life, in its entirety, could be communicated, and where the Catholic identity of impressionable eighteen- to twenty-three-year olds could be nurtured and safeguarded. This way of life included head, heart, and hands; that is, doctrine, worldview, traditions, emotions, morality, piety, worship, service, social engagement, and every other aspect of Catholic identity and practice.

There was no question that Catholic universities existed, and many still exist, to serve the cause of the Catholic church in relation to Catholic young people in America. A great preponderance of those associated with such schools at every level (trustees, administrators, faculty, staff, and students) were committed to the Catholic faith and expected their schools to be faithful in transmitting it. Certainly this remains the vision of the Catholic university that is held by the Roman Catholic hierarchy, as evidenced by Pope John Paul II's 1990 encyclical *Ex Corde Ecclesiae*. Here the pope argued that those who teach theology at Catholic schools must do so in keeping with the faith tradition that they represent and to which they are responsible. "One consequence of its essential relationship to the Church is . . . the institutional fidelity of the University to the Christian message."[37] Academic freedom in Catholic universities is not absolute but rests within these confessional boundaries, because Catholic universities exist to serve the church and not themselves.

Benne's analysis of the University of Notre Dame concludes that despite the transformation of the Catholic role in American life and major changes in Catholic higher education, Notre Dame still retains much the same vision, even while striving to be a major "mainstream" American research university. (Not every observer is quite as sanguine about the survival of an authentically Catholic vision at Notre Dame.) Benne is most impressed with the various ways in which Catholic values and practices are both taught and modeled in cocurricular life, while expressing some concern about slippage at the faculty level, due to the hiring of too many non-Catholics, some of whom are hostile to the university's core vision.[38] Still, he is able to describe Notre Dame as a fairly effective bearer and communicator of a comprehensive religious tradition from one generation to the next. Richard Malloy, a professor and campus minister at St. Joseph's University, argues that it is not easy to communicate Catholic values to a body of students, many of whom are only culturally Catholic when they enter the Catholic university. Surely this is the case at Notre Dame as well, for few young people of any tradition are immune to the secularizing impact of contemporary culture.[39] But when schools such as Notre Dame and St. Joseph's find ways to communicate the Catholic tradition and imprint it on such students without compromising appropriate standards of academic excellence, their work clearly serves the church even while also advancing the work of the academy.

Why can't other church-related colleges do the same thing? This appears to be the driving question behind *Conflicting Allegiances,* a provocative collection of essays edited by Michael Budde and John Wright in 2004.[40] The underlying vision motivating this work will be familiar to anyone who has read Alasdair MacIntyre or Stanley Hauerwas, the Duke University theological ethicist. Emphasizing such postmodern themes as narrative, character, and community, the book argues that most church-related or "Christian" colleges and universities have accepted the forms of thought prevailing in "liberal" higher education. By "liberal" they mean political liberalism. The term takes in much of the modern way of organizing Western societies. This social/political order has included a co-optation of the churches, which often serve as tame expressions of liberal (American, democratic, secular, individualistic) values rather than demonstrating any countercultural allegiance to the lordship of anything resembling the biblical Christ. Instead, what is needed is for Christians to form themselves into coherent faith communities whose polity reflects biblical patterns rather than the prevailing patterns of American culture.

Conflicting Allegiances represents an extension of that thesis into the realm of Christian higher education. It is a thought experiment in which various scholars attempt to imagine what Christian higher education would look like if its polity was this kind of church rather than the "general public" of a liberal, secular, American democracy or the tamed churches that are one expression of that public. The writers speak as if such schools are entirely a thought experiment, as perhaps they may seem to be from the perspective of weary warriors in post-Christian or accidentally pluralist universities. Their point is well-taken insofar as they argue that the more universities take their cues from secular sources rather than their founding churches or a coherent Christian vision, the more their Christian identity will erode. But neither they nor we have to go entirely into the land of imagination to find schools that are at least partially successful at serving as agents of transmission of an entire ecclesial faith tradition. To do so, though, it helps to not be too comfortable in Babylon, too cozy with the powers and "worldview" of the culture as we find it, either here or anywhere else. The paradox, of course, is that the more successful our schools are by prevailing standards, the more our status and prestige will rise, which only increases our taste for more of the same—at the risk of our soul.

Toward an Intellectual Vision and Theological Identity for Baptist Higher Education

I did not offer a discussion of how Union University is doing in relation to this fourth and most comprehensive proposal because it raises broader questions of whether any Baptist college or university can function as the transmitting agent of our entire ecclesial tradition.[41] It is not at all clear that our tradition is sufficiently coherent to be transmitted *by anybody*, whether the university or any other agency. It is also not clear whether our student bodies constitute a sufficiently coherent community that a tradition can be transmitted *to* them; somebody must be there on the other end of a tradition-transmission process with a readiness to receive it. This leads us directly to the question of whether there can be a governing intellectual vision and theological identity for Baptist higher education, the presentation of which is the goal toward which this essay has been moving. And it suddenly plunges us into some pretty deep waters related to challenges facing our people as a whole, challenges that go far beyond the ivory tower and the issues facing Baptist higher education. To signal my conclusion, it seems to me that *only if Baptist universities contribute to the reform of the Baptist people through our education of the coming generation will our schools ultimately be able to be effective transmitters of any kind of meaningful ecclesial tradition*. But such a reform will require Baptist universities to throw their windows open to some fresh winds blowing our way from the broader tradition of the Christian church. Let me explain what I mean.

Douglas Henry, Michael Beaty, Scott Moore, and other Baptist scholars at Baylor are among those who are raising important questions about whether certain *design flaws* (my phrase, not theirs) in common understandings of Baptist theology make it likely that Baptists will inevitably, in Henry's somber words, "die the death of continued accommodation to culture,"[42] including the secularization of their universities. Burtchaell's searching analysis of the erosion of Christian identity at Baptist universities has contributed to my concern that our problem is not that we have failed in our implementation of an essentially sound theological and ecclesial vision, but that the vision itself may be flawed. I do not argue, with Mark Noll, that Baptists have made no "distinctly Baptist contribution to the life of the mind."[43] Instead, I worry that the distinctive contribution we *have* made has in many ways not been a constructive one.

After twenty-six years in Baptist life, I have now come to share what I read as the great uncertainty of many fellow Baptist scholars about whether our most important Baptist distinctives are adequate to accomplish our God-given mission as a people, including but not limited to our educational mission; this uncertainty is stimulated not just by the current higher education debate but by my entire experience of life in our denomination. Therefore, the proposal I make here about the identity and vision of our Baptist universities has everything to do with the identity and vision of our Baptist churches and the future of our entire fractured denomination.

Before offering my proposal I must begin with critique of where we are. Let's start with Burtchaell's analysis. He argues that many Baptist schools end up disengaging from their originating Baptist vision (as well as the churches, people, and beliefs of their denomination) for six reasons.[44] These reasons follow, along with my comments about their impact on our schools:

(1) The survival of Baptist colleges has "required the recruitment of non-Baptist students to such an extent as to make it difficult to sustain a Baptist ethos on the campus." *Problem: the lack of a critical mass of Baptist or even Christian students interested in a core Baptist or Christian vision, and therefore the lack of a coherent community of learners to whom a tradition could be transmitted.*

(2) Most Baptist educators sought to create nonsectarian schools that were "necessarily Christian but not necessarily Baptist." This "encouraged the view that the Christian faith included few essential and simple components and it discouraged an overzealous inquiry into their meaning."

Problem: the intentional or unintentional failure to develop a full-blown theological tradition that would then be available for reflection, discussion, and transmission.

(3) Baptist ecclesiology was sufficiently conversionist and individualistic that Baptist colleges could not understand themselves as "representing a functioning church actively seeking to develop its faith. There was little conviction that they might need to be functionally Baptist, not just Baptist-founded, Baptist-sponsored, Baptist-related." Baptist universities cannot serve the Baptist church as Catholic universities serve the Catholic church because there is no Baptist church, only autonomous and endlessly diverse Baptist churches. *Problem: the lack of a sense of peoplehood or corporate identity sturdy enough to be transmitted across generations by the Baptist university or anyone else.*

(4) Baptist commitments to the sole authority and sufficiency of the Scriptures has privileged biblical interpretation as the chief intellectual task and skill, and yet Burtchaell argues that "Baptists have not produced many outstanding biblical academicians . . . [and] their exegesis has been undisciplined" by any "shared communal understanding of the Scriptures." *Problem: the lack of an agreed-upon authoritative method of resolving differences between diverse and often idiosyncratic biblical interpretations, leading to intellectual and theological fragmentation and conflict.*

(5) Baptist commitments to soul competency, in which "the individual is the sovereign, or at least autonomous, interpreter of Scripture," has led us to fail to realize that "the elaboration of faith is a shared intellectual task" in the community of faith, and thus the authoritative boundaries established by our various covertly established hermeneutical traditions (or idiosyncratically arrived at by the soul-competent individual) cannot be fully inspected and critiqued. *Problem: the lack of a recognized process or authoritative agents responsible for retrieving, assessing, revising, and transmitting tradition, all essential parts of the traditioning process.*

(6) Our rejection of the authority of any kind of creedal formulations has meant that "the contemporary generation is sovereign and not accountable to any persons or texts between the New Testament and the present." But because the transmission of faith is always tradition-bound and has at least an implicit creedal dimension (which simply means that as a community we set theological boundaries, we confess that we definitely believe THIS and we refuse to believe THAT), this anticreedalism just means that our "clandestine tradition . . . does not permit enough open and conscious deliberation for it to be adequately cultivated as every generation has need." *Problem: the lack of historical*

awareness, lost access to resources of the church's tradition, and difficulties in setting doctrinal boundaries.

In recent papers, Henry, Moore, and Beaty affirm various of these concerns related to Baptist distinctives, while raising other issues.[45] Henry and Moore hone in especially on the philosophical underpinnings of Baptist emphases on liberty, soul competency, and the autonomy of the local church. Moore, for example, argues that free-church Christians, such as Baptists, are implicit Cartesians.[46] Descartes helped inaugurate modernity in offering his famous formulation, "I think, therefore I am," and Baptists function as faithful modernist Cartesians when we say, "I read the Bible and it says this *to me*, therefore this *is* what the Bible says and no one has the right to tell me anything different." A common slogan in some Baptist circles is "being Baptist means freedom." But Henry argues that our understanding of this Christian liberty, at least as far back as E. Y. Mullins, takes its cues "too uncritically from modernity's misguided notions of freedom, and thus . . . regard[s] liberty as a right disjoined from the good." Beaty, following Martin Marty, points out that this also makes Baptists very American; in fact, one could say that we live in a "baptistified" culture that glorifies liberty and autonomy above all values.[47] It is a dubious contribution. If Baptists had paid more attention to the historic Christian tradition, we would have been able to locate the significance and *telos* of freedom in a way that better protected us from "the hyper-individualistic form of autonomy emblematic of modernity."[48] Henry traces the "cultural captivity" of our churches, colleges, and Christians, at least in part, to this misunderstanding of freedom, so that "with fewer and fewer exceptions, twenty-first-century Baptists are virtually indistinguishable from the mainstream culture."[49]

It should also be added here that this distorted understanding of Christian liberty helps to make sense of the controversy that fractured our denomination beyond recovery and damaged our educational institutions. Especially beginning in the 1960s, theological and to some extent ethical slippage away from classic Christian orthodox beliefs in our colleges and seminaries was detected by concerned participants and observers. Criticism of this slippage often evoked the freedom defense on the part of those criticized. The response to this response eventually became a hard-line "conservative resurgence" that sought to arrest it by employing an often very narrowly interpreted Bible. *Precisely because they/we were all Southern Baptists*, neither the conservatives nor the moderates were generally well-informed or deeply rooted in the broader tradition of the church, a tradition that might have shown us how to draw the right kinds of boundaries. Thus, the conservatives (in the name of the Bible) sometimes attacked what did not deserve to be attacked, while the moderates (in the name of freedom) sometimes defended what did not deserve to be defended. How desperately we needed at that time the perspective that could have been offered by the wisdom of the Christian tradition in its broadest and richest formulations. How desperately we still do need that wisdom.

I want to argue that as a starting point the normative theological identity of any institution of Christian higher education, including Baptist universities, should be classic, orthodox, ecumenical Christianity—the understanding of the Christian faith that is rooted in the authoritative, trustworthy, and truthful Scriptures and articulated in the classic orthodox creeds that are a shared treasure of the church universal.[50] This turn to the broad tradition of the church universal, and the development of a new kind of ecumenism built upon it, is one of the major theological and ecclesial developments of our time.[51] This cannot fairly be described as a narrow or "tightly drawn" confessional boundary, nor can its turn to the creeds and confessions be fairly described as wholly alien to the Baptist tradition.[52] But it is true that self-conscious and consistent reflection on this classic ecumenically orthodox Christianity is alien to our customary way of doing things as Baptists—and this is to our great detriment.

As one paradigm, a Baptist college could follow Timothy George's practice at Samford's Beeson Divinity School and emphasize a normative role for the Apostles' Creed, the church's earliest and most basic creedal statement and one still employed in many churches today. If this rather spare confession were treated as the theological boundary-setter for an institution of Christian higher education, it would create a tent big enough to include classic Roman Catholicism, Eastern Orthodoxy, and Protestantism—a tent, in other words, much bigger than that now employed in most of our Baptist colleges and universities, especially in their religion departments. How refreshing it would be to have such rich diversity on our faculties. How often it would spare us tedious intramural debates about petty issues that only a very narrow range of Christians actually still care about. One can only imagine the constructive trickle-down effect that would mean for our churches. Yet this tent would *not* be big enough to include modernist or in some cases postmodernist revisions of classic Christian theology—which would, indeed, make it a smaller tent than that now employed in some of our Baptist colleges and universities.[53]

Given the grave problems that we face in general, and especially the problems that we have in transmitting a coherent theological and ecclesial tradition, I have wondered whether the preservation of Baptist universities *qua* Baptist universities really matters in the twenty-first century. Certainly there is little that *all* Baptists now have in common, and given the diverse streams of tradition that have shaped who we are as a people, this result is perhaps not a surprise. Of course, in recent years we have gone through a messy series of conflicts, the support of our denomination for higher education seems to be fading, and the identities of our schools are all over the map. Why not just go for ecumenical orthodoxy or perhaps an evangelical identity, and leave the Baptist label behind?

While I am open to finding more compelling reasons from within the Baptist theological tradition, such as those that William Hull outlines in his chapter for this volume, my reason for thinking that Baptist identity should be preserved is primarily strategic at this point. A theologically coherent school with a sustainable religious identity needs a particular sponsoring body to which it primarily relates. It should at least attempt to keep a critical mass of faculty, staff, students, administrators, and trustees from that tradition. Therefore, Baptist colleges and universities should seek to preserve their Baptist identity, as should Catholic, Lutheran, and Dutch Reformed schools in relation to their particular traditions. But the particular should relate to the universal with due respect, as Henry argues. We must humbly identify our tradition as one expression of the Christian tradition, and we must bring our understanding of our tradition into submission to that broader tradition.[54] All efforts to promote Baptist distinctives must be made within the context of ecumenical orthodoxy, including the rethinking of those distinctives where necessary.

Rooted in this kind of reformist appropriation of ecumenical orthodoxy, Baptist universities should seek to serve our sponsoring churches (and the church universal) in the transmission of the finest available version of the Baptist expression of the Christian tradition. At their best our schools will be sufficiently coherent in our Baptist tradition as to transmit that tradition with authority and cogency, while also being hospitable environments for students who do not come from the majority Baptist tradition but who will recognize the family similarities to another branch of the great tradition of the church.

The transmission of such a Baptist Christian ecclesial tradition includes all elements that were discussed in part 2 of this chapter. It includes the entire ethos of our Baptist tradition, such as its morality, spirituality, and theology, with constant inflows of fresh resources drawn from broader ecumenical orthodoxy. The creation of a pious campus ethos is certainly an appropriate aspect of this project, including chapel programming, dorm activities, mission trips, and student-life principles for living in community. It also includes the communication of the social and political vision of the Christian faith, along with constant reflection on its adequacy and occasional practice in social and political engagement. It involves the teaching of the conflicts, as well as the consensus, to be found within our Baptist tradition and the great tradition.

Certainly any coherent religious tradition has an intellectual dimension, and therefore the Baptist Christian university needs many loci for the communication of this content. This should include not only Bible classes but also various curricular and cocurricular means of transmitting our essential theological, moral, and ecclesial convictions. It certainly requires the presence of compelling administrative and faculty leaders who both embody and communicate the tradition.

Whether the intellectual project of the Baptist Christian university should be understood as "the integration of faith and learning" or the inculcation of "the Christian worldview" is debatable. As one surveys the landscape of classic Christian thought, it is clear that there have been both separatist (Tertullian) and integrationist (Clement) visions for how Christians should relate to non-Christian thought forms and perspectives. At our most confident, the church has happily "plundered the Egyptians," making use of whatever fits with Christian faith while being unsurprised that the entire corpus of human learning does not always fit very easily with Christian convictions. The classic Catholic formulation is that "grace perfects nature," and if this is so, then the stance toward even secularized academic disciplines need not be quite so relentlessly critical as it often seems in the integrationist or worldview model.

On the other hand, much depends on how deep and pervasive the alienation becomes between Christian convictions and the beliefs and practices prevailing in a given culture at any given time. This helps explain how Thomas Aquinas could be relatively sanguine about the works of culture while Pope John Paul II sounded much more strident notes in many of his writings. The church in Germany discovered to its horror during the Nazi years that with some worldviews there can be no Christian compromise, and that the relentless inculcation and strenuous fight on behalf of a Christian principle (such as the sanctity of *all* human life) sometimes is all that stands between a society and the abyss. In general, it is enough to say that the Christian intellectual task is to transmit its own tradition and to interpret contemporary realities accurately in light of that tradition. A more formal statement of intellectual vision for our Baptist colleges and universities might be something like the following: *Our vision is to offer students an excellent, culturally relevant education, exposing them to the full range of thought and behavior in contemporary life, with all subjects taught in a manner that reflects intelligently on the connections, tensions, convergences, and contradictions between such thought and behavior and the Christian tradition, especially in its Baptist expression.* Clearly, such an approach does not have to mean adopting the Reformed theological perspective or educational strategy. It does require critical engagement with the intellectual, social, and political currents of every time and place from the perspective of the Christian intellectual tradition in its Baptist expression.

Can Baptist universities be places in which this kind of theological identity and intellectual vision are pursued? Frankly, the jury is still out. I believe that Baylor and Union University are both Baptist schools that for the past ten years have been trying to do something like what I am proposing here, with Baylor moving more in the direction of an ecumenical and "critical mass" environment and Union taking the more "orthodox" and explicitly "evangelical" approach. There are certainly sufficient numbers of Baptists in places like Texas and Tennessee to educate, certainly enough to sustain a critical mass in our Baptist universities if we want it and if we have a coherent vision to offer them. Students emerging from many of our churches and homes have the raw ingredients of the piety needed to enliven a truly Christian university, and they are quite remarkably open to the riches of the broad church's intellectual tradition. They are often very much aware of the corrosive currents of modern culture and are looking for resources to resist them.

Baptist universities rooted in an orthodox ecumenical vision, critically aware of the particularities of Baptist identity, and effective in intelligently bringing this kind of Christian faith to bear on all aspects of contemporary life and thought can be successful in twenty-first-century higher education. We can meet the felt and real needs of students while transmitting a compelling and comprehensive version of the Christian tradition to the next generation. In so doing we could make a profound contribution to the life of our fractured people, now scattered both within and outside the Southern Baptist Convention. In fact, I believe that if our fractious, wounded, and yet beloved people are to find renewal, that renewal will probably come from universities that pursue a vision like the one I am proposing here. It would not be the first time that the renewal of the Christian church emerged from the halls of the Christian university.

Chapter Three

Building on a Shared Identity within a Shared History

William E. Hull

It is not easy to talk about "The Purpose of Baptist Higher Education" in these troubled times. When I mentioned my assigned topic to a faculty colleague, he responded, "Why do we even need a distinctive *Baptist* approach? Shouldn't the education we offer simply be excellent rather than parochial?" With a mindless anti-intellectualism running high within our denominational ranks, some educators have begun to experiment with other Christian traditions,[1] only to discover from the exhaustive reports of George Marsden, Mark Noll, and James Burtchaell that the situation is not really any better in those camps.[2] All of Christian higher education is squeezed between a secular relativism on the left and an ideological rigidity on the right. Our denominational enterprise is certainly beset by enemies on every hand, but at least they are *our* enemies whose ways have been well known to us for generations;[3] thus I doubt if we need to borrow any new briar patches in which to do our work.

The genius of Baptist higher education has always been its close connection to the life of our churches. From this source we have drawn many of our students, a significant portion of our funding, and a sizable public constituency. In a thoughtful study of six schools in five different Christian traditions, Robert Benne emphasized that "sponsoring churches . . . supply the persons, ethos, and vision that are needed to shape the identity of the school and guide its mission."[4] While it is important to maintain good relations with those denominational entities that broker our relationships with a host of cooperating churches, Baptist polity is so decentralized that these mediating agencies, such as state conventions, do not have the power to sustain our meaningful connection to Baptist life if such is not widely desired and continually reaffirmed by the affiliated congregations.[5] It is no longer enough just to have Baptist trustees who elect a Baptist president who secures Baptist funding.

Instead, if there is to be a future for Baptist higher education, it must be grounded in a shared vision of what it means to be Baptist that is embraced both by our schools and by a critical mass of our churches. In recent years, many of our most thoughtful leaders best equipped to work on forging such an understanding have neglected this challenge either because they think that the age of denominations is coming to an end or because they think that the Baptist mind is hopelessly divided regarding its own identity. But as Glenn Hinson, one of our more ecumenical scholars, has repeatedly emphasized, "I think it is critical to the future of Baptists (as to the future of Christianity) to say, 'This is our tradition, and it distinguishes us . . . from many other traditions.'"[6] Or as Carol Holcomb put it, "Baptist colleges must find their identity within their own tradition or simply indulge in self-hatred and allow themselves to be colonized by a foreign Christian ethos that is neater, cleaner, and less ridden with baggage."[7]

In quest of a vision that both our schools and our churches can accept because it embodies those central distinctives constitutive of our shared identity, I shall briefly recount the core of our Baptist story, then ask how this expression of the Christian faith—our denominational DNA, if you please—is relevant to the educational enterprise in which we are engaged. Indeed, I would hope to show how these allegedly "parochial" features might even make American higher education more "excellent" because they effectively address some of the key concerns troubling the academy today. I ask only that these suggestions be received in the spirit of modesty with which they are offered, not as a comprehensive philosophy of education or a sweeping blueprint for institutional reform, but as a way of deserving the name Baptist by being faithful to who we really are.[8]

Remembering the Baptist Story

Baptists were conceived and gestated in the enormous ferment stretching from the Renaissance through the Reformation, which launched the modern era in Western civilization. Building on the fearless witness of Wyclif and Hus, Luther dared to set his solitary convictions shaped by Scripture above the collective consensus of the ruling church and to follow those existential commitments wherever they might lead. When the second wave of this Reformation reached England in the late sixteenth century, those determined to rid the Anglican church of the last vestiges of "popery" came to be called Puritans because of their concern for the "purity" of the faith. Frustrated by long delays and meager results, the more impatient of these reformers organized themselves into voluntary congregations and covenanted together to put into practice without delay the marks of a true church, thus earning such countercultural epithets as Separatists, Nonconformists, Independents, and Dissenters.[9]

Violently persecuted as sectarians, one such group from Lincolnshire under the leadership of John Smyth sought asylum in Holland where they were influenced by Mennonites in the Anabaptist tradition. In 1609 they accepted the New Testament practice of believer's baptism and applied it to thirty-seven of their members, thereby becoming the first of what would be called Baptist churches in the historical sense of that term. Note two features of this originating impulse that are often neglected or misunderstood. First, while deeply indebted to the Protestant principle, Baptist identity was even more radical than that, for it represented an effort to reform the Reformation. Our movement arose not in protest against a corrupt Catholicism, but in protest against an incomplete Protestantism. Second, to contest the established church was not simply a matter of tinkering with ecclesiastical machinery. Rather, it represented a frontal challenge by ordinary citizens to the authority of the monarch, to the cultural norms of society, and to the exclusive prerogatives of a clerical hierarchy. Indeed, the very existence of Baptists was subversive of the status quo existing in the Old World since classical antiquity.

Proof of this startling claim was provided when Baptists moved to the New World only to find themselves bitterly harassed for two centuries (1633–1833), not only by Anglicans in the South, but by their Congregationalist cousins in the North.[10] The banishment of Roger Williams from the Massachusetts Bay Colony by the Puritans in 1635 may be taken as prototypical of just how alien the Baptist idea was until the full implications of the American Revolution began to be grasped early in the nineteenth century. But even then, as Baptists entered a period of rapid growth spurred by the Second Great Awakening, spokesmen such as John Leland functioned to confound both the cultural and religious elites of the day by insisting on the right to think for oneself no matter what the results might be.[11]

This iconoclastic impulse[12] has continued to characterize the worldwide spread of Baptists to the present day.[13] It is striking to observe the close correlation between patterns of growth and their political context. In Old World countries dominated by established churches, such as England, Scandinavia, and Continental Europe, Baptists are weak or in decline. In New World countries with a strong tradition of religious liberty, such as the United States, Baptists are strong but growing only modestly. In Third World countries, however, where a fierce struggle for religious freedom is under way, such as Brazil, Nigeria, and Korea plus China and Russia, Baptist life is most vital and growth most rapid.[14] It is not accidental that Baptists seem to flourish best in places where non-elites are pushing the envelope of freedom.

Now that we have summarized the story that highlights some of our most basic Baptist genes—voluntarism, religious liberty, the right of self-determination, the uncoerced conscience—I wish to select three components of this denominational identity as foundational for our educational vision: responsible dissent, revolutionary democracy, and relational discipleship.

Responsible Dissent

First, our very nature as nonconformists is rooted in a sober awareness of human fallenness that feeds a discontent with the status quo even, or especially, as regards religion. Baptists emerged as deconstructionists before their time, keenly aware that the elites of their day enforced monopolistic thinking, not merely to ensure social stability, but to exercise control. By protesting the power moves lurking behind the exalted language of creeds, oaths, and edicts, Baptists were making an invaluable contribution to that sense of agency which encouraged ordinary people to take destiny into their own hands rather than bowing to an inscrutable fate or to the dictates of an entrenched aristocracy.[15] Nothing is more foundational to the populist paradigm of higher education pioneered by Baptists on the American frontier than this sense that every individual has both the right and the competence to question one's inherited lot in life and to seek a better way.

But some are quick to say that Baptists in America can no longer function as dissenters because they have moved from the margins to the mainstream of our national life. William McLoughlin states the case well: "By entering the mainstream the Baptists ceased to be critics of American society; their piety relaxed, and they became the captives of the culture against which they had fought so long."[16] This critique has cautionary value, but it overlooks the way in which the biblicism of Baptists nourishes a deep desire to recover and replicate the normative expression of apostolic faith found in the New Testament, a faith that forever challenges principalities and powers no matter how successful its adherents become. Insofar as Baptists bear witness both to their story and to their Scriptures, they will be summoned to the essential task of responsible dissent.[17]

Is any task more essential to the cultivation of an inquiring mind?[18] Each advance in human understanding is almost always preceded by a prolonged period of protest against conformity to the status quo, as a host of intrepid iconoclasts can readily attest. The very nature of the creative impulse is fraught with struggle, harboring a dialectic of discontent over things as they are. As Picasso put it, "Every act of creation is first of all an act of destruction."[19] And yet, despite the crucial importance of challenging convention as an antidote to scholarly groupthink, academics on all sides find the professoriate taking refuge in rigid stereotypes of professorial thought police enforcing political correctness. In the name of such polarizing labels as "conservative" and "liberal," agenda-driven ideologues attempt to stifle opposing viewpoints by resorting to inflammatory accusation, deliberate boycott, and media-driven uproar.[20] At a time when the academy ought to be showing our nation how to protect its hard-earned freedom of speech, it has instead used intimidation to place a host of sensitive issues off-limits even to courteous, reasoned debate.[21]

The Baptist vision of responsible dissent stands in sharpest contrast to these increasingly restrictive tendencies in the academy. Its enormous importance for higher education has been well expressed, appropriately enough, by the now embattled president of Harvard University:

> In many ways, this commitment to seeking truth through contrasting positions is what is best about great universities. . . . If one has to identify a single source for the human progress that has transformed the lives of every one of us, it is the idea of skeptical inquiry; of confronting belief with evidence; of submitting ideas and convictions to the possibility of falsification—and in no other type of institution is that process more central.[22]

Let me seek to apply this insight to the curriculum and do so in a way that claims the Baptist right of dissent. For years, our preferred model, which we borrowed from Evangelicals at schools such as Wheaton and Calvin, has been to integrate faith and learning, typically described as understanding each academic discipline from the perspective of a Christian worldview.[23] Each term in the formula is weighted with difficulties. To "integrate" means to complete or make whole by combining equals,[24] but in this case are the uniting partners sufficiently of the same order to permit such a fusion? Further, does the Christian faith, either in Scripture or in church history, have only one worldview, or is its universality seen precisely in its amazing adaptability to many worldviews?[25] Again, do the academic disciplines have a stable worldview, or do their perspectives endlessly evolve or even mutate amid the many "paradigm shifts" that academics love to claim?[26] Certainly both faith and learning are essential to a wholistic education, each having a valuable contribution to make to the other, but to "integrate" them is, in my view, both a theoretical and practical impossibility.

Instead, my suggestion is that Baptists belong at the opposite end of the spectrum with a model that seeks not to *integrate*, but to *interrogate* the curriculum with the Christian faith. Rather than using one theological worldview to shape one disciplinary worldview as most compatible with the Christian faith, let the competing theological and disciplinary worldviews continue to interact with each other rather than trying to elide selective elements into a monolithic structure. In the two-thousand-year sweep of the Christian story there have been remarkable synthesizers such as Augustine and Aquinas, Luther and Calvin, but has there ever been a worse time than the present to bring closure to higher education's open-ended quest for truth? The best thing we can teach our students now about the knowledge explosion that has created information overload is not how to give the right answers but how to ask the right questions.

So what kind of questions about the curriculum does being Baptist prompt us to ask? A short sampling might include the following:[27] Does this discipline reflect a diversity of viewpoints which are allowed to challenge one another in free debate? Does it encourage a vigorous critique of views held by the professor and empower students to make meaningful choices rather than expecting assent to an established position? Does it avoid a totalist and therefore potentially totalitarian approach to its intellectual domain by renouncing epistemological triumphalism in advancing its claims? Does it probe the reigning orthodoxy in its own field as relentlessly as it probes dogmatic certainty in the field of religion? Does it utilize its findings to empower the marginalized rather than to benefit the privileged, especially those in big business and big government who sponsor its research? Does it stimulate the kind of moral and spiritual reflection that fosters a quality of life characterized by growth toward maturity? Does it embolden passive learners to become active leaders willing to work creatively and courageously for human betterment?

Revolutionary Democracy

Second, Baptist dissent at its best was not merely iconoclastic but was animated by the confidence that such protest could inaugurate a new age of spiritual freedom. Already the Protestant Reformation in Europe had been the harbinger of a new mood of self-determination in religious matters, but the Baptists resolved to carry that principle to its logical conclusion, which would require liberating the faith from coercive control by any earthly power, especially the heavy hand of the autocratic state. Consider just how audacious that enterprise proved to be. By defying the right of kings and magistrates to regulate religion, Baptists were challenging the Constantinian paradigm that had prevailed in Christendom for more than a millennium.[28] Indeed, they were inverting the hierarchical pyramid of top-down authority that had ruled Western civilization since its origins and replacing it with a bottom-up polity that anticipated the democratic revolutions of the modern era.

So momentous was the transformation to which Baptists lent their witness that it would not be an exaggeration to describe their hope as eschatological in nature.[29] By this I do not mean the expectation of an imminent Parousia to end history—although millennialism did surface during the excitement of the Great Awakenings—but rather the inauguration of a whole new order in human affairs discontinuous with the old.[30] The distinguishing practice of believer's baptism, which was a *re*-baptism in its earliest expression, represented both a rejection of the inherited past and the acceptance of a fresh start not only in the life of the individual but in the understanding of the church as well. Furthermore, the insistence of rebels such as Roger Williams that the state had no right to coerce or control the individual conscience[31] demanded the development of a pluralism-of-equals that eventually became essential to the acceptance of American diversity.[32] As the first president of the Southern Baptist Convention, William Bullein Johnson, put it, "The right which I exercise in holding *my* views of divine truth, I cheerfully accord to all others to hold *theirs*."[33]

Note the profound relevance for our day of the Baptist determination to free not only the practice of religion, but even the dictates of conscience from domination by the state. Only a few years ago we thought that the new century and millennium would begin a year early on January 1, 2000, with a computer crash, but instead, it began almost a year late, on September 11, 2001, with a World Trade Center crash. Just as the Cold War of the West with communism defined the last generation, so the assault by Middle Eastern terrorists seems certain to dominate the next generation. Suddenly, and by surprise, we have a whole new geopolitical agenda that profoundly affects everything we teach. Samuel Huntington has taught us to call it a "clash of civilizations"[34] that pits the two most powerful religions in the world against each other in a cultural, ideological, and political "holy war," or *jihad*. With as many as 4.5 million male "students" as young as seven years of age being tutored in terror as future "holy warriors," or *mujahedeen*, in ten thousand mosque-based schools called *madrassas* in Pakistan alone, this conflict will be with us for years to come.

For our purposes, it is amazing to observe how remarkably this conflict reenacts the originating struggles of Baptist identity. Once again we have an assertion of religious absolutism by a clerical hierarchy of *ayatollahs* that enjoys the protection of theocratic states noted for their autocratic ways that have largely disenfranchised the majority of their citizens, especially women. Lacking a system of checks and balances not only *within* government, as with the separation of the executive, legislative, and judicial branches, but also *between* government and other forces in society, such as a free press, free schools, and free churches, a fanatical fringe of Islam has been allowed to run wild for lack of what I have identified as the distinctive Baptist contribution to democracy.

Listen to the way in which a British Roman Catholic, Andrew Sullivan, has grasped the centrality of this issue:

> The issue of religious fundamentalism . . . was the central question that led to America's existence. The first American immigrants, after all, were refugees from the religious wars that engulfed England and that intensified under England's Taliban, Oliver Cromwell. . . . Following [John] Locke, the founders established as a central element of the new American order a stark separation of church and state . . . [which] led to one of the most vibrantly religious civil societies on earth. . . . It is this achievement that the Taliban and bin Laden have now decided to challenge. . . . What is really at issue here is the simple but immensely difficult principle of the separation of politics and religion. . . . We are fighting for religion against one of the deepest strains in religion there is.[35]

Despite the centrality of religious freedom to the American experience, the lure of theocracy is ever with us. For Jews, the Zionist impulse which led to the re-establishment of the nation of Israel had strong theocratic implications. For Catholics, the waves of immigrants from Old Europe imported Constantinian notions of theocracy to our shores while, for Protestants, the resurgence of a neo-Calvinism has had a similar effect. Emerging from their fundamentalist rootage, evangelicals such as Jerry Falwell and Pat Robertson have done much to keep the theocratic hope alive in that broad coalition called the religious right. Black church leaders turned to the federal government for relief during the civil rights movement and are tempted by the largesse of "faith-based initiatives" to form even closer alliances today.

All about us the historic "wall of separation" between church and state is being breached, especially in this fearful time when praying to God, displaying the Ten Commandments, and rallying around the flag have become virtually indistinguishable. Even some Baptists are aggressively working to "establish" their favored expression of Christianity as a privileged religion in the public square, not by monarchical edict, but by executive order, congressional legislation, judicial decree, and constitutional amendment.

In the present world crisis, a great deal of serious intellectual work needs to be done to ensure that Christianity is not perceived as an American religion or even as a Western religion but as a global religion without allegiance to any country or culture. If our religious interests are no broader than our national interests, then they serve only to deepen the divisions that condemn the world to perpetual strife. As never before, this is a time to concentrate on the commonalities that unite the three great Abrahamic faiths, chief of which is the monotheism that they all emphatically affirm.[36] For if there really is only one God, then this universal deity must be the God of us all, friend and foe alike. Unless we cleanse religion of tribalism and nativism, we will soon be back to the internal and external religious wars that wracked Europe for a century (1556–1648) and spawned a scientific secularism that is still with us today. The historic Baptist understanding of religious liberty is not some denominational oddity, a mere hiccup on the side of history. Rather, it offers an essential contribution to the post-9/11 geopolitic by enshrining the insight that the awesome spiritual power of religion must never again be linked to the equally awesome temporal power of the state if any semblance of democracy is to survive.

Relational Discipleship

Third, by dissenting against the established church, by repudiating the protection and privileges afforded by the state, and by forsaking a guaranteed supply of new members through infant baptism, the Baptists chose to occupy a precarious position which made urgent their need for mutual reinforcement to compensate for the traditional bulwarks of support now denied them. This they found in a sweeping redefinition of the church primarily as a decentralized fellowship dominated by personal relations rather than as a centralized institution dominated by an ecclesiastical hierarchy.[37] This profound bondedness to one another caused the community to function as a spiritual democracy long before that polity found widespread political expression.[38] The sense of solidarity fostered by their life together gave balance to the individualism necessitated by the free exercise of an autonomous conscience. So strong were the ties that bound their hearts in Christian love that it provided the essential context for the development of their discipleship.

The rejection of any officially sanctioned status has not penalized the Baptists, however, but actually serves to strengthen our witness because it challenges every member to work in concert as a priesthood of believers rather than relying on clerical authorities or on political props to ensure success. Emil Brunner shrewdly recognized that our insistence on voluntary affiliation carries with it the inevitability of competition for adherents which "has had a beneficial effect in that it has compelled the churches to exert themselves. Only by remaining vital could they exist at all."[39] Social scientists are increasingly emphasizing the importance of this dynamic in building a "supply side" or "marketplace" model of religion.[40] That is, in a regulated religious environment, established churches tend to become lazy monopolies because they need not compete for "customers," whereas, in a free market, churches successfully compete for "customers" only by offering more and better religious services. All of this is to say that Baptists put primary stress upon the quality of relationships that exist in each local expression of their life together.

Since the *koinōnia* central to Baptist religious life can have a wide variety of secular applications, let us look now at how it speaks directly to a great need in higher education today. From the founding of the colonial colleges until the late nineteenth century, a belief in the unity of truth meant that education aimed to develop the total person, especially the formation of character as well as of intellect. When our Baptist forebears chartered the Rhode Island College (now Brown University) in 1764, they inserted in its charter this purpose statement: "Institutions for liberal Education are highly beneficial to Society, by forming the rising Generation to Virtue [,] knowledge and useful Literature & thus preserving in the Community a Succession of Men duly qualify'd for discharging the offices of Life with usefulness & reputation."[41] Symbolic of the centrality of virtue to the entire curriculum was the tradition that the president teach every student a senior capstone course on moral philosophy which sought to unify the educational experience within a Christian framework.

But with the rise of the research universities, the scientific method of study gradually separated fact from value and morality from religion with the result that, in less than a half-century, character formation vanished from the curriculum.[42] While some schools have sought to bridge this chasm through such cocurricular activities as service learning, most campuses today find themselves without a moral compass at a time when their students are confronted on every hand with the seductions of ethical anarchy. In his 2004 Hester Lecture, Thomas E. Corts eloquently reminded us of just how subversive the prevailing culture has become to Christian values and just how saturated our students are in the ethos of that culture.[43] As lurid portrayals of promiscuity laced with hard-core profanity fill movie, television, and computer screens, a trivialized and even debauched vision of life seeps into the subconsciousness of students by stealth where it lurks to overwhelm the occasional glimmer of goodness that may come from classroom or chapel.

Well known for his scathing satires of New York and Atlanta,[44] the novelist Tom Wolfe has recently aimed his rapier thrusts at the contemporary American campus in a sprawling, brawling tale called *I Am Charlotte Simmons*.[45] He was drawn to the subject when he realized that college has "more and more replaced the church as the source of new . . . ethical outlooks" at a time when, "with a few exceptions, universities have totally abandoned the idea of strengthening character. . . ."[46] In breathless prose he recounts how a teetotaling, God-fearing virgin makes her way from the mountains of North Carolina to the prototypically elite Dupont University in Pennsylvania on the strength of her perfect 1600 SAT score. Expecting to live the life of the mind, she is instead confronted on every hand with binge drinking, predatory sex, and relentless peer pressure to participate. The plot is every parent's nightmare:

how can my child retain her very identity in such an environment? Alas, in Wolfe's telling, the fervent Christianity of Charlotte's "momma" disappears as an influence in her daughter's struggle to determine who she really is.

In graphic fashion, Wolfe has described one of the most urgent challenges facing the American academy today, namely, how to overcome the Cartesian cleft between fact and value[47] so that education and ethics will again work in partnership as contributors to the formation of character. Otherwise, the most desirable trees of knowledge in the groves of academe will continue to offer forbidden fruit with its bitter legacy of shame and guilt resulting in a conflicted life of alienation east of Eden (Gen. 2:15-17; 3:1-24). The central thrust of the Baptist response is not to offer a philosophical solution to the cognitive problem of competing epistemologies but to contend that a wholesome sense of identity and integrity is best nurtured through the development of responsible relationships in small, close-knit communities of character.

Readers of this volume know as well as I do the many ways in which we seek to implement this ideal on our campuses, but let me mention just three, lest we come to take them for granted. First, to give insecure entering students living away from home for the first time a fighting chance to preserve the values brought with them from family and church, we may prohibit the sale of pornographic magazines in the bookstore, or block X-rated sites on the Internet, or deny all-night visitation privileges in single-sex dorms, or refuse to permit alcoholic beverages on campus. But the loss of freedom from these so-called restrictions is nothing compared to the loss of freedom students experience when overwhelmed by peer pressure from fellow students. Second, Baptist schools typically offer core courses in the crucial freshman year for classes of 25–30 students staffed by permanent full-time faculty who post and keep office hours, while many public universities offer their foundational work in sections of 250 students taught by temporary graduate instructors who disappear after class to work on their dissertations. Third, we tend to stress the kind of teaching and learning, best described in the writings of Parker Palmer, that seeks to transform the class itself into an academic expression of *koinōnia* where love replaces fear, mutual respect replaces faculty elitism, sharing replaces competitiveness, and hospitality replaces loneliness.[48] It is in this kind of climate that individuals can express bold dissent while deeply valuing those with whom they disagree.

Conclusion

When Jacques Derrida died, the nimble-minded and eminently quotable Stanley Fish "was called by a reporter who wanted to know what would succeed high theory and the triumvirate of race, gender, and class as the center of intellectual energy in the academy." He answered like a shot: "religion," because "that is now where the action is."[49] Is it coincidental that the runaway best-selling fiction (*The Da Vinci Code*), nonfiction (*The Purpose-Driven Life*), and cinema (*The Passion of the Christ*) are all explicitly religious? Or that religion came to dominate the 2004 presidential campaign? Or that any wars soon likely to be fought are almost certain to be religious wars?

Some of this enormous ferment is a manifestation of good religion, but much of it is a manifestation of bad religion, which means that hosts of students will be asking hard questions which only a wide range of well-trained scholars are prepared to answer. Baptist educators are well positioned to make a vital contribution to this global dialogue if only we will rise above our fratricidal strife and regain a strong vision of our normative identity. We need not claim that our heritage offers the only way, or even the best way, but that it is *our* way, given us by the providential Lord of history. So let us make the best of it for such a time as this.

Chapter Four

Fostering Dissent in the Postmodern Academy

Bill J. Leonard

I

In 1890, William Whitsitt, president of the Southern Baptist Theological Seminary, Louisville, wrote:

> I am casting about to begin writing a work on American Baptist History. It is an Herculean task, and I must keep it all to myself. Baptist History is a department in which "the wise man concealeth knowledge." It is likely I shall not be able to publish the work while I live, but I can write it out in full and make arrangements to publish it after my death, when I shall be out of the reach of bigots and fools.[1]

Whitsitt knew whereof he spoke. By 1899 he had resigned his position under pressure from those Landmark leaders whose theology of Baptist succession he challenged with his historical investigations. Today, few would dispute Whitsitt's findings that Baptists did not begin to practice immersion until 1641, some thirty years after their beginnings in Amsterdam. Yet the conflict that surrounded his research anticipated controversies that have swept over Baptist institutions for more than a century. Indeed, Baptist history in the United States is replete with examples of conflicts that from time to time descend upon Baptist-related schools nationwide. Issues are diverse and divisive, creating upheavals for school trustees, administrators, and faculty, and often spilling over to students, alumni, and church constituencies. During the last century, such controversies occurred over the teaching of evolution and the historical-critical method, dancing on campus, the acceptance of government funds, faculty publications, adherence to confessions of faith, required chapel, and institutional governance.

Baptist higher education in America began as early as 1764 when Rhode Island College (later Brown University) was founded. A bold, but ultimately unsuccessful, attempt at a national Baptist college was undertaken in 1821 with the inauguration of Columbian College in Washington, D.C. Other state Baptist schools soon followed. Historian Donald Mathews observed, "By the 1830s Methodists and Baptists were energetically establishing educational societies throughout the South in an attempt to broaden the scope and constituency of Evangelical [and denominational] education."[2] During the 1830s and 1840s Baptists founded colleges to educate their ministers and extend benefits of economic and communal success to their churchly constituency.

Other Baptists resisted this effort, however. In the "Black Rock Address" (1832) Old School (Primitive) Baptists argued against Baptist-based higher education, outlining the difficulties these schools would encounter. They opposed "sectarian colleges"—denominational schools—because the existence of such institutions implied "that our distinct views of church government, of gospel doctrine and gospel ordinances, are connected with human sciences, a principle we cannot admit."[3] They feared that Baptist identity would be swept away or watered down if it became associated with the liberal arts. They also objected to the creation of "divinity" or religion faculties or programs since teaching theology or religion suggested that God's truth was "a human science on a footing with mathematics, philosophy, law, etc." They feared that Christian distinctiveness would be undermined by making Christianity simply another academic subject. The "Black Rock Address" repudiated the idea that those "called to preach" should be required to have any sort of formal theological education, suggesting instead that God would allow "no man to preach his gospel, till he has made him experimentally acquainted with that gospel, and endowed him with the proper measure of gifts suiting the field he designs him to occupy."[4] They believed that God, not theological faculties, would take care of the "called." These Old School Baptists were insightful in their awareness of the dangers Baptists would face in their programs of higher education. They anticipated then some of the very issues that we continue to discuss and debate today. Many of the concerns they raised are evident (often with a vengeance) in questions such as these: How can Baptist identity be maintained amid the pluralism required by a liberal arts education? How is a religious studies curriculum distinct from and parallel to other segments of a liberal arts curriculum at a Baptist-related school? What is the nature of ministerial education for a generation more concerned about the generic Christianity of nondenominationalism than the sectarian distinctiveness of a vanishing denominational system?

Earlier controversies in Baptist higher education in the South were moderated—a relative term—by the cultural hegemony that Baptists maintained inside southern culture and by their loyalty to denominational programs. Indeed, as I have written elsewhere, the links between southern culture and the Southern Baptist denominational system forestalled or localized many controversies that descended on seminaries and colleges throughout much of the twentieth century.[5] Baptist schools received young people from Baptist churches, educated them in a context of the liberal arts with required religion classes, mandatory chapel, Baptist campus ministry, spring revivals, and summer missions. Graduation sent them back to their respective churches to serve as laity or clergy in service to the community and the kingdom of God. Those called to ministry moved on to a Baptist seminary where they were taught by Baptist professors who prepared them for service in Baptist churches, missions, and educational institutions or for other "denominational service." A relatively intact denominational culture meant that there was general consensus as to what it meant to be Baptist, and the Baptist system created both protection and vulnerability for denominationally controlled schools.

In the South, debates often involved internal struggles over the nature of Baptist history and polity as represented in Landmarkism, a successionist movement that set agendas for churches and schools regarding the nature of the church, baptism, communion, localism, and history. Professors were sometimes disciplined over issues related to biblical authority, the nature of salvation, excessive Calvinism or Arminianism, and other positions deemed outside the Southern Baptist "norm." External struggles regarding new science, philosophy, and theology spilled over into Baptist life in debates over evolution, the historical-critical method of biblical studies, German theology, the social gospel, and other signs of liberalism. Yet, as intense as many of these debates became, they were generally moderated by the constituency's commitment to Baptist denominational identity in the context of southern regionalism. Southern culture carried with it a kind of de facto establishment with Baptists as the "unofficial official" religion throughout the region. However, controversies and conflicts often set the conservative middle of the constituency against the "orthodox" right and the "progressive" left. In distinct but parallel ways, these latter two groups often criticized the centrist majority, a group too bound to denominational loyalty and tradition to stand up for either doctrinal orthodoxy or social justice.

Maintaining traditional Baptist identity today is complicated by the essential collapse of Anglo-Baptist culture in the South during the last thirty years. Transitions shaped by racial integration, ecumenism, pluralism, evangelicalism, nondenominationalism, and secularism have contributed to a variety of "disconnects" in the traditional Baptist system.[6] These tensions arose during the 1970s and 1980s through certain efforts of the "orthodox" party to establish a "course correction" that would retake or restructure the entire denominational system of the Southern Baptist Convention—national, state, and regional. Much of the initial effort was focused on the issue of liberalism in Baptist-related schools of higher education. The "orthodox" party required conformity to a particular type of confessionalism centered on the doctrine of biblical inerrancy and made certain blanket condemnations of Baptist-related educational institutions as arguments for the need for a correction in the direction of the convention and its agencies.[7]

The "orthodox" party successfully captured control of denominational agencies by appointing trustees committed to their type of conservative agenda. When these trustees gained a majority, they moved to replace school administrators and set in motion policies that would remove nonconformist faculty on a short-term and long-term basis. By the mid-1990s this effort had created significant changes in the faculties of the six denominational seminaries.

These developments in the national SBC have produced varying responses from state Baptist convention-related colleges and universities across the South to these denominational realities. Some institutions have redefined, indeed, renegotiated their traditional relationships with their parent Baptist bodies, changing their charters and gaining institutional control of their respective boards of trustees. Certain schools—Samford and Baylor, for example—revised their charters in order to select their own trustees but retained financial and familial ties to their denominational constituencies. Others—Richmond, Furman, and Wake Forest—relinquished all formal connections to the state conventions. Still other schools—Mercer, Mississippi College, and Carson Newman College—retain their traditional relationships and continue to negotiate with an increasingly divided state constituency. Others, most recently Louisiana College, have been caught up in controversy regarding orthodoxy, institutional control, and confessional conformity, all of which have created significant upheaval and unrest on campus. For many schools that continue to be owned, operated, and funded by state conventions, conflict and tension may erupt at any moment.

Ironically, while these denominational controversies continue, large segments of the Baptist constituency, churches and students alike, have moved away from denominational loyalty altogether, seeking a more nondenominational and evangelical Christianity. This has introduced an increasingly more complicated reality for many Baptist-related schools that seek to define themselves less as sectarian/denominational institutions than as generic Protestant evangelical institutions. The burgeoning evangelical, nondenominational influences often lead schools into the mainstream of Christian evangelical life, which creates a new set of tensions with some of their traditionalist Baptist constituency. Indeed, the impact of nondenominational, mega-church, and emerging church cultures in the United States now presents major challenges for traditional congregations, denominations, and church-related schools across a wide theological and ideological spectrum. Social historians and other analysts now describe a very different religious culture in the South in the 2000s than existed in the 1980s.[8]

From an historical perspective these apparently unending controversies often revolve around two questions of institutional identity: What does it mean to be a Christian-oriented, church-based institution, and what does it mean to be a Baptist-related institution? Many contemporary Baptists worry that their distinctions as a denomination will be or have been lost because of the incipient pluralistic character of the modern or postmodern university. In other words, the nature of a university requires an acceptance of diversity in curriculum and constituency that tends to undermine the "Baptistness" of the institution, to lessen the perceived importance of the institution's historic Baptist origins, and to weaken the institution's connections with Baptist communions. As student bodies and donor bases become more diverse, as faculties engage more persons with limited Baptist or even limited Christian commitments, and as denominational connections are called into question or abolished, how will schools relate to their early Baptist "heritage"? If confessional requirements are not essential for defining Baptist identity, then what is?

Likewise, many Baptist institutions struggle with just how far to go in affirming a distinctively Christian identity. Does the appellation "Christian university" apply to schools that are intentional about the promotion of a distinctively Christian ethos in belief and practice throughout campus life? If so, then which type of identity—Catholic/Protestant, Evangelical/Old Line, denominational/nondenominational, confessional/nonconfessional—will define the Christianity that is at the center of the university experience? Will a certain generic Christianity suffice in order to allow for a breadth of faculty and student dialogue? Does a "Christian university" have a particular mandate to address health care, staff salaries, and working conditions in peculiarly "Christian" ways?

Many believe that the primary, perhaps the only, choice lies between blatant secularization of the college campus and the explicit Christianization (if not Baptistification) of a school's educational ethos. But are there other choices than becoming Brown or Wheaton? How might the Baptist past inform the individual and institutional future?

II

Before we attempt to answer these questions that arise from contemporary attempts to delineate Baptist identity, it might be fruitful to study theological and political dissent among Baptists, particularly the relationship between dissent, believers' church, and individual conscience in early Baptist life. Such dissent did not exist for itself, but was a direct outgrowth of Baptist commitment to a church composed only of believers, those who could testify to a work of grace in their hearts. Likewise, such dissent was clearly related to Baptists' concern for the freedom of conscience and the nature of uncoerced faith. A concern to define and protect freedom of conscience led Baptists to oppose established religion and to develop principles of religious liberty that anticipated modern and postmodern pluralism. These aspects of early Baptist identity might be helpful in addressing the unending quest for what it means to be Baptist in the postmodern era, especially in terms of higher education at Baptist-related colleges and universities, and might inform religious conversations on campuses where questions of diversity, pluralism, and "voice" seem unending.[9]

Baptists began as a community of dissent. They challenged establishment hegemony in a variety of ways. As nonconformists, they refused to varying degrees to abide by the imposition of religious uniformity demanded by the state-based church of their day. They believed that individuals should not be compelled to support financially and devotionally a church in which they had no voice, and they sought to separate themselves from any church that compelled belief by virtue of birth, status, or culture.

Anglican Daniel Featley's critique of seventeenth-century Baptists illustrates their basic nonconformity. He provides the following list of Baptist distinctives:

> First, that none are rightly baptized but those who are dipt.
> Secondly, that no children ought to be baptized.
> Thirdly, that there ought to be no set form of Liturgy or prayer by the Book, but onely by the Spirit.
> Fourthly, that there ought to be no distinction by the Word of God between the Clergy and the Laity but that all who are gifted may preach the Word, and administer the Sacraments.
> Fifthly, that it is not lawful to take an oath at all, no, not though it be demanded by the magistrate.
> Sixthly, that no Christian may with good conscience execute the office of civil magistrate.[10]

Worse yet, they proliferated their views throughout the land. As Featley noted, "the presses sweat and groan under the load of their blasphemies."[11]

Clearly Baptists represented an establishmentarian's nightmare. Every article in this fascinating list reflects degrees of nonconformity among Baptists in terms of theology, worship, and civic activity. In short, Baptists, like other sectarians in seventeenth-century England, were political and religious dissenters. Their Anglican detractors insisted that they were yet another reason for the necessity of the Clarendon Code and other acts against Puritans and other nonconformists.

A similar dissent was evident among Baptists in the American colonies in response to the Puritan establishment. Roger Williams, the erstwhile proto-Baptist, was thrown out of godly Boston in 1636 and into the "howling wilderness" of the New England winter for preaching "the same course of rigid separation and anabaptistry which Mr John Smith at Amsterdam had done."[12] He also exercised political dissent by insisting that the Native Americans were the sole owners of the American land and should be justly compensated for it. In exile, Williams was saved by the Narragansett Indians from whom he purchased land to found Providence Plantation, a place he hoped would "be for a shelter for persons distressed of conscience. . . ."[13]

For these early Baptists, then, dissent was grounded in the freedom of conscience, individual and communal. Indeed, references to conscience as a foundation of dissent regularly punctuate early Baptists' responses to religious and political establishments. Baptist leader Leonard Busher wrote in a 1614 treatise entitled *Religions Peace: or, A Plea for Liberty of Conscience*: "No king nor bishop can, or is able to command faith; That is the gift of God, who worketh in us both the will and the deed of his own good pleasure."[14] He warned, "And as kings and bishops cannot command the wind, so they cannot command faith; You may force men to church against their consciences, but they will believe as they did afore, when they come there; for God giveth a blessing only to his own ordinance, and abhorreth antichrist's."[15] He suggested that "Bishops should know, that error and heresy cannot be killed by the fire and sword, but by the word and Spirit of God."[16]

Busher also delineated seventeen reasons for refuting efforts to persecute dissenters. He argued that the church's persecution of dissenters provided a "negative witness" to those outside the church, threatening the evangelical dynamic of the gospel. It also gave impetus to "Jews, Turks, and Pagans" to persecute Christians, an observation no less meaningful in the twenty-first century than in the seventeenth. Likewise, he concluded that "through forcing men to church by persecution, the true-hearted subjects are forced out of the land, and out of the world. Some [are] banished, others burned, hanged, and imprisoned to death."[17]

Thomas Helwys's classic work, *A Short Declaration of the Mystery of Iniquity* (ca. 1612), was perhaps the earliest Baptist document to articulate issues of conscience directly. One of his most quoted passages begins, "Let the King judge, it not most equal that men should choose their religion themselves, seeing they only must stand themselves before the judgment seat of God to answer for themselves, when it shall be no excuse for them to say, we were commanded or compelled to be of this religion by the king or by them that had no authority from him."[18]

John Smyth's views on conscience are evident in an article included in *Propositions and Conclusions*, written in 1612 by schismatic Baptists who remained in Amsterdam and sought admission to the ranks of the Mennonites. It declared,

> That the magistrate is not by virtue of his office to meddle with religion, or matters of conscience, to force or compel men to this or that form of religion, or doctrine: but to leave Christian religion free, to every man's conscience and to handle only civil transgressions (Rom. Xii), injuries and wrongs of man against man, in murder, adultery, theft, etc., for Christ only is the king, and lawgiver of the church and conscience (James iv. 12).[19]

Helwys apparently went beyond Smyth in extending liberty of conscience to non-Christians and atheists alike. He wrote, "Let them be heretics, Turks, Jews, or whatsoever, it appertains not to the earthly power to punish them in the least measure."[20]

Some seventeenth-century Baptist confessions also address issues of conscience. These include the General Baptist *Standard Confession* of 1660 and the Particular Baptist Second London Confession of 1688. The *Standard Confession* asserts, "That it is the will, and mind of God (in these Gospel times) that all men should have the free liberty of their own Consciences in matters of Religion, or Worship, without the least oppression, or persecution, as simply upon that account."[21] It affirms Baptists' desire to "be subject to the higher Powers, to obey the Magistrates," but quickly adds, "But in case the Civil Powers do, or shall at any time impose, things about matters of Religion, which we through conscience to God cannot actually obey, then we with *Peter* also do say, that we ought (in such cases) to obey God rather than men; Acts 5.29."[22]

The Second London Confession, a hallmark of English Baptist Calvinism that parallels the Westminster Confession, states clearly that "God alone is Lord of the Conscience, and hath left it free from the Doctrines and Commandments of men which are in any thinking contrary to his Word, or not contained in it."[23] However, as a solidly Reformed document, Second London cautions: "So that to believe such Doctrines [that are contrary to his Word, or not contained in it], or obey such Commands out of Conscience, is to betray true liberty of Conscience; and the requiring of an implicit Faith, and absolute and blind Obedience, is to destroy Liberty of Conscience, and Reason also."[24]

Similar phrases are utilized in the Orthodox Creed of 1679 written by General Baptists who apparently flirted with Calvinism.[25] It states:

> The Lord Jesus Christ, who is king of kings, and lord of all by purchase, and is judge of quick and dead, is only Lord of Conscience; having a peculiar right so to be. He having died for that end, to take away the guilt, and to destroy the filth of sin, that keeps the consciences of all men in thraldom, and bondage, till they are set free by his special grace. And therefore he would not have the consciences of men in bondage to, or imposed upon, by any usurpation, tyranny, or command whatsoever, contrary to his revealed will in his word, which is the only rule he hath left, for the consciences of all men to be ruled, and regulated, guided by, through the assistance of his spirit. And therefore the obedience to any command, or decree, that is not revealed in, or consonant to his word, in the holy oracles of scripture, is a betraying of the true liberty of conscience. And the requiring of an implicit faith, and an absolute blind obedience, destroys liberty of conscience, and reason also, it being repugnant to both, and that any man, can make that action, obedience, or practice, lawful and good, that is not grounded in, or upon the authority of holy scripture, or right reason agreeable thereunto.[26]

This is perhaps the strongest and clearest statement in any of the Baptist confessions delineating the relationship between conscience, scripture, and uncoerced faith. Its opposition to the "requiring of an implicit faith" seems as relevant in twenty-first-century Saudi Arabia and North Carolina as in seventeenth-century Britain. (By the way, the Orthodox Creed is the only one of these seventeenth-century English Baptist confessions that supports the use and orthodoxy of the Apostles', Nicene, and Athanasian creeds.)

These references help to clarify what Baptists thought the role of conscience ought to be in Baptist life, in the church and in the public square. First, it appears that for these early Baptists conscience was closely related to uncoerced faith. Faith that was required, decreed, or otherwise based in "blind obedience" was no faith at all. Second, this understanding of the radical nature of conscience did not exist for itself but was somehow bound up in the overall work of Christ and faithfulness to the word of God. Like Luther, Baptists could declare that their consciences were "captive" to the word of God. The individual could indeed determine the meaning of scripture and challenge the prevailing hermeneutics of religious establishments and tradition. This approach to Baptist identity has led me to suggest that the genius of the early Baptists, at least in part, may be found in their belief that "the people can be trusted to interpret Scripture aright through the inner guidance of the Holy Spirit within the context of a community of faith."[27] And third, inside the community of faith, conscience and dissent were inseparable from the idea of a believers' church and the authority of Christ mediated through the congregation. Indeed, one of the things that made seventeenth-century Baptists dissenters was their understanding of the nature of the church over against that of the Anglican establishment with its mandated episcopal authority. Yet conscience also meant that those inside the church could claim Baptist identity while interpreting scripture in ways that were contradictory—Arminianism and Calvinism, for example.

Baptist concern for dissent and conscience is distinct in that it is founded on an experience of God's grace through Jesus Christ. Thus, dissent and conscience existed within a community of believers. Baptists spoke of a regenerate church membership. As the *Orthodox Creed* noted, "those who are united unto Christ by effectual faith, are regenerated, and have a new heart and spirit created in them through the virtue of Christ his death, resurrection, and intercession, and by the efficacy of the holy spirit, received by faith."[28]

Baptists believed that the congregation of believers appealed directly to the authority of Christ without the mediation of bishops, presbyteries, conferences, or other judicatories. Paul Fiddes suggests that the foundation of the "Baptist experience" begins with the belief that

> the presence of the kingdom of God which can be known in all the world is experienced in the church as the rule of Christ in the congregation. The liberty of local churches to make decisions about their own life and ministry is not based in a human view of autonomy or independence, or in selfish individualism, but in a sense of being under the direct rule of Christ who relativizes other rules. This liberating rule of Christ is the foundation of what makes for the distinctive 'feel' of Baptist congregational life. . . .[29]

There was, in short, a covenant relationship between Christ and the community of faith. Smyth's 1612 confession from Amsterdam gives evidence of this idea early on in this assertion: "That the church off CHRIST is a company off faithful people I Cor. 1.2. Eph. 1.1. separated from the world by the word & Spirit off GOD. 2 Cor. 6.17. being knit unto the LORD, & one unto another, by Baptisme. I Cor. 12.13. Upon their owne confession of the faith. At. 8.37. and sinnes. Mat. 3.6."[30] "Knit unto the Lord" and to one another by baptism is a powerful description of a covenant community of believers. God made covenant with the redeemed, and they made covenant with one another.

Yet the role of conscience and the autonomy of independent faith communities are implicit in the same confession in the following statement: "That as one congregation hath CHRIST, so hath all, 2 Cor. 10.7. and that the Word of GOD cometh not out from any one, neither to any one congregation in particular. I Cor. 14.36. But unto every particular Church, as it doth unto all the world. Coll. I.5.6. And therefore no church ought to challenge any prerogative over any other."[31] Congregations, duly constituted by "faithful" baptized believers, were bound by a communal conscience that was responsible only to God. Members were bound by covenant with God and each other to be faithful to Scripture as they saw it, even when it set them over against other like-hearted congregations. While later Baptists surely qualified this radical autonomy at least a bit through associational relationships, they continued to assert the importance of communal conscience.

These dissenting ideas regarding congregationalism and conscience had implications for Baptist responses to hermeneutics, church polity, religious liberty, and ultimately pluralism, but they created an inevitable tension between individual and communal appropriation of conscience. That is, while Baptists assert the importance of the relationship between the individual and the community of faith, they have a theology and polity in which individual conscience can set the one member against the community, and one local congregation against other congregations, while all remain faithful to various Baptist identities and convictions. Recent religio-political divisions in the United States have revealed frustrations at both ends of that spectrum as some have bemoaned the rabid individualism evident in those who (it is said) use the idea of the priesthood of all believers as a kind of carte blanche for believing anything they wish and still remaining Baptist, and those who demand uniformity to creed, confession, or ideological positions and exclude those who disagree.[32] From the beginning of their history, Baptists anchored conscience and its resulting dissent solidly in their theological understanding of the nature of the church as a believers' community in which the authority of Christ was directly received. Yet this kind of personal and communal autonomy meant that Baptists could and did divide over multiple ways of interpreting Scripture and of being Baptist, raising an ever-present possibility that conscience could lead to divisions inside the church.

In the public square, Baptists' understanding of church, conscience, and dissent produced what in many cases turned out to be even more radical results. In fact, one might suggest that in their concerns for freedom of conscience and religious liberty in the general society, Baptists anticipated religious pluralism more immediately than any other Protestant communion. Many Baptists in England and America insisted that God alone was judge of conscience, and therefore no religious or political establishment could judge the nonconformist, the heretic, or even the atheist. The belief that liberty could be extended to heretics and atheists was radical for its time and came to highlight Baptist identity in the New World. Ever our teacher, Roger Williams asserted in *The Bloudy Tenent of Persecution for the Cause of Conscience Discussed* (another reference to conscience), "That a civil sword, as woeful experience in all ages hath proved, is so far from bringing or helping forward an opposite in religion to repentance, that magistrates sin grievously against the work of God."[33] Williams likewise anticipated pluralism with his suggestion that non-Christians could function as effective citizens of the colonies. He asked "whether or no such as may hold forth other worships or religions, Jews, Turks, or anti-christians, may not be peaceable and quiet subjects, loving and helpful neighbours, fair and just dealers, true and loyal to the civil government." He concluded that, "It is clear they may, from reason and experience in many flourishing cities and kingdoms of the world."[34]

Dr. John Clarke, Williams's contemporary and the founder of Newport colony, was also an outspoken proponent of freedom of conscience and religious liberty. In a treatise known as *Ill Newes from New England; or, a Narrative of New-Englands Persecution,* Clarke acknowledged his Baptist commitments, writing that "a visible believer, or Disciple of Christ Jesus . . . is the only person that is to be Baptized, or dipt."[35] Of conscience, Clarke declared, "No such believer, or Servant of Christ Jesus hath any liberty, much less Authority, from his Lord, to smite his fellow servant, nor yet with outward force, or arme of flesh, to constrain, or restrain his Conscience, no nor yet his outward man for Conscience sake."[36] The charter of Rhode Island incorporated these ideals, noting,

> No person within said Colony, at any time hereafter, shall be in any wise molested, punished, disquieted, or called in question for any differences of opinion in matters of religion, . . . but that all and any persons may, from time to time, and at all times hereafter, freely and fully have and enjoy his and their own judgments and consciences in matters of religious concernments throughout the tract of land hereafter mentioned.[37]

Thus, Rhode Island became, in the eyes of many New England Puritans, a "rogue's harbor," a seedbed for dissenters and religious perverts from throughout the colonies. Thomas Cobbet, the Puritan anti-Baptist, knew exactly what would happen if such a Baptist vision of church and society prevailed. He wrote that if the dissenters "are to be let alone unrestrained and [un]punished, both civil government and state and churches here [in New England] would soon be blown up and we should become a very chaos."[38] And he was right, in a way. Rhode Island seemed a religiously chaotic place if ever there was one. Quakers came in droves, Jews established America's first synagogue, Baptists divided among Particulars, Generals, Six Principle, and Seventh-Day, and even the infamous woman teacher/preacher Anne Hutchinson, exiled from Boston, found sanctuary there.

Conscience and religious liberty did not mean silence or nebulous syncretism, however. Baptists debated, dissented, and argued with their opponents (and each other) unashamedly. And that is the paradox. Baptists spoke of ideas freely, strongly, passionately, but began by asserting the right of others to do the same. Conscience is not merely tolerated by an actual or de facto majority; it belongs to every individual. Yet the right to belief according to conscience does not mean that everyone is right. Baptists have not hesitated to express their disagreement with those—Quakers, for example—with whom they differed. Williams's anti-Quaker tract "George Fox Digg'd Out of his Burrows" is a case in point. Baptists seemed to have known through experience that it was only through religious liberty that this kind of debate was possible, since heretofore there had been a thin line between disagreeing with one's theology and silencing it.

III

The response of these seventeenth-century Baptists to their social and ecclesial contexts may have implications for contemporary educational institutions with Christian and Baptist roots as they confront the changing religious landscapes. The dilemma is nothing new; it has simply become more intensified. Restorationist historian Richard T. Hughes asks the central question: "How is it possible for Christian institutions of higher learning to develop into academic institutions of the first order and, at the same time, to nurture in creative ways the faith commitments that called these institutions into existence in the first place? More than this, how is it possible for Christian colleges and universities to weave first-class academic programs from the very fabric of their faith commitments?"[39] Hughes observes quite a spectrum. At one end, Hughes says, are those "Christian educators in America [who] have established numerous Christian colleges and universities, only to see those institutions eventually abandon their Christian orientations in the interest of a purely Enlightenment-based search for truth." At the other end are those schools that "cling so tightly to a particularistic, *a priori*, Christian worldview that they place limits on the search for truth, largely abandon the Enlightenment-based presuppositions of higher education, and thwart any possibility that they might eventually take their place in the larger American culture as serious colleges and universities of the highest order."[40]

This discussion is nothing new, but it intensified in the United States through the 1980s and 1990s, especially as Baptist schools began to reexamine their relationship with their parent Baptist bodies, some deepening those connections confessionally, even dogmatically, and others distancing themselves from formal connections to varying degrees. Many are caught somewhere in the middle. Some Baptist-related schools find themselves with Roman Catholic pluralities in the student body and a growing number of faculty who are neither Baptists nor necessarily Christian in their religious orientation. Some institutions are caught in a kind of time warp where their larger, funding constituency retains a more traditional Baptist identity, while their students, even those who are members of Baptist churches, wear denominational affiliations loosely, if at all. Certain Baptist-connected schools have begun to speak of a more "evangelical" future as providing a distinctively Christian institutional future. Some are trying to sort out how to appeal to Christian students and churches while also attracting faculty who may have varying Christian commitments or none at all. Old symbols for defining religious identity such as required chapel, campus ministry, and direct connections with the denomination are dropping away or being significantly redefined.

Likewise, Hughes points out that there are many ways in which denominational schools might respond to these issues that are distinct from the Reformed-based agendas that have received attention from many school administrators. These include the Mennonites, for whom "the driving force for higher education is not the sovereignty of God over all creation, but a vision of radical discipleship," often connected to service and even to dissent. Lutherans have often grounded their educational philosophy in the tradition of the "two kingdoms" centered in the world and the kingdom of God.[41] Catholics, Hughes suggests, are "incarnation and sacramental" in their approach to education, in ways that lead them to ask "how Christian scholars—and graduates of Catholic institutions—can bring the presence of Christ into a world filled with suffering, poverty, and injustice."[42] Perhaps a major difference between Catholic and Protestant institutions, especially Baptist institutions, is a sacramental presence of chapels or churches on the Catholic campus. Catholics bring Christ's real presence into the center of campus whereas Baptists tend to minimize the sacramental and replace it with the verbal (the spoken or preached word). Thus efforts to replicate Notre Dame on a Baptist-connected campus cannot possibly succeed without a drastic change in theological and liturgical orientation.

Perhaps one Baptist way (no doubt one way among many) for responding to the changing nature of campus life would be a reassertion of those early Baptist ideals of dissent, conscience, and believers' church. That is, Baptists should be at the forefront of the quest for "voice" on college and university campuses, not as a tepid, grudging response to nebulous political correctness, but because "voice" is endemic to the nature of Baptist identity, perhaps even its most profound distinctive. Baptist schools might lead the way in drawing on this heritage to encourage and facilitate dialogue, dissent, and cultivation of conscience, not because that is the secular wave of the future, but because their tradition recognized the value of these ideals earlier than any other modern Protestant communion. Two examples, one negative, the other positive, must suffice. They are related explicitly to the Southern Baptist Convention, but no doubt could be found in other Baptist-related schools.

In their first edition of the Baptist Faith and Message, approved in 1925, the denominational confession of faith, Southern Baptists seemed to celebrate diversity in the quest for truth, while anchoring it to their Christian heritage. The section on "Education" asserts, "Christianity is the religion of enlightenment and intelligence. In Jesus Christ are hidden all the treasures of wisdom and knowledge. All sound learning is therefore a part of our Christian heritage. The new birth opens all human faculties and creates a thirst for knowledge."[43] In this document Christ is the door to "wisdom and knowledge," and the faith of the believers impels them to seek education.

After numerous controversies in Baptist-related educational institutions, many a direct outgrowth of issues of dissent and conscience, the 1963 revision of the Baptist Faith and Message took a different approach to education. The article declared:

> In Christian education there should be a proper balance between academic freedom and academic responsibility. Freedom in any orderly relationship of human life is always limited and never absolute. The freedom of a teacher in a Christian school, college, or seminary is limited by the pre-eminence of Jesus Christ, by the authoritative nature of the Scriptures, and by the distinct purpose for which the school exists.[44]

In a little less than forty years for Baptists, Christ ceased to be the door to all truth and learning and became the wall that "limited" the teachers' "freedom," and set the boundaries for conscience and the possibility of dissent. In a sense, therefore, Baptist-related schools, at least in the South, have mirrored that dichotomy in their approach to divisive issues and "voice" on campus. The third revision of the Baptist Faith and Message (2000) combines both of the statements with brief editorial changes.

Yet there is another historic circumstance that illustrates the way in which certain Southern Baptist schools were forced to come to terms with dissent and conscience because of their commitment to and rhetoric in support of evangelism and a believers' church. It began with efforts to desegregate schools affiliated with Baptist state conventions in the American South. Dissenters could not get a hearing from trustees and administrators when they called for admission of African Americans to Baptist higher education, so they turned evangelism on its head by insisting that Southern Baptists could not in good conscience send missionaries to Africa to evangelize native peoples and then refuse to admit them to their schools in the United States, should they qualify and seek admission. Wake Forest University in North Carolina and Mercer University in Georgia experienced similar situations. Will Campbell details the events at Mercer in the book *The Stem of Jesse*, a title that references Jesse

Mercer, the founder and namesake of the school. Campbell recounts the story of the admission of Nigerian Baptist Sam Oni to Mercer in 1963. He cites the letter sent to the university president by John Mitchell, admissions director. It stated:

> Mr. Oni was converted through the work of a young man who was graduated from our university. Would this young Christian understand that the doors of the university which prepared the missionary who brought the Gospel are closed to his converts? Indeed, he has a closer relationship to our university than the Negro of Macon, Georgia. He is one of our constituents.[45]

The admissions director held the university's feet to the evangelical fire. Baptist converts who could not be admitted to Baptist schools to expand their educational possibilities negated the very heart of the church's mission. On April 18, 1963, the Mercer board of trustees voted thirteen to five (with three abstentions) "that Mercer University consider applicants for admission based on qualifications, without regard to race, color of skin, creed, or place of origin."[46] Sam Oni became the first black student at Mercer, but others, specifically African Americans, would follow. The color line at Mercer was broken, at least in part, because of the commitment of Baptist dissenters to freedom of conscience as well as evangelical imperatives.

Today Baptist-related schools and Baptists in other kinds of schools ought to consider dissent, conscience, and believers' church as resources for responding to the controversies in American private higher education. They would thereby acknowledge a heritage in which pluralism was not simply tolerated but demanded; where dialogue between ideologies was strong and divisive, but where, ideally, no one was silenced and everyone had voice. They also would demonstrate that pluralism does not mean compromise with conscience and that their commitments to individual and communal faith should be respected amid the many voices sounded out on any one campus. That is, they would make clear that their concerns for pluralism and voice are grounded in their understanding of the nature of faith in Jesus Christ. They would acknowledge with the rest of the college or university that the campus may nurture church communities, but that a college or university is not a church and that the term "Christian university" must be used with caution both in terms of providing a context for multiple voices and for the school's own moral commitments.

This approach could be its own kind of "witness," especially in situations where representatives of both the left and the right are working to silence dissent that seems to them unorthodox in one way or another. It may mean that on some campuses, Baptists relinquish their traditionally privileged status. It does not mean that Baptists representing multiple ideologies and sub-groups should remain silent about their convictions regarding politics, ethics, and theology on the campus and in the world. Indeed, individual Baptists on any given campus will surely exercise conscience and express dissent very differently even as they claim a common faith in Christ. Some conservatives strongly believe that secularism represents the new de facto religious establishment and that they are called to be counterculture in their witness against abortion, same-sex unions, and the displacement of Judeo-Christian traditions in the public square. Others believe that gospel liberation impels them to challenge efforts by a religious majority to restore or perpetuate an implicit religious establishment in a privileged Protestantism while defending the right of conscience regarding abortion rights and gay rights. Still other Baptists may eschew the temptation to demand or retain a traditional privilege in the campus and in the culture, while reasserting a concern for radical freedom and radical discipleship, forcing them to challenge secularist and fundamentalist agendas and ideologies in the free marketplace of ideas.

This is not without danger, especially since the energy in many private schools is for dogmatism left or right that minimizes voice or redefines the nature of dialogue. Fiddes writes insightfully about British universities in ways that may inform the American situation. He notes that in spite of the "advantages of a non-confessional stance of theology in the universities, we in Britain have also paid a price for it. Theology in some university faculties has become detached from the life and mission of the church. It has become a field of study using the same methods of investigation and research as other humanities, and has often obtained respectability by becoming simply identified with religious studies. . . ."[47] He concludes:

> In a variety of ways, then, a 'non-confessional' approach to theology at university level may result in the sundering of academic theology from the experience and practice of actual church communities. A better way forward is surely a 'multi-confessional' one, enabling students to reflect on a plurality of ways of life in community, across the separated Christian families. In such an approach the distinctive life-style of Baptist communities, marked by a particular Baptist experience, will have a part to play.[48]

Increasingly, Fiddes's call for a "multi-confessional" approach has implications for non-Christian individuals and communities on campus, expanding the complexity of voice in ways the founders of Rhode Island anticipated years ago.

For me, that "particular Baptist experience" is inseparable from issues of dissent, conscience, and unashamed faith. So, to return to Helwys's radical insight, bring on the "heretics, Turks, Jews or whatsoever," along with the unashamedly Christocentric Baptists (many of whom surely were deemed heretics themselves). In the words of Featley's memorable line, let the "presses sweat and groan with the load" of our twenty-first-century "blasphemies." And through it all let us all confess with humility the words appended to the conclusion of the First London Confession, 1644: "(We confess) that we know in part, and that we are ignorant of many things which we desire and seek to know; and if any shall do us that friendly part to show us from the Word of God that we see not, we shall have cause to be thankful to God and them."[49] Now there is pluralism worth exploring, one more time.

Chapter Five

Blending Baptist with Orthodox in the Christian University

David S. Dockery

> Clearly this is a critical time to redefine the meaning and mission of Christian Higher Education to understand the distinctive reason for our existence. What role does learning play in the Christian life? How does faith in God enhance an unfettered quest for truth? Our need now is not for a general philosophy of education, but for an explicit theology of education rooted in the imperatives of the Christian Gospel. In a time of spiritual confusion and moral anarchy, Baptists have been driven back to the Bible and to their core confessions of faith, which is where the church always goes when under furious attack.[1]

With these words, William E. Hull, then provost of Samford University, concluded the Hester Lectures on Southern Baptist Higher Education in 1996. In this chapter, given originally as one of the Hester Lectures in 2004, I attempt to advance the conversation and the challenge issued to us by Hull a decade ago. The focus of this essay is not a discussion about a general philosophy of education, but is indeed a call for *an explicit theology of and for Baptist higher education rooted in the imperatives of the Christian gospel.*

What Is Theology?

The very term "theology" scares many people. It sounds formidable, esoteric, abstract, and technical. Many people are suspicious of the word "theology," thinking it is irrelevant to our life with God or, even worse, a sort of human presumption. I have found the suspicion of theology to be present among many people, not just academics, but pastors and numerous laypeople alike. The suspicions are often right, at least in part, because theology frequently has been studied in the wrong way, which has led to mis-thinking, or even hurtful thinking at many places.

Theology is not just an attempt to articulate our feelings about our dependence on God, as the influential German theologian Friederich Schleiermacher said over two hundred years ago.[2] On the other hand, it's not merely an attempt to state the objective truth, to put the truth in proper order, as the great Presbyterian theologian Charles Hodge suggested when he attempted to articulate theology in nineteenth-century scientific terms.[3] It seems best to me as a Baptist to think of theology in a twofold way: (1) as *developing a mind for truth* so that we can indeed "articulate the faith once for all delivered to the saints," and (2) as *developing a heart for God* so that our lives are built up in the faith. Ultimately, a distinctive Baptist theology will have Christ at its center, the church as its focus, and the influencing of culture as a key element of its vision.

I believe theology can render service to Baptist higher education in many ways. It satisfies the mind so that we can know God, so that we can know the living Christ. Theology is vitally important for both the teaching and culture-engaging task (1 Pet. 3:15). Theology is necessary as a touchstone for understanding what we believe and for recognizing the principles by which our lives are to be shaped. Such beliefs and practices come from serious theological reflection. Baptist theology therefore also points to ethics. Certainly it is possible to act one way and to think another, but it is not logically possible for us to do so for long, for even the biblical writer has admonished us, "as a person thinks in his heart, so he is." Since the goal of Baptist higher education is to help our students live in the world with a lifestyle that issues in glory to God, then we must think—and think deeply—not only of personal ethics, but of the implications of the biblical faith for social, economic, and political ethics as well. Such necessities touch the heart of the life and mission of Baptist higher education.

Baptist Shaping Traditions

But before moving further into our topic, it might be helpful to reflect upon the significance of that heritage. Baptist higher education can be traced in this country to the first Baptist institution in Rhode Island in 1764. This institution was followed by schools like Colby (1813), Colgate (1819), and others that began shortly thereafter (see chap. 1).

Several Baptist historians have tried to understand the shaping traditions that have influenced us as Southern Baptists. These would include what is often called the Charleston tradition, the Sandy Creek influence, the importance of the Landmark tradition, and the Texas revivalist tradition. Each of these has had a substantial stamp upon the life and work of Baptists across the South and throughout our country. However, if we are looking for the birthplace of Southern Baptist scholarship, looking for serious interest in higher education, it is to the Charleston tradition that we can readily turn. That is not to say that some educational influences are absent from the others, for certainly Union University where I serve had the Landmark stamp on it in the middle of the nineteenth century (and I might add that the shadow continues to extend over West Tennessee and other parts of the Mid-South region). The Texas revivalist tradition birthed Baylor University, and the recent work edited by Donald Schmeltekopf and others on the Baptist and Christian character of Baylor University points to some of those early shaping influences.[4]

Out of these various geographical trajectories we can further point to important theological traditions in our 160-year history as Southern Baptists. At this point I would list at least ten. We are heirs of (1) the British heritage, (2) the Princeton influence, (3) pietism, (4) revivalism, (5) the confessional tradition so identified with Charleston and the founding of Southern Seminary, (6) the role of experience as identified in E. Y. Mullins and W. T. Conner, (7) the church-based theology so well exemplified in the middle of the twentieth century by Hershel H. Hobbs and W. A. Criswell, (8) the many influences of contemporary European theology, (9) the North American evangelical trajectories, and (10) what many would identify in Southern Baptist life today as the "conservative resurgence." As you can tell, there is great diversity in the heritage that has shaped us. Out of these, I think we find pointers to the struggles within which most of us live on a day-to-day basis. Thus, some wonder if there is a way to identify what it means to be a Baptist in moving toward a theology of/for Baptist higher education.

Timothy George, taking an insider's perspective, has said that the Baptist heritage is formed by orthodox Christian convictions, by the influence of the evangelical tradition, by a connection to the sixteenth-century Reformation, and by a consistent use of the great historic confessions. From these four overarching markers he suggests we can connect Baptists with other Christians. In addition, he has identified four key Baptist distinctives, which include the regenerate church, baptism by immersion, religious liberty, and church-state issues.[5]

Viewing the Baptist heritage from an outsider's perspective, Mark Noll has suggested six distinctives of Baptist life: (1) believer's baptism instead of infant baptism, (2) voluntary ecclesiology instead of inherited/parish ecclesiology, (3) local organization of church life instead of state control or even denominational control, (4) biblical authority as priority over tradition, (5) populist biblical interpretation instead of interpretation by bishops or academics, and (6) Christian ordinances practiced as matters of obedience instead of sacraments practiced as means of grace.[6]

When we think about the particular challenges flowing from our heritage and tradition to engage the culture, to carry on the great Christian intellectual tradition, and to develop a theology of Baptist higher education, we recognize at least six issues with which we must come to grips. First, the emphasis on localism, populism, and voluntarism, all of which have frequently acted to spur renewal and mobilization for ministry, has often carried with it a lack of appreciation for formal intellectual life. Second, the stress on conversion and piety has sometimes stood in the way of sanctified intellectual development and cultural engagement. Third, the influence of Landmarkism has often kept us from appreciating the breadth of the Christian intellectual tradition through the centuries. Fourth, the general culture of the South has sometimes carried with it an embedded anti-intellectualism. Fifth, while seeking to address the previous four challenges, a form of liberalism has been adopted which often grew out of reactions to our populist, revivalistic, and pietistic heritage. And sixth, the pitfalls of fundamentalism associated with some aspects of the current conservative resurgence in the Southern Baptist Convention (SBC) must also be avoided. With Bill Leonard in his *Baptist Ways*, we recognize the great variety in our heritage, yet we want to focus on the core or center of our Baptist heritage and beliefs that can help us move forward in this project.[7] Thus, we must take a good look at who we are and where we are in order to think about developing a theology of and for Baptist higher education. I believe this will call for us to (1) reappropriate the best of our Baptist heritage, (2) clarify our confessional commitments, and (3) engage the broader evangelical movement in Britain and North America.

Basic Baptist Beliefs

In 1994 the SBC unanimously adopted a resolution which acknowledged that "Southern Baptists have historically confessed with all true Christians everywhere belief in the Triune God, Father, Son, and Holy Spirit, the full deity and perfect humanity of Jesus Christ, His virgin birth, sinless life, His substitutionary atonement for sins, His resurrection from the dead, His exultation to the right hand of God, and His triumphal return; and we recognize that born again believers in the Lord Jesus Christ may be found in all Christian denominations."[8] The resolution recognizes common Christian convictions shared by Baptists with other orthodox Christians who stand in continuity with the consensus of the early church on matters such as the truthfulness of Holy Scripture, the doctrine of God, and the person and work of Jesus Christ.

Leon McBeth was most likely right when he observed that Baptists have often used confessions not only to proclaim Baptist distinctives, but also to show how similar Baptists were to other orthodox Christians.[9] Thus the Orthodox Creed of 1678 incorporated the Apostles' Creed, the Nicene Creed, and the Athanasian Creed in Article 38, declaring that "all three ought thoroughly to be received and believed. For we believe that they must be proved, by undoubted authority of Holy Scripture and are necessary to be understood of all Christians." It should not be ignored that when Baptists gathered in London for the inaugural meeting of the Baptist World Alliance in 1905, they stood in that assembly and recited in unison the Apostles' Creed, which is certainly a foundational framework for developing a theology of and for Christian higher education in general, if not for Baptist higher education as well.

Thus, our first steps involve the need to cultivate a holistic orthodoxy based on a high view of Scripture and congruent with the Trinitarian and Christological consensus of the early church. Only in this way will we avoid the dangers of fundamentalist reductionism on the one hand and liberal revisionism on the other. I would suggest that our shared Baptist work cannot move forward without confessional convictions or confessional boundaries. This, however, does not mean we should expect or demand uniformity of belief or conviction. Inherent in an historically informed understanding of orthodoxy is the need for some flexibility and variety lest we place straightjackets around our community and around Scripture itself. The world in which we live with its emphasis on diversity and plurality may well be a creative setting for us once again to pray for a far-reaching renewal of Baptist higher education.

Connections to Orthodox Christianity

We must ground our unity not only in the biblical confession that Jesus is Lord, but also in the great tradition flowing from the Apostles' Creed to the confessions of Nicea in 325 and Chalcedon in 451. Likewise, we must claim the best of our Baptist confessional heritage as well, beginning with the *Standard Confession* of 1660 and the London confessions of the seventeenth century to the Baptist Faith and Message. Such historic confessions, though neither infallible nor completely sufficient for all contemporary challenges, can provide guidance in seeking to balance the mandates for right Christian thinking, right Christian believing, and right Christian living.

Such historically grounded confessions can also help us think rightly about faith and how we relate to one another in love, pointing out for us the important differences between primary, secondary, and tertiary issues in Christian theology and practice. Although it is not always clear in distinguishing these, a useful guide is that the truths of Scripture and the consensus of the Christian tradition as shared by Christians at all times and all places are to be considered essentials as primary doctrines. Secondary matters tend to be those things that are distinctive to a particular denomination, as well as those matters on which biblical Christians equally anxious to interpret and follow Scripture reach different conclusions. These secondary or tertiary matters are certainly important and are matters about which we should have beliefs or convictions, but they are not likely to be the broad foundational matters on which we can build a theology of and for Baptist higher education. For example, a bedrock primary doctrine essential for us to confess is that salvation is by grace alone, but the different Calvinistic or Arminian expressions of that truth are secondary, not primary. Confessing that Christ will return is a primary doctrine, but defining the nature of the millennium is a secondary or probably even a tertiary matter. The great confessional tradition, though not the final authoritative word, can serve as a tremendously helpful resource for us in distinguishing primary issues from second- and third-order doctrines.

These examples perhaps help us understand that in essentials, faith and truth are primary and we may not appeal to love or grace as an excuse to deny any essential aspect of Christian teaching. In secondary matters, then, love is primary, and we may not appeal to personal conviction or zeal as an excuse for failure to exercise grace or demonstrate love. Faith instructs our conscience. Love respects the conscience of others. Faith shapes our liberty; love and a concern for others in the context of Christian community limits its exercise. At the heart of our exploration for a theology of Baptist higher education we must find an affirmation of the Bible's truthfulness.

As we take the next step in thinking about a theology of Baptist higher education, it is important not only to affirm these central consensus beliefs of the Christian faith, but we must also exclude errors on the right and the left. Errors on the right, such as a dictation view of scripture or fundamentalist separatism or legalism, must be recognized as faulty thinking in the same way that Paul called out the Judaizers in the book of Galatians. On the other hand, views of so-called Christian existentialism, liberation, or process thought, as well as other thinking less faithful to Scripture, must also be excluded. In our day we must reclaim such bedrock convictions in the midst of a growing secularized academy. This move will call for us to swim upstream, but I believe for us to be faithful to the Christian and Baptist character of our institutions that we can do no other.

Thinking Theologically

I'm sure some are at this time asking, "Does this mean that all involved in Baptist higher education are to be theologians in the sense of being uniquely summoned to the task of leading in theological thought?" Certainly I would like to encourage all faculty and staff at our Baptist institutions to be theologians, but not theologians in the technical sense of that term. What I believe is needed today is for administrators, trustees, faculty, and staff once again to think lofty thoughts about God and to live accordingly—that is, to live according to God's Word and Holy Scripture. Some theologians suggest that essentially theology is thinking about God. If they are right, and I believe they basically are, then to abdicate the theological domain to specialists alone either because of a lack of interest or because of the technicalities involved is not only harmful to the work of Baptist higher education, but I believe also that it is unpleasing to God. The truth is that every believer in the world of Baptist higher education is in some sense a theologian, for all believers who know God have the responsibility to see and understand the revelation of God for their foundational beliefs, while integrating these beliefs into their calling as academics.

Theology is certainly not the whole of academic life, but there must be a place for the true intellectual love of God, for Jesus has told us to love God with our heart, soul, strength, and mind, and love our neighbor as well. This should not lead to some cold intellectual approach to the faith unaccompanied by affection. For too many, theology is a kind of intellectual aloofness or uncommitted intellectual curiosity. But before we can develop a theology of and for Baptist higher education, I would suggest that we think about the relationship of theology to Baptist life or to the church, and also to understand the responsibility of higher education in preparing future church and denominational leaders.

We need to understand history for what is distinctive about Baptists theologically, which understood historically is our contribution to the understanding of the church. For Baptists the church is central to God's working in history. The church is central not only to history, but also to the gospel and Christian living as well. Thus, theology is more than God's words for me as an individual; theology is God's words for us—the community of faith. It is vitally important that we understand theology not merely in individualistic terms. We need to move to a corporate and community understanding of these ideas. For these reasons in the early years of Baptist higher education, institutions placed their focus first in terms of service for the church and then more broadly for society.

We need to acknowledge that the discipline-specific separation or fragmentation in which we find ourselves in today's academy often results in a twofold problem: (1) a kind of lone-ranger individuality, and (2) a suspicion of and hostility to the theological enterprise. Certainly the academy at large, and sometimes even the Baptist academy, does not encourage, and in fact at times seemingly discourages, creative and collaborative efforts of theologians. Unfortunately, there is seldom sufficient cross-fertilization between serious theological thinking and the rest of the academy. These groups read different books, listen to different experts, identify different problems, consider different issues, contribute to different journals, and congregate in different groupings as they pursue diverse and sometimes competing agendas.

My concern is not to be another sour voice on the contemporary scene. Too many people today look at these issues and see the glass half empty. What we need is a renewed eschatological vision for the people of God, with a recognition of the important place that Baptist higher education can have in God's overall plan and a fresh appreciation for the significance of a theological foundation for this work. Granted the lack of theological acumen on the part of many in the academy is due to many factors beyond the control of professional theologians; nevertheless, it is important that we recognize the relationship between faithful theology and faithful Baptist academics.

Despite the fact that academic theology has produced vast amounts of materials requiring technical specialization, as is the case in other areas of knowledge, theology, if it is to serve the various disciplines across the academy, cannot afford to become some sort of esoteric endeavor done only for the initiated few. It is germane and important to have theological societies in serious theological debate, but unless Baptist theology operates consciously as the servant of both the church and the academy, little long-term value is forthcoming. One is reminded somewhat facetiously of the ghost of the cultured voice, as C. S. Lewis describes him in his work *The Great Divorce*. Upon refusing to repent of his snobbish spirit, of open-ended intellectual inquiry in order to enter the heavenly city, the ghost cuts off conversation with his host to return to the gray city by saying, "Bless my soul. I'd nearly forgotten, of course I can't come with you, I have to be back next Friday to read a paper. We have a little theological society down here."[10]

The responsibility of making theology helpful to the academy rests both with professional theologians and with other thinkers across the disciplines as well. Theology must be understandable to nonprofessional theologians. Too often what theologians write is unintelligible for many outside the discipline. Lest anyone misunderstand, I think that serious theological research and investigation must continue, but that can't be the end of the theological enterprise. In the past, theologians of the church wrote so that literate people could understand, and it must be acknowledged that Augustine, Aquinas, Luther, Calvin, and Wesley are often much easier to read and understand than many contemporary theologians. Today we need theologians who can write in ways that are sharp, powerful, and right on target. In this vein the reformers and early Baptists frequently commended the biblical writers for their clarity, simplicity, and brevity, and sought to emulate them in their own writings. If theology is to impact the church and inform others in the world of Baptist higher education, theologians must learn to communicate in understandable ways, for as someone has humorously said, "It may be impressive to say scintillate, scintillate, globule divific, feign would I fathom thy nature specific, loftily poised in the ether capacious, strongly resembling a gem carbonaceous." But it is much more understandable to say, "Twinkle, twinkle, little star, how I wonder what you are, up above the world so high, like a diamond in the sky."[11]

Likewise, theology in the academy must be relevant and applicable to other disciplines. Yale theologian Miroslav Volf, in his recent work *Practicing Theology: Beliefs and Practices in the Christian Life*, has encouraged us to think of theology as "a way" in the manner the early church thought of the Christian life as the way of life.[12] This is not in any sense to downplay or denigrate the importance of serious Christian scholarship. We recognize that the various disciplines of theology are indeed indispensable to an accurate understanding of truth. Without the scholarship of experts in philosophy, archaeology, history, languages, and other related fields, theological study itself would be seriously impoverished. Yet, when these specializations are pursued as an end in themselves and not molded into a unified view of truth, they can possibly get lost in the cacophonous voices across the academy. I hope that no one hears me suggesting that we should subvert the validity and importance of scholarly disciplines. Quite the contrary! But such scholarship does not finally touch the higher function of theology nor inform the work of Baptist higher education unless it sets forth a perspective that depends upon the regenerated mind and exposes the radical difference between Christianity and the competing philosophies within the broader academy.

We must admit that some theologians unduly complicate the Christian faith or distract us from aspects of helpful Christian thinking and living. Similarly theology can enable all aspects of Baptist higher education to recover a true understanding of human life. In this sense faculty, staff, and students can once again gain a greatness of the soul. Theology can help us recover the awareness that God is more important than we are, that the future life is more important than this one, and that a right view of God gives genuine significance to our calling as academics.

Theology can help those called to serve in Baptist higher education to better understand what we believe and why we believe it. We can appreciate our heritage and enliven our future hope. When this takes place, I believe Baptist colleges and universities can be strengthened. The gospel in its fullness can be proclaimed. Without the foundation of solid theology there can be no effective long-term educational efforts that are truly and distinctively Christian, much less truly and distinctively Baptist.

Our fundamental assumption in this task is that there is truth available to us, and it is found in God's revelation of himself in creation, history, experience, and ultimately in Christ as made known to us in Holy Scriptures. While we unhesitatingly affirm these truths, a warning needs to be voiced. No single group, church, or denomination, however orthodox or evangelical (or Baptist), strictly and faithfully follows this revelation from God. While the church has characteristically sought to be faithful to Scripture, the depth of meaning in the biblical text is rarely fully understood at any one moment in history. Theology in any tradition is often the art of establishing central and classic texts, which may mean that the other texts unfortunately are ignored or not given significant weight.[13] No single theologian, church, or denomination has escaped or can escape this frailty, though there is certainly continuity throughout the centuries, particularly in the teachings concerning the person and work of the Lord Jesus Christ, which I believe provides the ultimate foundation for our work in Baptist higher education.

The Christian Intellectual Tradition in History

Thus, understanding theology in the context of the great Christian intellectual tradition of the church at large and within the stream of Baptist life can provide insight for today and guidance for the future. In this way theology can help us engage the wrongheaded thinking often evident in today's academy. Knowledge of the past keeps us from confusing what is merely a contemporary expression from that which is enduringly relevant. Theology helps present to the church and the academy a valuable accumulation of enduring insights along with numerous lessons and warnings, both positive and negative. Thus, theology done with the focus on the church and done for the good of the academy will always have one eye on the historical past of the Christian tradition.

Such awareness of the church's history provides a bulwark against the pride and arrogance that would suggest that "we"—yes, even we Baptists—are the only group or tradition that carries on the orthodoxy of the apostles. Knowledge of such continuities and discontinuities in the past will help us focus on those areas of truth that are timeless and enduring, while encouraging authenticity and humility as well as a dependency on God's Spirit. Hopefully this awareness will cause us not just to accept things in accordance with our tradition or do things in accordance with our own comfort zones, but will again and again drive us back to the source of our theology in the New Testament with fresh eyes and receptive hearts and help us both understand the distinctives of Baptist higher education and relate constructively to those outside the Baptist and Christian tradition. Some might be asking, "Do these theological commitments stifle honest intellectual exploration?" The answer is no, but our challenge is to faithfully preserve and pass on the Christian tradition while encouraging honest intellectual inquiry. I believe these two things can coexist, even if in tension, in an enriching dialectical dependence.

So our choice is not an unquestioning acceptance of Baptist tradition or open-ended inquiry. The unquestioning acceptance of tradition can degenerate into traditionalism. To quote the brilliant Yale scholar Jaroslav Pelikan, "If tradition is the living faith of the dead, traditionalism becomes the dead faith of the living."[14] Such traditionalism is often characterized by inflexible and at times anti-intellectual dogma at every point and in every discipline. This approach fails to engage our society or to influence our culture.

On the other hand, free inquiry unanchored to theology and tradition often results in unbelieving skepticism, advancing the directionless state that characterizes so much of higher education today. Such an approach cannot sustain the Baptist tradition and its truth claims. I believe we have a better option. Within the world of higher education in general, Christian higher education has something different, even distinctive, to offer which will help engage our culture, will strengthen our love for God and our love for study, by emphasizing both tradition and honest intellectual inquiry.

I believe guidance and balance in these matters will come as we are faithful in integrating an informed theological foundation with all areas of learning. For Baptist academics to address these matters we must hear afresh the words of Jesus from what is called the Great Commandment (Matt. 22:36-40). Here we are told not only to love God wholeheartedly with our hearts and souls, but also our minds as well. Jesus' words refer to a wholehearted devotion to God with every aspect of our being, from whatever angle we choose to consider it—emotionally, volitionally, or cognitively. This kind of love for God results in taking every thought captive to make it obedient to Christ (2 Cor. 10:5), a wholehearted devotion to distinctively Christian thinking (or as T. S. Eliot put it, "to think in Christian categories").[15] This means being able to see life from a Christian vantage point; it means thinking theologically across the curriculum.

Beginning Steps

The beginning point for such a task is the confession that we believe in God the Father, maker of heaver and earth. We recognize that "in him all things hold together" (Col. 1:15-18), for all true knowledge flows from the one creator to his one creation.

A theologically informed approach to Baptist higher education must offer a way to live that is consistent with reality by offering a comprehensive understanding of all areas of life and thought, every aspect of creation.

The starting point begins with God and brings us into the presence of God without delay. The central affirmation of Scripture is not only that there is a God, but that God has acted and spoken in history. God is Lord and King over this world, ruling all things for his own glory, displaying his perfections in all that he does in order that humans and angels may worship and adore him. Such thinking provides a coherent way of seeing life, of seeing the world distinct from deism, naturalism and materialism, existentialism, polytheism, pantheism, mysticism, or deconstructionist postmodernism. Such a theistic perspective provides bearings and direction when confronted with secularistic and pluralistic approaches to truth and morality. Fear about the future, suffering, disease, and poverty are informed by Christian thinking grounded in the redemptive work of Christ and the grandeur of God. What is needed among those of us who serve in Baptist higher education in the twenty-first century is a renewed commitment to Holy Scripture and to our confessional heritage. But not only this, we need to renew our commitment to relate to one another in love and humility, bringing about true fellowship and community, resulting not only in a rebirth of orthodox foundations, but also a rebirth of Baptist orthopraxy before a watching world.

If Baptists lived in the kind of love and unity that the Lord Jesus Christ called for, it would do wonders for converting sinners and enlarging the church of Jesus Christ. So, the choice is not between truth or piety, orthodoxy or orthopraxy. Someone recently asked me if I would prefer a person with a warm heart and a mushy head, or a straight-thinking orthodox person with a cold heart. My answer was that I would prefer neither. In that sense we need to think of the call for a theology of Baptist higher education not just as an attempt to articulate our feelings about our dependence on God, as the pietists might say, or to describe the great truths of the faith in proper order, as the rationalists might say. Rather, as I said at the beginning of this essay, it is an attempt to *develop a mind for truth* so that we can articulate the faith once for all delivered to the saints and to *develop a heart for God* so that our lives are built up in the faith.

I'm sure that some may be thinking that such commitments as described in this chapter are potentially divisive and thus should be de-emphasized in their importance. But these theological commitments are the very backbone, the underpinnings, of Baptist higher education, the very essence of what it means to be both orthodox and Baptist. Without healthy theology, those of us in the church and the academy are prone to be tossed back and forth by waves, blown here and there by every wind of teaching (as Paul describes in Eph. 4:14). A healthy understanding of theology for Baptist higher education will help mature the head and heart, enabling believers to move toward spiritual health, resulting in the praise and exaltation of God.

Those who teach and study in Baptist institutions must take to heart the words of the Apostle Paul: "Do not be conformed to this world, but be transformed by the renewing of your minds" (Rom. 12:2). What I am calling for is intellectually challenging. It is not the easiest road for us to travel, but it is one faithful to the best of our heritage, and it provides no room for mere anti-intellectual piety, much less some vague spirituality, in Baptist higher education. We are to have the mind of Christ; this certainly requires us to think and wrestle with the challenging ideas of history in the issues of our day. For to do otherwise will result in a generation of God's people ill-equipped for faithful thinking and service in this new century. Christian thinking is needed to confront an ever-changing culture. Instead of allowing our thoughts to be captive to culture, we must take every thought captive to Jesus Christ.

This calls for serious theological thinking as we have indicated, affirming our love for God and our love for study, the place of devotion and the place of research, the priority of affirming and passing on the great Christian traditions and the significance of honest exploration, reflection, and intellectual wrestling. These matters are in tension but not in contradiction and are framed by faith-informed commitments. Rightly understood, then, theologically informed Baptist higher education is not contrary to either faithful teaching or Christian piety. It provides a foundation for a new discovery and creative teaching as well as the framework for passing on the coherent truth essential to the advancement of the Christian faith.

Concluding Considerations

In summary, I would suggest that a theology of/for Baptist higher education can help us develop connecting and unifying principles for Christian thinking, grounded in the truth that God is creator and redeemer. A call for a theology of and for Baptist higher education will encourage curious exploration and serious wrestling with the foundational questions of human existence. I believe such a commitment to a theology of Baptist higher education will help us develop a comprehensive and historically informed view of what it means to be a part of the great Christian intellectual tradition as we shape the Christian educational enterprise for this new century. A theology of Baptist higher education will help us be aware of contemporary cultural, social, and religious trends. What we are suggesting will require us to live in tension, reflecting a theological outlook while simultaneously having particular discipline-specific emphases across the curriculum. This living in tension will not entirely please those who see truth as a battle in which it is perfectly clear who stands with the forces of light or darkness. Sometimes the issues with which we wrestle are filled with ambiguities, for at this time, as the Apostle Paul reminds us, even with the help of Holy Scripture and Christian tradition we are finite humans who still see as through a glass darkly.

Ultimately, a theology of Baptist higher education grows out of a commitment to sphere-sovereignty whether in the arts, the sciences, the humanities, education, business, health-care, or social arenas. Thus, a theologically informed Baptist higher education must surely subordinate all other endeavors to the improvement of the mind in pursuit of truth, taking every thought captive to the Lordship of Jesus the Christ. We would be naïve not to recognize the times in which we live and the context and culture for which our students are preparing to serve. A theology of Baptist higher education rooted in Scripture and grounded in the best of our Baptist heritage can equip the work of Baptist higher education for times of duress and trial, whether that comes through means of persecution, whether in the face of faithless scholarship or in the midst of the church's internal bickering and divisions. What is needed is a bedrock, nonnegotiable commitment to a belief in a triune God; in one mediator between God and humanity, the man Christ Jesus, who was God incarnate. This commitment represents a belief in a totally truthful and authoritative Bible, and the message of God's justifying work by grace through faith revealed therein; and it is rooted in a focus on the church, and lives in hope of the return of Christ, resulting in a commitment to a life of prayer, holiness, obedience, and growth in Christ.[16]

This kind of theology can shape Baptist higher education for a promising future. It is built on a center of bedrock truths that are not culturally confined or easily expunged without great peril. What I believe is needed for this time is an ancient kind of orthodoxy, a primitive but passionate core of theological truths that nurtured persecuted believers in the past, and will be the only thing to comfort once the flames of suffering are stoked again. If persecution is coming back, then our orthodox commitments must also return—commitments that are firm but loving, clear but gracious, ready to respond to issues and challenges that the culture and world present to Christ-followers, but not necessarily responding to every contextual skirmish or intramural squabble.

As William Hull said a decade ago, the best time to advance is when our backs are to the wall. These commitments Hull claimed, as noted at the beginning of this essay, are based on the intuition that our cultural exhaustion may signal the beginning of a new humility, that our moral frustration may be the harbinger of a new seriousness—in other words, that our desperate alienation from the roots of our humanity may itself provoke the advent of a new *kairos*, that this explosive yet empty age may indeed become the incubator of a new era when the search for wholeness can begin all over again.[17] May God renew his church, renew our Baptist life, and renew Baptist higher education as we seek to develop a theology of and for Baptist higher education even as we pray for one another at the beginning of this century. May these commitments not be easily lost or forgotten, but may they remain firmly rooted in our minds and hearts for years and decades to come for the glory of God.

Part Two

Faculty and Students and Baptist Higher Education

Chapter Six

Who Will Our Students Be in a Postmodern, Postdenominational, and Materialistic Age?

Richard Franklin

The study of large groups of students is intriguing, complicated, exciting, and extremely beneficial. Many academicians, particularly those in the disciplines of sociology and psychology, do a good job of keeping up with the latest developments and current thinking about young people, and through their research they often make significant contributions to our understanding of the traits, motivations, and aspirations of college students. Although professionals and practitioners charged with the responsibility of nurturing students on campus attend conferences, read journals, and participate in personal and professional development in their functional areas, their research contributions are minimal compared to many of their faculty colleagues. If I were a betting person, I would wager that not many university administrators, even those within student life, have spent much time learning about the students who voluntarily come to our campuses to get a college education. I have been in the student-life profession for over thirty years, and I must confess that even I most often take a micro view of the students who are already on campus rather than a macro view of who they are and what forces have shaped them before they arrive at our doors.

These conditions exist in spite of the fact that many courses in student personnel services and higher education curricula attempt to foster a macro view. Most graduate-trained student-life professionals have had at least one course focused on the American college student, and we certainly should have had a course devoted to student development theories, including theories of cognitive, psychosocial, and faith development, and of typology, as well as theories about other ways students grow and mature during their collegiate years. But most of these courses stress fundamental characteristics of students that do not change significantly from cohort to cohort. They often do not address the differences that arise in each incoming generation of students as a result of the changing social, economic, and political environment in which they were reared and in response to specific great historical events, such as those of September 11, 2001.

Let me draw an analogy from sports, and since at the time I write this we have just experienced March Madness, basketball will provide a good example. Not much has changed in the basics of basketball in many years. The floor is still ninety-four feet long and fifty feet wide. The goal rim diameter is eighteen inches, and the goal is still fifteen feet from the foul line. The width of the foul lane is still twelve feet. Most baskets still count as two points, and the free throw still counts as one point. It still takes five fouls for a player to be forced to leave the game. Although within the last decade a three-point basket was added to the game to make it more exciting, the rules of the game have remained largely unchanged. But what *has* changed are the players. Would anybody deny that they are faster, quicker, taller, stronger, and generally more skilled than in the past? Their physical attributes and understanding of the game make possible new coaching strategies that would have been impossible with less talented players. As a result, the way the game is played has changed, even though the fundamentals of the game have not. In a similar way, students today pass through our gates and enter our "courts" with the same fundamental needs as their predecessors to develop cognitively, socially, and spiritually, but like today's athletes they have different capabilities, motivations, and expectations than those of students ten or even five years ago. All of this is to say that we in higher education can serve our students more effectively if we have a better understanding of who they are and what their expectations are when they arrive on our campuses.

Neil Howe and William Strauss have been forerunners in presenting a model for understanding the upcoming generation of students, labeled Millennials, based on a peer personality of the cohort. Among their works are *Generations: The History of America's Future 1584 to 2069*, *13th Gen: Abort, Retry, Ignore, Fail?*, and *Millennials Rising: The Next Great Generation.*[1] Howe and Strauss define generations as "a cohort group whose length approximates the span or a phase of life and whose boundaries are fixed by peer personality."[2] The peer personality is defined as a "generational persona recognized and determined by (1) common age location; (2) common beliefs and behavior; and (3) perceived membership in a common generation."[3] While all three components of the peer personality are important, the third is perhaps the most important in that members of a generation must perceive themselves to be distinct from other generations.

It is not my intent to either delve into or critique the Howe and Strauss model but to acknowledge their work and the significant contributions they have made to understanding today's college students. While there are a few other models available, almost every work and study in this area acknowledges the contributions of these two researchers, and much of what follows is attributable to their work. In particular, I commend Howe and Strauss's 2003 book entitled *Millennials Go to College: Strategies for a New Generation on Campus*.[4]

To gain a greater understanding of the generation of students called Millennials on a more macro scale, it will be useful to look at the demographics, characteristics, learning styles, aspirations and expectations, ethics and values, and religious beliefs and worship styles that make this generation distinctive.

Demographics

Most definitions of the Millennial generation identify the parameters of the cohort by birth dates between 1982 and 2002. The members of this generation are called Millennials because the first of them entered college in 2000 and the final stage will enter college in 2020. Their generation will be the largest cohort in American history, as it is estimated that around eighty million people have been born since 1981. The anticipated influx of immigrants could raise the number to more than ninety million, which would mean the cohort of Millennials would be more than 30 percent larger than the cohort of Baby Boomers. The diversity of the college-bound Millennials is unprecedented. During the period from 1980 to 2000 Caucasian enrollment as a percentage of the total college population decreased from 81.5 percent to 69.4 percent, but the African American enrollment doubled and the Hispanic enrollment continued to grow. In addition, the percentage of women enrolled increased from 51.5 percent to 56.1 percent, and the Asian American student numbers increased 300 percent.[5]

According to the National Center for Education Statistics, there were approximately 6.9 million Millennials enrolled in higher education in 2002, and they represented around 44 percent of all college students. By 2012 that number is expected to swell to 13.3 million, or 75 percent of all students. In 2012 the number of students from other generations will have decreased by slightly more than 50 percent, and the Millennials will have increased by almost 94 percent over the 2002 level.[6] They are here, they will keep coming, and they are coming in droves. The questions we must ask ourselves are "Who are they?" and "Are we ready for them?"

Characteristics

Howe and Strauss indicate that Millennials are unlike any previous generation of youth to hit the American scene. They are more numerous and affluent, better educated, and more ethnically diverse. They demonstrate positive social habits that older Americans have often not associated with youth, such as habits of teamwork, achievement, modesty, and good conduct. Their attitudes and behaviors are different from the preceding generation, the jaded and cynical Generation X, and they counter trends associated with Baby Boomers. In fact, this new generation is challenging the negative stereotype of the young. Among other characteristics, they are optimistic, rule-following, accepting of authority, and not distrustful.[7]

A 1998 Harris Poll conducted for Northwestern Mutual Life Insurance Company to assess the college graduating class of the new millennium reached the following conclusions:

- Almost 100 percent of Millennials believe they will get where they want to be in life.
- They most often cite technology as their biggest advantage as members of the Millennial generation, followed by better career prospects and more educational resources and opportunities.
- The large majority (85 percent) say they are different from their parents.
- They trust grandparents most, then parents; they trust Generation X the least.
- The attributes Millennials admire most about a person are honesty and integrity.
- They admire their mothers more than anyone else, followed by their fathers.
- Almost all Millennials (96 percent) expect to marry, at an average age of twenty-six, and 91 percent plan to have children, an average of three.
- Almost 75 percent have volunteered in the past year, and an even larger 92 percent say they will likely volunteer for a charitable organization in the future.
- Almost 90 percent believe in God, 75 percent believe in life after death, the majority attend religious services, and almost half say religion will be more important in their future.
- A third of Millennials identify themselves as Democrats, 31 percent as Republicans, and 24 percent as Independents.
- Nearly 75 percent say they expect a person of color to be elected president in their lifetime, and 63 percent expect to see a woman elected president.[8]

Of course, while not every Millennial shares all the core traits that identify their cohort, Millennials are still part of a group that is defined by distinct commonalities or traits that set their group apart from others. Again, Howe and Strauss identify these commonly shared distinctives that, over the years, will clearly reveal the Millennials as being

- Special. From precious-baby home videos of the mid-1980s to the media glare surrounding the high school class of 2000, now in college, those of the older generations have inculcated in Millennials the sense that they are, collectively, vital to the nation and to their parents' sense of purpose.
- Sheltered. From the surge in child-safety rules and devices to the post-Columbine lockdown of public schools, Millennials are the focus of the most sweeping youth-protection movement in American history. Of course, this increase in efforts to shelter and protect them may be the result of their parents' perception that, because of current political and social circumstances, their children are perhaps more endangered and vulnerable than any previous generation.
- Confident. With high levels of trust and optimism and a newly felt connection to parents and the future, Millennials tend to expect good things for themselves and for their country.
- Team-oriented. From the television character Barney and soccer to school uniforms and group learning, Millennials are developing strong team instincts and tight peer bonds.
- Conventional. Taking pride in their improving behavior and quite comfortable with their parents' values, Millennials provide modern proof of the traditional belief that social rules and standards can make life easier.
- Pressured. Pushed to study hard, avoid personal risks, and take full advantage of the collective opportunities adults are offering them, Millennials feel a "trophy kid" pressure to excel.
- Achieving. With accountability and higher school standards rising to the very top of America's political agenda, Millennials are on track to becoming the smartest, best-educated generation in U.S. history.[9]

Roger Casey, a 1983 Furman University graduate and now the dean of faculty at Rollins College, offers this humorous insight into some of the traits that distinguish this generation from others:

> Remember learning to ride a bicycle? For me, growing up in South Carolina in the 1960s it was a red, pawn-shop special with pedal brakes. Dad ran behind with one hand on the plastic banana seat, letting go without my

> knowledge at some point. Of course, I fell and skinned my knee. "Get back on," he encouraged. Contrast that scene with the education of the Millennial. First there is the bike itself: a European or Japanese import that costs a little less than did the '72 Malibu I bought as a freshman at Furman. Next, Mom and Dad have probably read *Teaching Your Child to Bicycle Safely*—or at least watched the DVD. Perhaps they've sent Junior to bike safety school or hired a training consultant.
>
> On the appointed morning of initiation, Mom, Dad, and little Millennial set off for the park, bike nestled on the roof rack of the SUV. The entire event is being recorded by video camera. Before mounting the bike, little Millie is encased in a suit of plastic armor: helmet, knee pads, shoulder pads, chin strap, gloves. Yet, like all of us, she falls. She cries because her arm hurts, so she gets a visit to the hospital for an MRI because no one wants to ruin her chances of being a violinist (lessons at 6) or a softball pitcher (practice at 3).
>
> As my story illustrates, Millennials are the most protected, structured, watched-after, achievement-driven generation in American history. They are, as one Millennial parent actually said to me, "our little investment."[10]

Parental support and engagement are critical to a student's success and well-being as well as to the effectiveness of an educational institution. Most colleges and universities cultivate parental relationships through parents clubs, webpages, family weekends, and parent orientation programs. We all have stories of how these "helicopter" parents are more seriously engaged now than perhaps ever before. I do not think my parents set foot on Furman's campus until my graduation, and they would not have dared call anyone about a concern I might have had. They did not know I had concerns because I did not tell them.

This is not the case with Millennial students. They are very well connected to their parents via technology, and it is not uncommon for a faculty member or administrator to receive a phone call from a parent just minutes after a son or daughter has left the office. Another comment from Casey illustrates this point: "Almost every phone call the office of the Dean at Rollins received last summer regarding fall course scheduling for first-year students came from parents, not students themselves. I'm amused when parents use the possessive 'our' to refer to a student's schedule, as in 'We received our materials about fall term. . . .'"[11] Admissions officers know that co-buying parents and students is a developing trend, and information pieces used to sell a school must have a message for parents as well as for students.

Learning Styles

Traits of team orientation and the strong desire to achieve characteristic of Millennials certainly have implications for the classroom. The July/August 2003 issue of *EDUCAUSEreview* includes an article on how learning takes place among Millennial students. The article notes that Millennials gravitate toward group activity, are fascinated by new technologies, spend less time watching TV and more time doing homework, and think it is cool to be smart. Their learning preferences are for group work, experiential activities, structure, and the use of technology. Their strengths include multitasking, goal orientation, positive attitudes, and a collaborative style.[12]

Linda Sax, director of the Cooperative Institutional Research Program that collects and analyzes data from the CIRP instrument that is given to thousands of entering college students annually, reports that students have grown increasingly optimistic about their ability to be successful in college. In 1971 only 26.7 percent of entering freshmen thought they would earn at least a B average in college, but by 2002 that percentage had jumped to 60.2. More students believe they will have a good chance of graduating from college with honors.[13]

The Millennials' optimism about their ability to achieve success is noted by George Hudson, professor of English at Colgate since 1960. He says, "I'm very fond of the younger generation. One thing I like so much is that they have such eager faces. I love to teach them; they are always responsive, writing notes to me outside of class about the assignments. They are remarkably open and really smart." On the other hand, because Millennials are accustomed to being successful, when they fail, they often expect special treatment. Hudson notes that he never would have gone to his professor's office asking for a better grade than the one he earned based on how much his parents paid for him to attend the school, but he said today it happens to him regularly.[14]

We are well aware that this Millennial generation is technologically savvy and sophisticated. They are probably the most digitally literate students ever to enter college. In fact, what we call technology they call a way of life, because they have known nothing else. It is not surprising, then, that they expect information technology to be used as a teaching and learning strategy. Don Tapscott, in *Growing Up Digital: The Rise of the Next Generation*, published in 1998, offers an interesting and informative insight into the technological abilities of our students.[15]

Work and Career

Brian O'Reilly, writing in *Fortune* in 2000, began his article "Meet the Future" by stating, "It's your kids. The Millennial generation has grown up with prosperity, the Internet, divorce and Columbine. They already know they don't want to live and work the way we do."[16] Millennials do not want to be consumed with work the way Boomers have been. They show little interest in climbing the proverbial corporate ladder, have disdain for office cubicles, and do not necessarily aspire to the corner office. Most are turned off by the obsessiveness of the extremely well-to-do and the inordinate amount of work required of entrepreneurs. Only a few of them consider Bill Gates a hero. A consultant who worked with O'Reilly on his project predicted that Millennials will first decide what kind of lifestyle they want and then look for the jobs and careers that will accommodate that lifestyle. She also predicted that many of them will not take conventional nine-to-five jobs but will contract with a company for project work, work hard for a few months, and then take time off to pursue other interests before beginning the work cycle again.[17]

Northwestern Mutual's 2004 study on Millennials found they are ambitious about careers that provide them an opportunity to help others. They want an opportunity to impact the world and to have coworkers who, like themselves, are also idealistic and committed. Working for a large or global company is not important, and neither is having a high-pressure work environment. Three-fourths of the students interviewed said that how they spend their time is more important than how much money they make, and half indicated they want to own their own business. Amazingly, 20 percent report that they already own their own business.[18]

Kenneth Judd, president of a productivity and performance training company, offers advice to managers on how to get the most out of Millennial employees, providing yet another glimpse into their work ethic and characteristics. He advises that since Millennials want to be part of the action of a company, managers should help them understand how a business operates. Managers should share their experiences and let their employees participate and learn. Similarly, managers should relate to Millennials personally, getting to know them and sharing the company vision with them. It should be easy for managers to encourage positive morale since Millennials are optimistic and do not tend to be cynical. Being positive and always honest are important to the future Millennial workforce.[19]

Ethics and Values

Millennials place a premium on parental and peer relationships. Technology has provided them the means to stay in touch, and we know they do stay connected with family and friends. Most often their heroes are their parents or grandparents. So it is not surprising that they share a desire for a warm and loving family life for themselves and their children. They want a stable family life and hope to avoid divorce and its effect on children. They value making money not as an end in itself, but as a means to improve family life and to provide for their children. Millennials believe that making money will never be more important for them than children and family life. They also believe they have a financial responsibility to care for aging parents. While they may fuss and fume about being too sheltered by their parents and may even disagree with their parents' values, they respect them for who they are and for what they have done to ensure their children's success.[20]

Rules are generally respected by Millennials as long as they understand the reason for the rule in the first place. They do not, however, see the world in black and white or in terms of right and wrong. In the Northwestern Mutual study most students surveyed thought that littering is absolutely wrong, but only about half responded that it is absolutely wrong not to report all of one's income to the IRS or to exaggerate their qualifications on a resumé or application.[21] Of course, most administrators and faculty members are painfully aware of incidences of academic dishonesty and particularly plagiarism. There is no doubt that students freely use and abuse resources on the Internet to their advantage. But there is evidence that plagiarism is on the decrease, perhaps simply because faculty are finally catching up with the technology and using the resources available to them to detect plagiarism.

While the Millennials have been sheltered by their parents and others, they have not been able to escape the influence of the media in shaping their sexual values. Engaging in sexual activity for some is as much a way of life as technology. Many of those who are not actively engaging in sexual intercourse are doing almost everything else. Naomi Riley, in the chapter entitled "Sex, Drugs and Rock 'N' Roll" in her book *God on the Quad*, quotes Ben Patterson, the chaplain at Westmont College, and comments on his report:

> In areas of [sexual] morality, students are very much affected by their feelings, more than any sense of dogma. . . . It's pretty scary around there how many professing Christian students who are really serious believers split off there. What they will do . . . in intimate relations [is] so off the edge. I was at [the evangelical] Hope College for four years and I talked to students periodically who wanted to clean up their sex lives, to get themselves in line with their faith. . . . It took me four years to realize what they meant by that. They weren't having intercourse, but they were doing absolutely anything else. And it just one day dawned on me. Oh heavens. I thought they meant they had very high standards, but they didn't. They went right up to that. That was the only thing left to do. . . . [Westmont students] are in the same place. They'll say, "I feel close. I'm not just doing it with anybody. I care deeply."
>
> I mention this issue because while I see many good and positive traits and characteristics in the Millennial generation, I fear that self-gratification and hedonism are values that are continuing to gain acceptance as a way of life.[22]

Religion and Worship

George Barna and his research group offer insight into Millennials and matters of faith and worship. Barna's 2001 book *Real Teens* reported that the top-ranked faith-related goal of teens is to have peace with God, but this goal is number seven in a list of outcomes desired by teens. There is a high level of spiritual involvement among adolescents, but they are the least likely to be involved in church life when they are older.[23] Richard Cimino and Don Lattin, in a study of the dimensions of faith among Millennials, found a number of patterns in matters of faith: "the continuing separation of spirituality and formal religious institutions; a 'pick and choose' approach to faith, which empowers seekers to borrow the most useful doctrines and of spirituality into other areas of life, including work and education; and the popularization of faith." Furthermore, they argue that "as entertainment media becomes the primary conveyor of common culture, it will compete with religious groups as the main bearer of spiritual and religious insight."[24]

The Barna research group in 2002 also found that while spirituality has been mainstreamed into teen life, it has not radically changed their lifestyle and values. In 1990, 31 percent of teens in the study reported they were born-again Christians, but in spite of increased dialogue about religious matters and high levels of church participation, the percentage remained virtually unchanged in a 2001 follow-up study. In fact, the percentage of teens who identify themselves as evangelicals has declined from 10 percent in 1995 to 4 percent today. Barna attributes the decline to the growing numbers who accept moral relativism and pluralistic theology as their faith foundation.[25]

The Barna study further indicates that Millennials are looking for an authentic experience with other people and with God: "Teenagers patronize churches and other event-oriented organizations because they are seeking a compelling experience that is made complete and safe by the presence of people they know and trust, and from whom they are willing to learn and take their cues. Music and other ambient factors may attract them once or twice, but those elements will not keep them coming back for more. There has to be sufficient substance, quality, hope, and genuine mutual concern and acceptance for them to return."[26]

Robert Webber, director of the Institute of Worship Studies and professor of ministry at Northern Baptist Seminary, in an editorial entitled "How Will the Millennials Worship?" explored the intersection of worship, culture, and evangelism among Millennials and suggested the following conclusions:

- The primary issue of the future is not the style of worship so much as its *authentic character*. It must be real, genuine, and sincere. Millennials can smell "phony" a mile away. Therefore, traditionalists must avoid "dead ritualism," and proponents of contemporary must avoid "entertainment" and "manipulation" worship.

- The future style of worship will draw from the Catholic (early church), Reformation, evangelical, and contemporary traditions. Local churches must be eclectic.
- Future worship will move toward the following style characteristics:
    - More use of ritual and symbol
    - More spaces for quiet and contemplation
    - More frequent celebration of communion
    - High participation
    - Convergence of musical styles
    - More use of string and wind instruments
    - Recovery of the Christian year as a spiritual discipline [27]

Conclusion

At the beginning of this essay I suggested the importance of knowing who the students are who are coming to our campuses today, the students some authorities have referred to as "the next great generation." If we in Baptist higher education are to be prepared to receive the students predicted to attend our colleges and universities, we will need to take into account the characteristics of Millennials outlined by Howe and Strauss, characteristics that distinguish them in some important ways from the previous generation of students. The authors write: "Now, with the arrival of the Millennials, campus life is due for another transformation. Policies needed to accommodate or manage college students in the '80s and '90s will become increasingly inappropriate." According to Howe and Strauss, we must adapt our institutions to a "new crop of students" who are, among other things, close to their parents, highly focused on grades and achievement, technologically accomplished and interested in math and science, desirous of a "regulated environment" and community participation, tending toward conformist thinking, ethnically diverse yet not preoccupied with issues of racial identity, and predominantly female. The Millennials are also a large generation committed to the value of a college education.[28] This fact alone means that we need to get to work now if we are to be ready when they arrive.

For those of us in Baptist higher education, the results of the Barna research group offer an even more sobering picture than that suggested by Howe and Strauss, at least with respect to the religious outlook and practices of this new generation of students. The pick-and-choose approach to institutional religion reflects a "what's in it for me" outlook toward the Christian faith, and this attitude toward religion paves the way for a significant number of students today to accept moral relativism and theological pluralism as normative in their lives. In this sense, the Millennials are surely a product of the contemporary culture in which we all live. For this reason, we in Christian higher education must constantly be attentive to who our students are, this generation we now call the Millennials, if we are to offer the kind of moral and educational leadership our institutional missions require of us and that our students need.

Chapter Seven

Religious Identity, Academic Reputation, and Attracting the Best Faculty and Students

Larry Lyon

About five years ago *The Chronicle of Higher Education* reported on a conference of scholars and senior administrators at Harvard discussing "The Future of Religious Colleges."[1] The irony of the meeting's being at Harvard is readily apparent. Having been founded by Puritan Christians in 1636 and soon given the motto *Christo et Ecclesiae*, Harvard experienced a gradual transformation over the next two and a half centuries. By the beginning of the nineteenth century the Calvinists had been ousted from control of the university and had been replaced by Unitarians. And by the end of the nineteenth century, President Charles Eliot had transformed Harvard from a religious college into a prestigious secular university. This shift in ideological allegiances at schools such as Harvard suggests to some that today's religious colleges or universities are on the horns of a dilemma: either they maintain a distinctive religious identity or they move toward a strong academic reputation. The purpose of this essay, then, is to assess empirically the often-assumed dilemma that national universities cannot attain (1) a reputation for academic excellence, (2) a nationally known faculty, and (3) an academically strong student body if they maintain their religious identity. While some of the history and the projections apply to all religious schools, the focus is primarily on national universities such as Baylor because these schools should experience the dilemma more acutely than the preponderance of Baptist colleges and universities across the United States today.

An Apparent Dilemma

George Marsden, professor of history at the University of Notre Dame, expressed the dilemma in the following stark and provocative way:

> Since almost all the most highly regarded schools in America, from Harvard, to Amherst, to Chicago, to Duke, started out as traditionally religious schools, but eventually abandoned their original faith, is it not inevitable that the same will eventually happen to a Wheaton, Calvin, a Baylor, or a Notre Dame—at least if they hope to be recognized among America's academic elite?[2]

The histories of the leading institutions of American higher education reflect this trajectory, suggesting that if religious colleges and universities aspire to be prestigious national universities, then the religious identity of such institutions must diminish. Alternatively, if they remain faithful to those religious convictions that called them into being, then they must accept academic mediocrity and dwell in the backwaters of academic culture.

A major sociological study of higher education—*The Academic Revolution*, by Christopher Jencks and David Riesman—concurs with the historical studies mentioned above, but adds an important distinction between local colleges and national universities. Jencks and Riesman note a correlation between the localism of colleges and the special interests they represent, such as serving a specific region, a single gender, or relying on a sectarian religious identity for their mission.[3] National universities, conversely, represent more broadly national interests such as quality academics and the capacity to prepare students for prestigious occupations. Jencks and Riesman predict that a truly national university "must be de facto non-sectarian to acquire [a high academic reputation], given the prejudices of able faculty and students" and that the religious institution "that wants to compete in this market is unlikely to have much success unless it reinterprets its denominational commitments in largely secular terms or else gives them the flavor of snob appeal rather than piety."[4] In a related work, Riesman compares American higher education to a snake, where the middle and the end are constantly trying to follow the head.[5] With this evocative metaphor, Riesman identifies the major national universities as the head of the snake, while religious colleges and universities—at best in the middle, but more likely to be near the end of the tail—try to keep up by following the secular standards embedded in the new academic culture. Should religious universities aspire to move toward the head of the snake, then the religious identity of such institutions must diminish. Alternatively, if they remain faithful to the religious convictions that called them into being, then they must accept academic mediocrity and remain at the tail.

Must Baptist Schools Secularize?

Although the conference at Harvard acknowledged the perception of a dilemma, one of the purposes of the meeting was to challenge this view. Indeed, the consensus among attending scholars was that the cultural climate is increasingly "hospitable to religious institutions" and the "future of religious colleges is bright."[6] Ironically, the optimism of the participants at the Harvard conference is shared by George Marsden, the Notre Dame historian who chronicled the decline of religion in higher education in his *The Soul of the American University: From Protestant Establishment to Established Nonbelief.* In his paper delivered at the Harvard conference, Marsden claims that "[r]eligiously-defined liberal arts colleges are finding that by having preserved some of their traditional ways they are now offering more of what people are looking for in higher education and hence are ahead of the game."[7]

Support for such optimism may be found by closely examining schools currently trying to achieve a reputation for excellence while maintaining their religious connections. Case studies of fourteen schools by Richard Hughes and William Adrian "offer proof that colleges and universities can become first-rate academically and simultaneously maintain viable faith traditions."[8] More recently, Robert Benne employs a somewhat different case-study methodology but reaches a similar conclusion about six schools that "are academically excellent according to any ranking system" while "the Christian account of life [is] made visible and relevant in all facets of each school's activities."[9] Still, these affirmations are made primarily about colleges and regional universities. Thus, while they may offer comfort for colleges, the dilemma may still face those institutions that want to be both intentionally religious and a national university.

In Jencks and Riesman's view, national universities that want to be near the "head of the snake" will be especially susceptible to losing their religious identity. Marsden makes a similar observation about what he calls "pace-setting" universities.[10] Jencks, Riesman, and Marsden share the view that these national or pace-setting universities have characteristics that may make a distinctive religious character problematic. National universities must serve multiple interests with diverse faculty and typically enroll large numbers of heterogeneous students. National universities will have strong research and publishing expectations for their faculty. Such expectations are grounded in the aims and interests of academic disciplines and guilds rather than the sponsoring church. Professional accrediting agencies often define the curriculum and the criteria for success. Thus, even if the "future of religious *colleges* is bright," it does not follow that the future of religious *universities* is equally bright.

In fact, most of the Christian institutions represented at the Harvard conference were not national universities and do not aspire to be national universities. Bruce Keith, in a recent study of academic prestige, insists quite correctly that "colleges and universities are assumed to differ markedly in their scope and direction, with colleges typically oriented toward teaching and universities emphasizing research. Thus, comparing the two in light of such different objectives is counterproductive and could be misleading."[11] Accordingly, while a Calvin or a Wheaton, or in our context a Mercer, a Samford, a Hardin-Simmons, or a Campbell, may be able to maintain a religious identity and still move toward a stronger academic reputation, it does not necessarily follow that a Baylor or Notre Dame can remain distinctively Baptist or distinctively Catholic while achieving a strong academic reputation as a national university.

Measuring the Effect of Religious Identity on National Universities

The most widely cited measure of excellence among U.S. universities, the *U.S. News & World Report's* (*USN&WR*) annual college rankings, indicates that among the eighty-three national private universities, twenty-five claim some religious identification or affiliation. Further, eleven of these church-affiliated national universities have a reputation of 3.0 (on a 5.0 scale) or better, placing them among the top fifty private universities in the nation. Does the existence of these church-related schools with strong academic reputations suggest that the dilemma is indeed more apparent than real? A common response to this question is to downplay the significance of a church affiliation for highly ranked schools such as Duke and Wake Forest. Case studies such as James Burtchaell's have supported Jencks and Riesman's assertion that many of these schools are, for all intents and purposes, secular, and their church-affiliated status reflects a bygone era.[12]

Determining Which Private Universities Are "Religious"

Table 7.1 gives a complete list of all the national private universities, including the twenty-five that are church-affiliated. It also includes the *USN&WR* indicator of each institution's academic reputation. With regard to church affiliation, however, we must acknowledge the assessment of historians like Marsden who refer to schools such as Southern Methodist University and Emory as schools that lost their religious mooring and then "drifted into the national mainstream."[13] Similarly, Burtchaell argues that many "universities no longer have a serious, valued, or functioning relationship with their Christian sponsors of the past."[14] Many of the schools that claim a church affiliation may not be significantly different from their secular counterparts and, therefore, they may not encounter special problems in achieving a strong academic reputation. Thus, it is important to distinguish between universities that clearly embrace a religious identity and universities that are only nominally church-affiliated. We assume that institutions that are clearly and closely connected with the religious denomination or tradition will possess a distinctive identity distinguishing them from secular institutions. In addition, we presume that this religious identity will emerge from the intentional and direct influence of the sponsoring religious tradition on the institutions in empirically observable ways. For this reason we refer to such institutions as "religious" universities.

Table 7.1
Private Universities Listed by *USN&WR*'s Measure of Academic Reputation and Classified by Church Affiliation and Religious Identification

4.9 Harvard	3.6 Rensselaer Polytech	2.8 *Loyola of Chicago (Catholic)***
4.9 Stanford	3.5 U of Rochester	2.8 U of San Francisco
4.9 MIT	3.5 Tulane	2.8 Howard
4.8 Yale	3.5 *Boston College (Catholic)***	2.7 DePaul (Catholic)*
4.8 Princeton	3.4 Boston University	2.7 TCU (Christian)*
4.7 Johns Hopkins	3.4 Syracuse	2.7 Hofstra
4.7 California Institute of Technology	3.3 George Washington	2.7 Stevens
4.7 University of Chicago	3.3 Lehigh	2.7 *Seton Hall (Catholic)***
4.7 Cornell	3.3 *Baylor (Baptist)***	2.7 *U of San Diego (Catholic)***
4.6 Columbia	3.3 Wake Forest (Baptist)*	2.6 Clarkson
4.6 Duke (Methodist)*	3.2 *Fordham (Catholic)***	2.6 University of Denver
4.5 Brown	3.2 SMU (Methodist)*	2.6 Polytechnic
4.5 Northwestern	3.1 *Brigham Young (Mormon)***	2.6 U of the Pacific
4.4 Dartmouth	3.0 University of Miami	2.6 Duquesne (Catholic)*
4.4 University of PA	3.0 New School	2.5 University of Tulsa
4.2 Rice	3.0 Yeshiva	2.5 MCP Hahnemann
4.2 Carnegie	3.0 *St. Louis (Catholic)***	2.4 Clark Atlanta
4.1 Washington U	3.0 Illinois Institute of Technology	2.4 Florida Institute of Technology
4.1 Vanderbilt	2.9 *Pepperdine (Church of Christ)***	2.4 Pace University
4.0 Emory (Methodist)*	2.9 American (Methodist)*	2.3 Adelphi

3.9 *Notre Dame (Catholic)***	2.9 Clark University	2.1 Union University
3.9 *Georgetown (Catholic)***	2.9 *Marquette (Catholic)***	2.1 University of Detroit
3.7 Brandeis	2.9 Drexel	2.0 *Andrews (7th Day Adventist)***
3.7 New York University	2.9 Northeastern U	1.9 U of La Verne (Brethren)*
3.6 Tufts	2.9 *St. John's (Catholic)***	1.8 *Biola (Christian)***
3.6 Case Western	2.9 Worcester Polytech	1.8 U.S. International
3.6 USC	2.8 *Catholic University (Catholic)***	1.7 Nova Southeastern

* Universities identified as church-affiliated by *U.S. News & World Report* survey

** Church-affiliated universities also classified as "religious" based on mission statement and curriculum requirements

Given our earlier characterization of a religious university, we posit three observable criteria to distinguish religious from nonreligious universities. Two of the criteria relate to the school's mission statement and the third to the curriculum:

(1) As Merrimon Cuninggim explains, the university's mission statement should acknowledge a specific link to a church or claim a religious heritage—for example, "We commit ourselves to create a climate patterned on the life and teachings of Jesus Christ as embodied in the traditions and practices of the Roman Catholic Church"[15] (St. John's University, New York)

(2) Michael Buckley maintains that the mission statement should mention an explicit religious goal—for example, "The mission of Biola University is biblically centered education, scholarship and service equipping men and women in mind and character to impact the world for the Lord Jesus Christ."[16]

(3) Mark Schwehn, among others, has argued that the core curriculum should require religion courses that reflect and support the university's religious identity—for example, Baptist Baylor University requires two religion courses, "Christian Scriptures" and "Christian Heritage."[17]

The determination of which criteria each school meets was based on a review of each university's most recent catalogue, specifically the mission statements and core curricula. While these measures are not sufficient to capture all the complex nuances of religious identity, they allow us to identify sixteen national universities that currently maintain their religious identity by meeting at least two of the criteria. The list was narrowed from twenty-five to sixteen by eliminating those church-related institutions that analysts argue are nominally but not seriously and distinctively religious. Many of those remaining on our list are schools that, according to case studies, have successfully resisted secularization. The sixteen religious schools identified in Table 7.1 are compared against the national model for secular private universities developed in the next section.

Measuring Academic Reputation

Historically, the desire for a stronger academic reputation has been the factor most often cited as the reason for the secularization of previously religious institutions in the academy. Although *USN&WR* uses multiple indicators of academic quality, such as smaller class sizes or higher retention rates, an institution's academic reputation—the goal of those who secularized their religious universities—is determined by a survey of academicians. All college presidents, provosts, and deans of admissions are surveyed, with an overall response rate of 68 percent. Each respondent is asked to rate peer schools' academic programs on a scale from 1 (marginal) to 5 (distinguished). Those who do not know enough about a school to evaluate it fairly are asked to mark "don't know." We hypothesize that if the dilemma discussed earlier does, in fact, exist, distinctively religious universities would have a difficult time attaining a strong academic reputation. Furthermore, we hypothesize that if these sixteen schools with a distinctive religious mission and curriculum were to be assessed by the academy as if they were secular, unhampered by their religious "baggage," their academic reputation would logically be higher than is currently reported by *USN&WR*.

Are Religious Universities Handicapped in Seeking Strong Academic Reputations?

Although a number of possible predictors of academic reputation were originally included (e.g., graduation rate, class size, student/faculty ratio, acceptance rate, alumni giving), our baseline comparison model is a simple (in conserving degrees of freedom) and powerful (in explained variance), one that includes only SAT scores of entering students and faculty salary as predictors. Theoretically, both variables are obvious and logical predictors of a school's academic reputation. In previous research, SAT scores of entering students have typically been highly correlated with academic reputation, and the salary of full professors (those most likely to enhance a school's reputation) has emerged as a strong predictor as well. High SAT scores mean "better" students, and higher faculty salaries help recruit and keep "star" faculty. Statistically, several regressions with various combinations of predictors were run, and SAT and faculty salary consistently emerged as the most powerful explanatory variables, with other variables adding little or nothing to the existing level of explained variance.

Table 7.2
Summary of OLS Regression Analysis for Variables Predicting Academic Reputation for Private Secular Universities (N=54)

Variable	*B*	*SE B*	β
SAT	.0045	.001	.710****
Faculty salary	.0157	.005	.269**

Note: Adjusted R^2 = .885 F=208.234**** (*$p < .05$; **$p < .01$; ***$p < .001$; ****$p < .0001$)

The final base-comparison model potentially includes all secular private schools that are Doctoral Level II or higher. As Table 7.2 illustrates, SAT and faculty salary combine to explain 88 percent of the variance in academic reputation of the fifty-four schools with complete data. Schools recruiting students with higher SAT scores and paying their senior faculty more garner stronger academic reputations on the *USN&WR* survey.

If the quality of students (as measured by SAT) and the quality of faculty (as measured by faculty salary) are known, then it is possible to predict a university's academic reputation. Again, the baseline model in Table 7.2 includes all secular private schools, producing an equation in which religious schools' SAT scores and faculty salary can be inserted into the secular model so that they are rewarded as if they were secular. In terms of academic reputation, this equation will estimate how religious universities would perform if they did not have a distinctive religious affiliation/identification.

When religious schools accrue academic reputation by the same algorithm as their secular counterparts, no statistically significant distinctions emerge between the two equations (i.e., the "secular" and the "religious" equations produce similar mean scores and standard deviations). Table 7.3 gives a comparison of both the predicted and actual reputations and the average (mean) residual for all the religious universities. No statistically significant differences emerge between religious schools' predicted and actual reputation, indicating that, overall, religious universities are neither hindered nor helped by their religious identification. Thus, we find little support for the proposition that a distinctive religious identity handicaps the quest for a strong academic reputation. Given their student SAT scores and faculty salaries, religious universities are performing as well as secular universities.

Table 7.3
Predicted Reputation for Religious Schools and Average Residual

	Actual Reputation	Predicted Reputation	Difference
Georgetown	3.9	4.1	-0.22
Notre Dame	3.9	3.9	-0.03
Boston College	3.5	3.8	-0.28
Baylor	3.3	2.8	0.50
Fordham	3.2	3.1	0.15
BYU	3.1	2.9	0.17
St. Louis	3.0	2.7	0.28
Pepperdine	2.9	3.3	-0.40
Marquette	2.9	2.6	0.26
St. John's	2.9	2.4	0.55
Catholic	2.8	2.8	-0.02
Loyola	2.8	2.8	0.02
San Diego	2.7	2.9	-0.24
Seton Hall	2.7	2.5	0.18
Biola	1.8	2.2	-0.44
		Mean Residual:	.03

Note: t-ratio = .521; p = .610

Can Religious Schools Recruit Top Students and Faculty?

With sufficiently talented students and faculty, religious schools apparently can impress the larger secular academic community. This implies that the proposition that distinctively religious schools are penalized because of their religious identity is incorrect. However, the process of acquiring an academic reputation is more complex than what is represented in the base model. Figure 7.1 illustrates how SAT and faculty salary can be considered a university's "human capital," which in turn depends on the university's "economic capital." For private schools this would be endowment, donations, and tuition. Therefore, given that faculty and students are often "for sale" (through scholarships and salary), a reasonable causal sequence is that the more money a school has, the better students and faculty they can recruit, resulting in a stronger academic reputation.

Figure 7.1
Causal Model Predicting Academic Reputation

Economic Capital →	Human Capital →	Academic Reputation
(donations, tuition, endowment)	(faculty and students)	(*USN&WR* measure)

Table 7.3 showed that given equal amounts of human capital (high-scoring students and highly paid faculty), religious universities suffer no handicap in converting that capital into academic reputation. However, it may be that the handicap of being religious occurs earlier in the causal chain. We now assess whether or not religious universities are hampered in their attempt to recruit faculty and students. This requires two separate regressions, one to predict faculty salary, and the other to predict SAT scores. Again, only secular, private, national universities are in the baseline model. For our first equation, endowment per student, donation per student, and tuition were significant predictors of SAT, explaining 80 percent of the variance (see Table 7.4).

Table 7.4
Summary of Simultaneous Regression Analysis for Variables Predicting SAT for Private Secular Universities (N=46)

Variables	*B*	*SE B*	β
Donation	.004396	.001	.404****
Tuition	.017300	.003	.468****
Endowment	.000077	.000	.273**

Note: Adjusted R^2 = .798; F=61.424**** (*$p < .05$; **$p < .01$; ***$p < .001$; ****$p < .0001$)

Similar to the model predicting academic reputation, Table 7.5 shows little support for the existence of the so-called dilemma. Religious universities are not at a significant disadvantage in student recruitment. Students recruited by religious schools are scoring only four points lower on their SAT than would otherwise be predicted if these schools were secular, a difference not large enough to lead to the conclusion that religious universities are disadvantaged in recruiting good students. However, a pattern not seen with academic reputation emerges with the SAT. Results in Table 7.5 indicate that the higher-ranked religious universities (Georgetown, Notre Dame, Boston College, and Baylor) are recruiting higher-scoring students than predicted when considering their financial base, while religious universities with lower reputations appear to be recruiting lower-scoring students than the model predicts, a pattern that is explored later in the essay.

Table 7.5
Actual and Predicted SAT Scores for Religious Universities and Average Residual

	Actual SAT	Predicted SAT	Difference
Georgetown (3.9)	1355	1277	78
Notre Dame (3.9)	1320	1258	62
Boston College (3.5)	1285	1233	52
Baylor (3.3)	1155	1041	114
St. Louis (3.0)	1120	1156	-36
Pepperdine (2.9)	1227	1289	-62
Marquette (2.9)	1120	1132	-12
St. John's (2.9)	985	1086	-101
Loyola (2.8)	1110	1161	-51
San Diego (2.7)	1160	1163	-3
Seton Hall (2.7)	1050	1138	-88
		Mean Residual:	-4

Note: *t*-ratio = .198; p =.847

We now turn to faculty. The previous procedure was repeated for faculty salary and again the results were similar to the regression for student SAT. Table 7.6 indicates that all three independent variables—endowment, donations, and tuition—are significant predictors of faculty salary, explaining about 70 percent of the variance.

Table 7.6
Summary of Simultaneous Regression Analysis for Variables Predicting Faculty Salary for Private Secular Universities (N=45)

Variables	*B*	*SE B*	β
Endowment	.00001436	.000	.417**
Tuition	.00156900	.000	.345****
Donation	.00040200	.000	.299*

Note: Adjusted R^2 = .707; F= 37.133**** (*$p < .05$; **$p < .01$; ***$p < .001$; ****$p < .0001$)

The model was then used to predict faculty salary for religious universities as if their financial base had the same influence that it does for secular universities. Table 7.7 suggests that, *with a financial base equal to their secular counterparts*, religious universities would pay their full professors ninety-eight hundred dollars more a year, which is approximately 10 percent more than they would pay if they did not have a religious affiliation. For the first time we find empirical evidence of a possible disadvantage for distinctively religious universities. Our model suggests that these universities pay more than we would predict to keep the faculty most likely to affect their academic reputation: the senior faculty. Two explanations of the relatively high cost for senior faculty at religious universities are considered in the following section.

Table 7.7
Actual and Predicted Faculty Salary (in thousands of dollars) for Religious Schools and Average Residual

	Actual Faculty Salary	Predicted Faculty Salary	Difference
Georgetown (3.9)	100.3	87.6	12.7
Notre Dame (3.9)	98.1	85.9	12.2
Boston College (3.5)	98.9	83.7	15.2
Baylor (3.3)	73.9	66.2	7.7
St. Louis (3.0)	78.4	76.7	1.7
Pepperdine (2.9)	84.9	88.7	-3.8
Marquette (2.9)	73.7	74.4	-0.7
St. John's (2.9)	94.1	70.3	23.8
Loyola (2.8)	85.3	77.1	8.2
San Diego (2.7)	96.6	77.3	19.3
Seton Hall (2.7)	86.2	75.1	11.1
		Mean Residual:	9.8

Note: t-ratio = 3.873; p =.003

Does Being Religious Help or Hurt?

When religious universities were treated in our mathematical model in the same way as secular universities in how they translate student SAT scores and faculty salary into academic reputation, their predicted academic reputation did not diverge significantly from their actual reputation. The caliber of students and faculty accurately predicts a school's academic reputation regardless of whether or not the school is distinctively religious.

A similar pattern emerges for student recruitment. Possessing a religious identity is not a disadvantage for these distinctively religious universities in their attempt to enroll high-scoring high school graduates. However, it is true that higher-ranked religious universities are recruiting higher-scoring SAT students than would otherwise be predicted by the universities' endowments, donations, and tuition, while schools with lower academic reputations are recruiting lower-scoring students than predicted by their financial base. The most likely possibility for this pattern is the independent effect of reputation on recruitment. Although academic reputation is the key dependent variable in this research, analysis not shown here indicates that if academic reputation were included as an independent variable in the prediction model: (1) it would indeed help explain how schools attract high-scoring high school seniors (i.e., the R^2 increases), and (2) the student recruitment disadvantage experienced by religious schools with relatively low reputations disappears (i.e., with reputation as a predictor, low-reputation schools experience no recruitment disadvantage in the model).

When exploring the significance of faculty salary, a different pattern emerges. Most national religious universities, regardless of their academic reputation, are paying more for their senior faculty than are secular, private, national universities with a similar financial base. There are at least two possible explanations for why religious universities might pay their faculty more than their financial resources would predict. One explanation has nothing to do with the religious nature of these schools. Most of these distinctively religious universities are in cities with exceptionally high costs of living, and the effects of these differences are much larger when the school is assessed individually rather than with all private schools aggregately. Controlling for the cost-of-living differences would allow for a better understanding of the relationship between faculty salary and academic reputation. Unfortunately, no broadly accepted source for "cost of living" data exists, and the available sources differ considerably in their measurements. However, adjustments by perhaps the most widely used measure, the local surveys compiled by the American Chambers of Commerce, completely eliminates the higher salaries paid by religious universities. In fact, all the cost of living comparisons we found reduced the salary difference paid to faculty at these schools.

The other explanation is tied directly to the religious nature of these universities. At some religious schools the effort to increase academic reputation occasionally trumps the desire to have faculty committed to the university's religious identity. These academicians may associate "religious" with restrictions on academic freedom, making religious universities less attractive to some senior faculty who have established a body of research at odds with church teaching. In these instances, a religious university may choose to pay a highly sought faculty member for whom the religious identity of the university is unimportant more than predicted in order to keep him or her from leaving the institution. A recent example is the current struggle between Catholic universities and the Catholic church over *Ex Corde Ecclesia*.[18] While these two explanations are not mutually exclusive, we suspect that cost-of-living differences account for most of the differences.

Overall, however, regardless of why religious universities pay their faculty more than their financial resources would predict, the causal models do not provide much support for the idea that religious national universities face a dilemma—that they must secularize in order to achieve a reputation for academic excellence. Our most direct test indicates that with equivalent levels of financial support, the predicted academic reputations of private secular universities and private religious universities would also be equivalent. Further, religious universities do not appear to be at a disadvantage in their pursuit of quality students. These findings suggest, then, that while secularization has often occurred in American colleges and universities, the current argument that it is necessity to secularize in order to achieve a strong academic reputation may be overstated, even for national universities.

This analysis certainly offers support for the optimistic assessment that emerged from the Harvard conference. Baptist institutions may still choose to follow the historical trajectory of most other "pace-setting" private universities at the "head of the snake" and lose their religious distinctiveness. However, it does not appear that national religious universities are faced with a real dilemma of choosing either academic excellence or a distinctively religious identity. The data suggest that our dilemma is indeed more apparent than real, and that secularization, while historically common, is not currently necessary in the pursuit of a strong academic reputation.

Part Three

Baptist Higher Education and Its Constituencies

Chapter Eight

Is Higher Education a Justifiable Mission of Baptist Churches and Baptist Bodies?

James C. Denison

The scene from the Golan Heights in Israel is one of the most breathtaking in all God's world. Standing 1,150 feet above sea level, the massive rock outcropping is the largest I've ever seen, gray with streaks of metallic brown, flat and imposing. And towering above it is a gigantic cliff, dwarfing the Huleh Valley below in every direction. High up on that cliff our tour group could see a cave, the famous "Gates of Hades." This cave leads to a natural shaft that runs down through the mountain and through this rocky plateau on which it stands, so deep into the earth that the ancient Greeks believed it was the entrance to the underworld.

As I looked in awe, my mind traveled back to a time when, as the Bible records, another man stood where I was standing this day. As that man looked around him, he was aware of the religious significance of the place. He knew it was at this "Cave of Hades" where the Greeks worshiped Pan, their god of nature, and he knew that Roman gods were worshiped here as well. Scattered around the place were fourteen temples to Baal, the Canaanite fertility god, where the pagan Syrians worshiped. And just a short distance away stood the brilliant white marble temple built by Herod the Great as an altar to the worship of the Roman Caesar, hence the name of the place, "Caesarea Philippi." He knew the emperor was worshiped here. Somewhere below was the origin of the Jordan River, the holiest river in all the Jewish faith, the water Joshua and the people walked through to inherit the Promised Land, and he thought of his own Jewish traditions of worship.

Standing on this gigantic rock, surrounded by temples to every kind of god known to several great cultures, this man heard a Galilean carpenter ask the small group of men gathered there, "Who do you say that I am?" And that man, standing where I stood, said, "You are the Messiah, the Son of the living

God." And he heard the Galilean say, "On this rock I will build my church," and—pointing to the cave towering above them, dwarfing this small group of men gathered below—"the gates of Hades will not prevail against it" (Matt. 16:16, 18).

Jesus Christ proclaimed that his church was to assault the gates of hell. Christians are under mandate to take the gospel to all the world, to "Jerusalem, in all Judea and Samaria, and to the ends of the earth" (Acts 1:8). The church of Jesus Christ was founded to "make disciples of all nations" (Matt. 28:19). Within the context of Baptist churches and of the Christian church, our mission is clear: to fulfill the Great Commission by making disciples of all nations.

The questions that inform this essay are simple: Is Christian higher education an appropriate part of this mission? Does such an undertaking as higher education play an effective and significant role in the church's work of reaching the world? Many admirable and noble activities do not play such a role, at least not in direct and demonstrable ways. For example, in my first pastorate I learned that a previous pastor had wanted years earlier to set up a welding shop on the church parking lot. Welding is a vocation for which we should all be grateful, but Truett Seminary does not teach welding as one of its ministry concentrations. And no church that I am aware of, my first church included, has chosen to make welding a part of its strategic mission and ministry.

Higher education is a good and noble endeavor, but is it peripheral to the mission of the church? Or is it central and crucial to the larger mission of Baptist churches and the church of Jesus Christ? Does such an activity distract the church from its calling to assault the gates of hell, or does it inform and empower it?

I became a Christian within an environment in which many would have argued that higher education is *not* a part of the church's mission. Without fully realizing it, I was influenced by three arguments against Christian education being part of the church's mission, all still prevalent in Baptist life today. Let's consider each church-centered objection to Christian higher education in turn and see if we can find grounds to defend the enterprise we are here to discuss.

Argument One
Christian higher education is irrelevant to the Great Commission purpose of the church.

The argument underlying this view is that Christians are here to win souls, not educate people. In this view, college and university education stands outside the missionary mandate of the church and is no more relevant to the church's purpose than law or medical schools. This conviction that the educational enterprise and the mission of the church are essentially different is reflected not only within the church, but within the academy as well. James Burtchaell, in his monumental study of the disengagement of many Christian colleges and universities from their Christian and denominational roots, describes the "marginalization of theological discourse" that occurred in institutions of higher education after the Civil War. The academic study of religion was shouldered aside for greater emphasis and investment in other intellectual and vocational disciplines.[1] Indeed, this argument sees a basic dichotomy between the missions of educational institutions and that of churches, so the idea of "Christian education" is irrelevant to both the church and the academy. In direct opposition to this perspective is the view of Stephen Evans:

> Those who are convinced in faith that the Christian narrative is true should see this narrative as one that enhances and stimulates fruitful inquiry. They should have the courage to stride boldly forward as scholars, confident that the God who is the source of all truth, and the Christ in whom are hid all the treasures of wisdom and knowledge, will bless and sustain their honest and humble efforts.[2]

Which perspective possesses the greater merit? Many Christians and Baptists not directly involved in Christian higher education would probably agree with the former argument rather than with Evans's perspective. For example, trustees of the International Mission Board of the Southern Baptist Convention have determined in recent years to cut off financial support for overseas educational institutions. One of their stated reasons was that these resources are needed for evangelism and church planting. In their view, Christian higher education is secondary and peripheral to such priorities.

Argument Two
Christian higher education may be appropriate for ministers, missionaries, and theologians, but it is unnecessary for the laity.

A second objection to Christian higher education follows the first: Christian higher education may be appropriate for some in ministry, but it is not essential for them and completely unnecessary for laypersons. The first assertion arises from the patristic endorsement of the clergy, the second from the Reformation emphasis on the priesthood of all believers.

In this view, Christians can fulfill the Great Commission without Christian higher education. In fact, it's best if they do. Such intellectual pursuit can damage faith and distract us from our evangelistic purpose. Just as colleges and universities can and do move away from their Christian heritage, so those who attend such institutions can be led away from the faith of their fathers. We need seminaries and other vocational training for our leaders, to be sure, just as we need military academies and medical schools for those who wish to become leaders in those professions. But not everyone needs to go to West Point to be able to hunt deer or attend medical school to bandage a scraped knee. A muffler shop doesn't need to teach its employees to rebuild engines.

How did the idea that Christian education was appropriate only for some ministers, missionaries, and theologians become widely accepted?[3] The earliest Christians subjected their message and ministry to biblical authority. Peter's Pentecost sermon stood upon the authority of Old Testament prophetic literature; Stephen's self-defense retold the biblical history of Israel; James used Old Testament prophetic texts in leading the Jerusalem Council to accept the Gentile mission; and Paul asserted that "All Scripture is inspired by God" (2 Tim. 3:16). Soon, however, church authority moved from the Bible itself to the Scriptures as they were interpreted by church leaders. Ignatius asserted the authority of the bishop over the church[4] and viewed a "college" of bishops as the ruling authority of the larger church.[5] Irenaeus considered the Roman church to be the "preeminent authority" in Christendom, and viewed her leaders as emanating from Peter and Paul through the bishops who succeeded them.[6]

By A.D. 250, Cyprian of Carthage had separated the "clergy" from the "laity" and made his famous claim, "He can no longer have God for his Father, who has not the church for his mother."[7] When Constantine embraced Christianity in 312 (historians will debate the sincerity of his commitment) and legalized his new faith, the Roman church was clearly understood to lead the Christian movement. In this view, since God gave the Scriptures through the church, he would lead the church to the proper understanding of his word. Creeds, councils, and papal declarations would become the means by which the Bible was interpreted and transmitted. In this view, religious education is appropriate and even permissible only for the clergy and is secondary to those involved in missions and evangelism for the larger church.

What's Wrong with Leaving Christian Education to Religious Professionals?

This perspective is flawed relative to the church's Great Commission purpose, for two reasons. First, trained professionals are not infallible. We can miss the intended meaning of the Scripture, despite our years of study, and sometimes even because of them. For example, the first Christian theologians faced the problem of finding ways to use the Old Testament in their new faith. Their typical answer was to find Christ in the Hebrew Bible wherever possible, and when passages and entire books had little or no intended application to the

Messiah, they found him there anyway. Clement of Rome (A.D. 30–100) said that Rahab's scarlet rope (Josh. 2:21) "made it manifest that redemption should flow through the blood of the Lord to all them that believe and hope in God."[8] Justin Martyr (ca. 100–167) insisted that the high priest's bells on his robe (Exod. 28:33-35) symbolize the twelve apostles, each of whom "ring out" the gospel of the Great High Priest.[9] Clement of Alexandria (150–213?) thought the different musical instruments in Psalm 150 each symbolize a different part of the human body.[10] In interpreting Jesus' triumphant entry into Jerusalem, Origen (185–251?) taught that Jesus' colt was the Old Testament carrying him to the cross.[11]

Mistaken interpretation has unfortunately not been reserved for the early centuries of Christian history. When oil wells were first dug in Pennsylvania, many New York ministers opposed the project, claiming that the wells would deplete the oil stored there for the predestined burning of the world (2 Pet. 3:10, 12). Church members and leaders rejected the use of winnowing fans in Scotland because "the wind blows where it wills" (John 3:8). Martin Luther reluctantly consented to the bigamous marriage of Philip of Hesse, reasoning that since men such as David and Solomon were permitted more than one wife, such practice must be biblical.[12] Because misinterpretation can easily happen today, I often tell my church members that they must judge everything they hear me say by Scripture. The only word God is obligated to bless is his own. Because all Christians need to be able to evaluate biblical interpretation, it is a crucial mistake to limit education to the professionals.

Second, restricting religious and Christian higher education to the clergy isolates biblical truth and ministry from the larger world. Imagine a hospital whose chief administrator is the only person allowed to speak with patients. Think of an automobile factory where only the foreman is permitted to handle car parts. Suppose that only the head coach touched the basketball. And you would have the picture of most churches if only the pastor were educated about religious issues. Because the gospel is the power of God unto salvation (Rom. 1:16), it must be studied and shared by the entire church if the entire world is to hear and believe. Limiting religious training and Christian higher education to the professionals is the surest way imaginable to keep biblical truth from reaching the world outside the church. My church members will speak with more non-Christians today than I will be privileged to meet in a month. If I am the only person permitted to dispense God's word, those who need it most will hear it least.

Jesus called his followers the "salt of the earth" and the "light of the world" (Matt. 5:13-16). Salt does no one any good in the saltshaker. Light is no help under a basket. The Bible cannot change the world if the world is never taken to it. Jesus wanted disciples to make disciples, Christians to multiply through personal evangelism and ministry. When we limit Christian higher education to the professionals, considering such endeavor for the larger church and society to be peripheral to our Great Commission mandate, we produce the opposite effect from that which we intend. Rather than reserving more resources for education and missions, we rob the church of resources crucial to such ministry.

Why are Lay Christian Believers to Be Priests?

As we know, the Protestant reformers sought to relocate authority with the Scriptures as they are interpreted by the individual believer. William of Occam argued that the revelation of God in Scripture is the authoritative basis for Christian faith, not the authority of the church. His position greatly influenced Luther, who studied under professors committed to Occam's theology. In fact, Luther called Occam his "beloved master." Luther in turn made the famous claim, "Only the Holy Scripture possesses canonical authority."[13] He discounted the claims of magistrates, church councils, church fathers, bishops, and even the pope to authority over the Scriptures.[14] John Calvin agreed: "God bestows the actual knowledge of himself upon us only in the Scriptures"; "Scripture has its authority from God, not from the church."[15]

Such conviction has characterized Baptists across our history. For instance, W. B. Johnson, the founder and first president of the Southern Baptist Convention, published in 1846 a book that opposed confessions of faith as a basis of Baptist union. In the introduction to his book, he listed five specific convictions that characterized Baptists in the South in the mid-nineteenth century: (1) the sovereignty of God in salvation, (2) "the supreme authority of the scripture," (3) "the right of each individual to judge for himself in his views of truth as taught in the scriptures," (4) democratic church government, and (5) believers' baptism.[16]

Later in the same century, the Baptist Union of Great Britain and Ireland affirmed their faith in "the Divine Inspiration and Authority of the Holy Scriptures as the supreme and sufficient rule of our faith and practice: and the right and duty of individual judgment in the interpretation of it."[17] From our beginnings, Baptists have argued that each believer has the right and responsibility of personal biblical interpretation. Growing out of our refusal to affirm creeds, we believe that God's Spirit is our sufficient guide in understanding the truth he inspired.

And so we encourage every believer to study Scripture personally. Contrary to the institutionalism of the Roman Catholic church, we have stood for the priesthood of every believer. We do not believe that the church determines the meaning of the Bible, or that church teachings and traditions are on a par with biblical authority. We do not submit to the dictates of denominational officials or decisions. Whenever a Baptist body takes a position on a particular theological subject, it speaks only for those present when the vote was taken. Its resolutions and decisions have no binding authority over any other person or church.

We do not require our members to obtain seminary degrees or acquire ministerial credentials before they interpret Scripture. We do not insist that they agree with their pastor or church leaders theologically. Our churches do not make binding decisions regarding matters of spiritual or theological conviction. There is no particular view of Genesis or Revelation you must affirm to teach the Bible at my church. I often tell surprised new members that their interpretation of God's word is just as valid as mine. And as necessary!

Why Do Baptists Have No Creeds but Scripture?

When people join my church from other denominations, they often ask to see our creed. I show them a Bible. When they look confused, I explain that Baptists must sign no statement of faith. Baptists do not recite the Apostles' Creed or the Nicene Creed in worship. Baptists do not insist upon the Westminster Confession of Faith as basic to our theology. We consider all man-made creeds to be secondary to biblical authority.

But what about our own confessions of faith? The preamble to the 1963 Baptist Faith and Message sets out the view the authors took of their statements:

> (1) That they constitute a consensus of opinion of some Baptist body, large or small, for the general instruction and guidance of our own people and others concerning those articles of the Christian faith which are most surely held among us. They are not intended to add anything to the simple conditions of salvation revealed in the New Testament, viz., repentance towards God and faith in Jesus Christ as Savior and Lord.
>
> (2) That we do not regard them as complete statements of our faith, having any quality of finality or infallibility. As in the past so in the future Baptists should hold themselves free to revise their statements of faith as may seem to them wise and expedient at any time.
>
> (3) That any group of Baptists, large or small have the inherent right to draw up for themselves and publish to the world a confession of their faith whenever they may think it advisable to do so.
>
> (4) That the sole authority for faith and practice among Baptists is the Scriptures of the Old and New Testaments. Confessions are only guides in interpretation, having no authority over the conscience.
>
> (5) That they are statements of religious convictions, drawn from the Scriptures, and are not to be used to hamper freedom of thought or investigation in other realms of life.[18]

The Baptist Faith and Message did not add conditions to salvation, state unchangeable theology, or limit interpretation or conscience. Clearly, "the sole authority for faith and practice among Baptists is the Scriptures." We don't sign anyone's faith statement, not even one of our own.

Back in 1911, historian W. J. McGlothlin made clear our relation to creeds and confessions:

> Being congregational and democratic in church government, Baptists have naturally been very free in making, changing, and using Confessions. There has never been among them any ecclesiastical authority which could impose a Confession upon their churches or other bodies. Their Confessions are, strictly speaking, statements of what a certain group of Baptists, large or small, did believe at a given time, rather than a creed which any Baptist must believe at all times in order to hold ecclesiastical position or to be considered a Baptist. In the latter sense there has been no Baptist creed.[19]

Indeed, the Baptist Faith and Message would be more properly titled "A Statement of the Baptist Faith and Message."[20] Not "the" statement or "the" creed we must believe. Jesus claimed, "All authority in heaven and on earth has been given to me" (Matt. 28:18). If he has all authority, we have none. Baptists believe in no creed but Scripture.

How Can Educational Preparation Be Beneficial for Laypeople?

Baptists' emphasis on individual priesthood can be carried to an extreme. We are called to make "disciples," reproducing followers of Jesus, not just church members. Our leaders are to prepare God's people "for the work of ministry, for building up the body of Christ" (Eph. 4:12). Our members are to "Love the Lord your God with all your heart, and with all your soul, and with all your mind" (Matt. 22:37). Even Jesus "increased in wisdom and in years, and in divine and human favor" (Luke 2:52). Intellectual preparation is vital to spiritual growth and service.

The Holy Spirit has a strange affinity for the trained mind. Moses was "instructed in all the wisdom of the Egyptians and was powerful in his words and deeds" (Acts 7:22). Josephus stated that he was "educated with great care. So the Hebrews depended on him, and were of good hopes that great things would be done by him; but the Egyptians were suspicious of what would follow his education" (*Antiquities* 2.9.7). When Saul of Tarsus was learning the larger Roman culture, he had no idea he would use such knowledge to win intellectuals to faith in Christ on Mars Hill (Acts 17). When he learned to master the Hebrew Scriptures, he did not know he would quote them across the Roman Empire. Matthew did not know that the stenographic skills he perfected in tax collecting would one day enable him to record the Sermon on the Mount. Intellectual preparation is vital to ministry effectiveness.

The late Pope John Paul II provided the best definition I have found of the "neighbor" we are commanded to love in ministry:

> When I say "neighbor," I obviously mean those who live beside us, in the family, in the neighborhood, in the town or village, in the city. But it also means those with whom we work, those who are suffering, are sick, know loneliness, are really poor. My neighbor is also all those who are geographically quite distant, or who are exiled from their own countries, are without, lack food and clothing, often lack liberty. My neighbor is all those unfortunates who have been completely or almost ruined by unforeseeable and dramatic catastrophes, which have thrown them into physical and moral want, often enough also into the sadness of losing their dearest ones.[21]

How are we to minister to such need, unless we acquire the skills required for such service? Christian higher education is crucial to the effective fulfillment of the Second Great Commandment and the Great Commission. It is clear that the church must maintain and even increase its support for such endeavors. Alan Wolfe documents a 1994 survey which indicated that only 9 percent of Americans in general and 25 percent of self-described evangelicals could say what the Great Commission was. Less than a majority could identify John 3:16.[22] When my church began helping our members identify and employ their spiritual gifts, by far the most common response we heard from our people was that they don't know how to do ministry. Their educational experiences, both in formal education and in our church, left them woefully unprepared to serve the kingdom.

Our members must be equipped not only to know Christ, but also to make him known; not only to receive the faith, but to reproduce it in the lives and faith of others. Christian higher education can and must play a vital role in such preparation for Great Commission engagement.

Argument Three
Christian higher education is irrelevant to our postmodern, postdenominational era.

Postmodernism makes "Christian" a subjective term, not an objective characteristic with independent merit or relevance. It would ask Baylor, for instance, to reject its distinctively Christian identity and character and admit that the Christian worldview is just one of many competing in a pluralistic and relativistic world. Postdenominationalism makes "Christian" more generic than Baptist universities admit or permit. It would call for Baylor to reject its distinctively Baptist identity and character and admit that the Christian worldview is more broadly evangelical and/or transdenominational than a Baptist commitment would permit.

Most of us know the story of the postmodern shift. It begins with René Descartes (1596–1650), who sought truth he could not doubt. He could doubt every part of his experience except that he was doubting, or thinking, and so he centered human experience in the autonomous rational process.[23] "Rationalism" followed his location of authority within reason. The empiricist reaction argued that personal experience is the true authority for knowledge. According to John Locke (1632–1704), the mind is not born with innate ideas (the Cartesian system) but as a blank slate, a *tabula rasa*.[24] David Hume (1711–1776) argued that experience cannot lead to certain knowledge. Our minds connect experiences into patterns on the basis of unprovable causal relations. We cannot use reason to defend reason.[25]

Immanuel Kant (1724–1804) combined the mind and senses into a larger whole: the senses furnish the data, which the mind organizes according to categories within itself, resulting in "knowledge."[26] However, this system yields certain knowledge only of the "phenomena" (sensory data), not of the "noumena" (objects beyond sense experience).[27] This distinction would be crucial for the later shift from the "modern" to the "postmodern" world. The Kantian synthesis created a crucial subjective result: I cannot claim objective authority for my interpretation of my sense data, the "phenomena." Truth is relative, not objective or absolute.

Who Were the First "Postmoderns"?[28]

Friedrich Nietzsche (1844–1900) is usually considered the "patron saint of postmodern philosophy."[29] In his view, the world is composed of individual fragments of reality. Our minds create concepts which rob this reality of its diversity and individuality. For instance, we form the concept "leaf" for leaves, an idea that can never do justice to the diversity of leaves. These concepts are illusions or convenient fictions.[30] "Truth" is solely a function of the language we use, and exists only within particular linguistic contexts.[31] The authority structure of the church, whether centered on the Bible or church dogma, is therefore unfounded and irrelevant.

Nietzsche's convictions parallel Friedrich Schleiermacher's (1768–1834) earlier assertions. According to this "father of theological liberalism," biblical texts are only reflections of the minds and experiences of their authors. The interpreter must move behind the text to its author's mind. The work of theology is therefore to "abstract entirely from the specific content of the particular Christian experiences."[32]

What Is the Postmodernist Idea of "Truth"?

According to Wilhelm Dilthey, hermeneutics functions in a circular fashion. We comprehend language by understanding its words, yet these words derive their meaning within their context.[33] Objective interpretation is neither possible nor desirable. Hans-Georg Gadamer (1900–2002) agreed that the interpreter must "fuse the horizons." Meaning emerges as the text and interpreter dialogue in a "hermeneutical conversation."[34] Since readers will conduct their own conversations with the text, objective meaning is obviously impossible. Ludwig Wittgenstein (1889–1951) came to view language as "game." Rules determine the use and meaning of words. Language is a social phenomenon, deriving meaning from social interaction.[35] Since each "player" works within personal and subjective rules, no objective authority is possible within any speech act.

"Structuralists" further developed this social dimension within language. Ferdinand de Saussure (1857–1913) ewed language as a work of music in which we focus on the entire piece, not the individual performances of the musicians. Texts provide structures of meaning in a meaningless existence.[36] "Deconstructionism" moved even further toward subjectivity: meaning emerges *only* as the interpreter enters into dialogue with the author. [37] The contemporary interpreter is to deconstruct the modern epistemological structures, along with their mythical claims to objective authority.

In recent generations, language philosophers have largely discarded the hermeneutical foundations that undergirded the premodern and modern eras. Claims to objective truth and absolute authority are dismissed, whether their source is the church, Scripture, or interpreted experience. The implications of this project for Christian higher education are historic and monumental.

Michel Foucault (1926–1984) served as the most significant bridge figure from Nietzsche to the postmodern world.[38] He asserted that humans use language to express and gain power. We name things to exercise power over them. We seek knowledge for the power it offers. Hermeneutics should therefore unmask the power drives that created the text before us. Jacques Derrida (1930–2004) believed there to be no fixed or universal reality.[39] We can make no objective knowledge claims, because there is no independent reality to describe. No "world" exists—only your world and mine. "Onto-theology," the attempt to articulate ontological descriptions of reality, must be rejected. Language possesses no fixed meaning; our words do not carry meaning ("logocentrism") but create it. For instance, I am typing these words either on a notebook computer, a fancy typewriter, or a strange box that makes annoying clicks, depending entirely on whether I, my grandfather, or my preschool friend is describing my actions. We cannot get beyond words to "reality," for words create that reality for us.

Richard Rorty (1931–), one of America's most popular philosophers, demonstrated the pragmatic usefulness of postmodernism for our daily lives.[40] He agrees with Foucault and Derrida that language is a matter of human convention, not the mirror of an objective reality. All language comes from its context and is thus subjective and relative. Rorty's contribution to postmodernism is his extension of this conviction to its larger pragmatic consequences. In his view, "truth" is what works for us. Language is to be judged by its pragmatic value, not by its supposed relation to objective reality. Language is only a tool for interpreting and coping with life. Language functions best when it creates community. As we tolerate and affirm other speech acts and those who make them, we foster acceptance. When we share common linguistic experience, we forge a common life. Since there is no objective reality outside our linguistic interpretation of our own experience, such community is our best hope for belonging and meaning.

This pragmatic language theory is seen to lead us to a kind of postmodern utopia. When we banish our power-driven, manipulative attempts to require and enforce one particular view of reality and truth, we are free to live in a society built on tolerance and mutuality. Such a postmodern hope offers a nonjudgmental alternative to the Christian worldview built upon our acceptance or rejection of a single way, truth, and life.

Os Guinness laments in a poignant way this contemporary rejection of an objective "truth":

> "We hold these truths to be self-evident," Thomas Jefferson and his fellow revolutionaries declared of the primary tenets of American democracy. Or as Mr. Jefferson wrote elsewhere, quoting a traditional Irish saying, "Truth is great and shall prevail."
>
> Today such sayings are "more a prayer than an axiom," one historian countered. Few things are less self-evident than truth. Truth, in fact, is said to be "dead"—or put more carefully, truth is relative, subjective, "socially constructed," and culturally determined; anything but objective, absolute, and universal. The result is politics by power plays in which "might makes right" and the one with the better lawyers, spinmeisters, muckrakers, and rumormongers wins. Do we seriously believe such a sea change has no consequences?[41]

This postmodern assault on the notion of truth, from Nietzsche to Rorty, constitutes a formidable challenge to higher education in general but particularly to Christian higher education as well as to the church. Clearly, a persuasive response is required.

What Can Christian Higher Education Offer in a Postmodern World?

George Marsden argues persuasively for the significance of academic leadership in helping the church avoid the cultural influence of this postmodern, relativistic age:

> Christian scholars who study the church or Christianity itself should recognize how Christian faith constantly becomes enmeshed with the cultural forces of the age. This adaptability of Christianity helps explain its worldwide impact; it also explains why it so often seems compromised. Not only do various "isms" reshape the church, but so do more impersonal forces such as those of the market, modern media, technology, or other forces associated with modernization. Accommodation to such forces is not always bad and is often necessary, but usually dangerous. The best education involves being not only critical, but self-critical. For that, the Christian perspective on the human condition and the deceptiveness of the human heart provides an excellent place to stand.[42]

Higher education has been radically affected by the postmodern shift to relative truth. No part of the academy has been immune from the influence of this movement, and the liberal arts have in large part been rethought and recast in view of this ontology, epistemology, and language philosophy. Left unchecked, this new academic environment will transfuse our entire culture with its rejection of moral absolutes and Scriptural authority. The church will find itself nothing more than one subjective option among many, its members believing that the foundational truths of the biblical worldview are only a convenient fiction that meets their pragmatic needs. No impetus for evangelism or missions will be viable in the minds of many, and our Great Commission mandate will be ignored or even dismissed as the unfair subjection of others to "our truth." David Wells describes in stark terms this general collapse of biblical authority:

> It has led the church to abandon the transcendent Word, the means by which it understands God, and in so doing it has rendered itself unable to see through this world. And it has led the church to look to the self for a substitute Word. It has assigned the self all the tasks that biblical and, in a Catholic context, churchly authority once exercised. . . . But the problem here is that the self doesn't have the strength to take over the functions of God's Word; it doesn't have what it takes to provide vision in the modern world because it is cut off from the true source and foundation of that world.[43]

Postdenominationalism is both the cousin and child of postmodernism. In a world absent objective truth, objective denominational convictions or distinctions hold no independent merit. Doubtless some distinctives within the Baptist tradition can and should be examined and challenged. But our basic, foundational emphases on political, soul, church, and Bible freedom are both biblical and essential. They meet the worthy test proposed by Richard Hughes: "The gospel can sustain the life of the mind since the gospel always points us to the God who stands in judgment on our narrowly conceived ideologies and our rigid orthodoxies. But the ideologies and orthodoxies themselves, unless they point beyond themselves to the living God, can do little to sustain the practice of Christian higher education."[44]

Hughes articulates exactly the postdenominational argument against Baptist higher education—unless, that is, the denominational distinctives which lie at the heart of Baptist higher education "point beyond themselves to the living God." In my view, our foundational freedoms not only reflect the biblical worldview, but they also enable its propagation.

Within the larger academic context, our churches must support institutional means of declaring, defining, and propagating these virtues and values. Postdenominationalism makes such higher education even more crucial than in previous generations, since we can no longer depend on the larger culture of the churches and denomination to foster and promote these values. If our colleges, universities, and seminaries will not define and defend these essential truths, we cannot expect our churches and their leaders to do so. The social bias against denominational distinctives as the imposition of subjective truth will always work against such support and propagation.

It is therefore no overstatement to say that Christian higher education has never been more important to Baptist churches and the church than it is today. In a culture that argues intellectually against truth, we must have intellectual leaders to help us defend and promote the essential, objective claims of the biblical worldview. Without medical schools, the quality of health in our country would quickly deteriorate. Without academic preparation and leadership, we will be ill-equipped to assault the gates of hell by making disciples. Christian higher education is therefore a crucial task for the church's ministry and future. As our churches help to enable academic excellence within a Christian worldview and context, we provide an alternative to the relativism that dominates the rest of the academy. The work of Christian higher education will not only offer our children an educational experience within the context of biblical faith—it will also provide an apologetic and transformational bridge to the larger academic world.

Conclusion

The tsunami tragedy in Southeast Asia in 2004 provides an analogy that may clarify the context of our current discussion. One huge wave washing over our churches is *professionalism*—to leave ministry to the ministers. Professionalism argues that Christian higher education is valuable for our leaders, but unwarranted as a significant value in our Great Commission investment and ministries. But, as we have seen, it is dangerous to trust theology only to theologians, or to limit the ministry only to vocational ministers. A second wave is *anti-intellectualism*—to believe members can do their ministry without academic assistance. Anti-intellectualism argues that intellectual pursuits often draw Christians away from their fundamental religious values. But, as we have seen, intellectual preparation is vital to spiritual growth and effective engagement with the needs of our culture. A third wave is *postmodern postdenominationalism*—to see Christian higher education as both subjective and outdated. But, as we have seen, both descriptors are fallacious. More than ever, the church needs intellectual resources with which to defend the biblical worldview and propagate essential faith distinctives.

Such waves can be damaging to the future of Baptist churches and their ministries. Or they can benefit us. They can cause us to reaffirm our historic partnership with Christian higher education in a way that encourages both. These rising tides can obliterate our shorelines or raise our boats. The choice is ours.

The sea wave analogy also calls to mind a story. When Allied armies advanced on the North African port of Eritrea during World War II, the fleeing Axis forces did an ingenious thing. They loaded barges with concrete and sank them across the mouth of the harbor, making it impossible for the approaching troops to enter. But the Allies hit on an even more inventive solution to the blocked port. They emptied several gigantic oil tanks, the kind that hold one hundred thousand barrels of oil and more, and sealed them watertight. They attached chains to each of them. Then at low tide their divers attached the other ends of the chains to the barges sitting on the bottom of the harbor. When the tides rose, the power of the sea was so great that the incoming waves lifted the sealed oil tanks and the cement-filled barges with them. It was then an easy task to dispose of the barges and reopen the harbor.

This power of the tides inspired Shakespeare to pen these inspiring words:

> *There is a tide in the affairs of men*
> *Which, taken at the flood, leads on to fortune;*
> *Omitted, all the voyages of their life*
> *Is bound in shallows and in miseries.*
> *On such a full sea are we now afloat;*
> *And we must take the current when it serves,*
> *Or lose our ventures.* (*Julius Caesar*, Act IV, scene II)

In support of Christian higher education, let our churches take the current when it serves, to the glory of God.

Chapter Nine

Can Baptist Institutions of Higher Education Meet the Needs of Increasingly Diverse Constituencies?

Albert Reyes

Introduction

I am a third-generation native Texan of Mexican descent and a third-generation Baptist Christian with connections to Hispanic Baptist congregations related to the Hispanic Baptist Convention of Texas, a fellowship of twelve hundred Hispanic congregations affiliated with the Baptist General Convention of Texas (BGCT).[1] My path to a personal relationship with Jesus Christ came through the people called Baptists. I came to faith in Christ at the age of nine and was baptized the following year under the ministry of William Thornton, a Texas Baptist who was serving as pastor of the Memorial Baptist Church in Rialto, California. I grew up in a Christian home with Baptist parents who demonstrated a love for Christ, devotion to the church, and expectations for their children to exceed their own experience in education. My father did not speak English when he began school in Corpus Christi, Texas, in the 1930s and eventually dropped out of school in the seventh grade. Later in life he completed a GED and began taking college-level courses. My mother graduated from Ray High School in Corpus Christi and later in life also began taking college courses. At the time I enrolled at Angelo State University in 1977 to major in business administration, my parents were encouraging me to pursue what had only been a dream for them.

During my undergraduate experience at Angelo State, I served in the ministry of Primera Iglesia Bautista of San Angelo, Texas, under the leadership of Fortunato Gonzalez. During my seminary years, I served other Hispanic Baptist congregations with pastors such as Ernest Rojas and Jonathan Hernandez. I also earned my way through seminary working full-time for six years at Sprint in the national customer service center in Dallas, Texas, during the long-distance postderegulation era of the 1980s. My church experiences also include membership in a number of Anglo Baptist churches. My earliest memories of participating in church with my parents were at Memorial Baptist Church, a predominantly Anglo-American congregation. My wife and I have been members at other predominantly Anglo Baptist churches in Arlington, Euless, and El Paso, and we are currently members of Trinity Baptist Church in San Antonio, Texas.

I am now in my thirty-first year of preaching the gospel, having answered a call to ministry in 1974 under the leadership of Rudy Sanchez, pastor of Primera Iglesia Bautista of Corpus Christi. Although my pastoral experience led me to serve in places like Mexico, Brazil, Spain, and North Africa, most of my experiences as a Baptist Christian have taken place in Texas, as a Texas Baptist, and nearly all of my ministry experiences have been impacted directly by Texas Baptists through the Texas Cooperative Program and the Mary Hill Davis Offering. Since 1999 I have served as president of Baptist University of the Americas, a theological university formerly known as Hispanic Baptist Theological Seminary in San Antonio. I have the honor and privilege of serving as president of the Baptist General Convention of Texas in the year I am writing this chapter (2005).

This personal history, colored by an Hispanic worldview and by my experiences as an Hispanic Texas Baptist, is foundational for a proper interpretation of my following response to the question that titles this chapter: "Can Baptist institutions of higher education meet the needs of increasingly diverse constituencies?" In other words, does this educational enterprise have as a central mission the education of the increasingly multicultural population of Baptists, and does it merit the financial investment and stewardship of increasingly multicultural Baptist denominational bodies? Whether or not we can answer the question positively is conditional on what we mean by "higher education," what we mean by "Baptist higher education," and exactly who we have in mind as the intended audience for the Baptist higher education enterprise.

Higher Education and Baptist Higher Education

What do we mean by "higher education"? Educators of public educational institutions acknowledge that the purpose of higher education is the transformation of the student.[2] Transformation of the student includes helping the student to develop independence as a learner, to embrace a commitment to lifelong learning, to integrate his or her values into a chosen profession, to become informed about a wide array of frames of reference, and to develop the ability to think critically.[3] So, if by higher education we mean undergraduate and graduate education of the highest caliber where academic freedom, discovery, exploration, and inquiry are encouraged, affirmed, and commended, this experience can empower our students to become mature and productive citizens. Lee Harvey and Peter Knight, in their book *Transforming Higher Education*, contend that empowerment of students as participants in the education process is possible if we encourage them to evaluate the education they are receiving, if we guarantee them a minimum standard of excellence they can expect, if we allow them to have greater control over their own learning experience, and if the educational process results in their enhanced ability to think critically.[4] A learning environment that accentuates academic freedom, discovery, exploration, and inquiry with the goal of student empowerment as described by Harvey and Knight is consistent with Baptist identity.

What do we mean by "Baptist higher education"? If what we mean by "Christian" in our Baptist institutions of higher education is different from what we mean by "Christian" in our churches and denominations, we would be compelled to reconsider our commitment to these institutions as a matter of integrity or reconsider educational ministry through our Baptist colleges and universities as a justifiable mission of our denominational body. However, if by "Christian" we mean that the educational enterprise is also Christ-characterized, Christ-centered, and therefore transformational both in the same ways that public educational institutions seek to be but also spiritually transformational; and if by "Christian" we mean that the life and work of Jesus Christ, as the living savior and redeemer of all of creation, intersects with the educational process designed to transform the lives of students, faculty, and administration in our institutions of higher education, we should be able to answer the question positively. Why would the Christian character of our Baptist institutions of higher education not be consistent with the Christian character of our Baptist churches and Baptist bodies? If we do not mean "Christ-centered" when we use the word "Christian" in our Baptist institutions of higher education, then we would be wise to use another adjective to describe higher education as the object of our educational ministries rather than invoking the name of Christ and all that is informed, implied, and transformed by the basic claims of the Christian faith. In other words, if our ecclesiology flows from our Christology, would not our educational institutions also be characterized by a Christological identity and fabric?

Many scholars have noted the struggle to reconcile Christian faith with the pursuit of knowledge in the academy. Mark Noll, in his 1994 book titled *The Scandal of the Evangelical Mind*, sets forth a compelling explanation for why the Christian faith is absent from the highest levels of academic pursuit. Noll argues that nowhere in the Western world can one find an institution of higher education at the graduate level that "exists for the primary purpose of promoting Christian scholarship defined in a Protestant, evangelical way."[5] George Marsden, in his 1997 book entitled *The Outrageous Idea of Christian Scholarship*, also notes the absence of any identifiable Christian schools of thought in mainstream academia in the United States. He asks, "What is it about the dominant academic culture that teaches people they must suppress reflection on the intellectual implications of faith?"[6] Bill Leonard asserts that throughout Baptist history, Baptists have struggled with the relationship between faith and learning and continue to struggle with the meaning of Christian education in the Baptist tradition.[7] Similarly, Richard Hughes, distinguished professor of religion at Pepperdine University, raises the question of how colleges and universities can become first-rate institutions of higher learning while engaging their faith. He focuses on one key question: "What resources does the [Baptist] tradition bring to the task of higher education?"[8] Hughes concludes that the Baptist tradition brings a wealth of resources to the Christian higher education enterprise, especially as it relates to the question of the integration of faith and learning.

The notion of the integration of faith and learning deserves our serious consideration. For some disciplines the integration of faith will be more challenging than for others. Stephen Evans has developed a "Relevance Continuum" demonstrating how faith and learning can have more relevant or less relevant applications. He suggests that some disciplines, like mathematics, are particularly challenging to relate issues of faith, while in disciplines such as philosophy and literature the application of faith is clearer. He also argues that when knowledge is applied, such as in business and law, one cannot avoid ethical questions and interactions with other worldviews.[9] Surely a benefit of an environment that allows and encourages discussion of how one's faith might be applied to learning adds value to the educational process that is absent at secular institutions where such discussion is not tolerated or certainly less tolerated. I strongly affirm Christian higher education if the "Christian" modifier unapologetically means Christ-centered, Christ-characterized, and transformational for all those who interact with the educational process. When Jesus was asked to articulate the greatest commandment in the Law, he replied, "Love the Lord your God with all your heart and with all your soul and with all your mind."[10] The Apostle Paul helps us at this point when he commends us toward transformation by the renewing of our minds (Rom. 12:2). The life of the mind, that is, the Christian mind, as described by Noll in 1994[11] and later by Hughes in 2003,[12] must be renewed by the life of the Spirit to give rise to the notion of Christian higher education.

Hughes argues that the core characteristic of Baptist higher education and the most potent intellectual resource available to any group of church-related institutions is the Baptist doctrine of "soul competency" coupled with an appreciation and respect for the Bible, which ultimately points beyond itself to God. Hughes defines "soul competency" as the individual soul being fully competent before God and every believer being free from human coercion because God alone is sovereign. Hughes also contends that the soul is competent because believers would rather obey God than men.[13] This doctrine leaves believers intellectually free to read the Bible and interpret it for themselves and to explore every aspect of knowledge and every truth as God's truth. Our Baptist identity and distinctives that have emerged over the years have blessed the educational enterprise we call higher education in the Baptist tradition by providing the kind of environment that encourages academic freedom, discovery, inquiry, and the pursuit of knowledge to the glory of God.

Hughes thus concludes that the Baptist tradition of higher education possesses rich theological resources for the life of the mind.[14] Of course, Baptists would be wise to also learn about the theological resources of other Christian denominations such as the Reformed, Lutheran, and Mennonite traditions that might also enhance the life of the mind. If this is what we mean when we say "higher education," then I strongly support the notion that it is a justifiable mission of Baptist churches and Baptist bodies.

The Intended Audience for the Christian/Baptist Higher Education Enterprise

Who are the people who represent the next generation of Baptists/Christians? How will Christian higher education be made available to them? How will Baptist/Christian institutions of higher education transform themselves to make Christian higher education available to this emerging generation over the next thirty or forty years? We must try to see ahead and ask ourselves what Christianity will look like by 2040 in Texas, the United States, and around the world. From a global perspective few scholars have attempted to think about the future with more insight than Phillip Jenkins, distinguished professor of religion and history at Penn State University. Jenkins has researched the history of Christianity worldwide and concludes that by the year 2050 two major shifts will have taken place: the center of gravity of Christianity will have moved firmly to the southern half of the hemisphere below the equator and only one in five Christians worldwide will be non-Hispanic White.[15] He questions the notion of "Western Christianity" and suggests that the next thirty to forty years will produce some of the most dramatic changes in the history of Christendom. It is, of course, already common knowledge that Christianity's most rapid growth is occurring outside of the United States in places like Latin America, Africa, and Asia and that some of the world's largest Christian churches are found south and east of North America. However, even in a post-9/11 era, in the minds of many American Christians, those changes seem too distant to affect what we have known as American Christianity with its vast array of churches, denominations, and educational institutions.

Vestiges of a tsunami of global change have reached our shores in only specific pockets of our nation. One indicator of those changes nationally is the news that in 2003, Hispanics became the largest minority in the United States for the first time in US history.[16] Even an unsophisticated observer of population trends would conclude that we are headed into an era of prolific demographic change. Juan F. Martinez, director of the Hispanic Studies Program and associate professor of pastoral theology at Fuller Theological Seminary, has indicated that the most radical and phenomenal changes we will see in the next twenty years affecting the United States demographically will be related to the issue of "global migration." Martinez contends that global migration—movements of peoples from south to north and east to west—will fundamentally change our previous understanding of American life of the past forty years.[17] In other words, the generation behind us will scarcely recognize the generation before us. Jenkins concurs with this assertion, suggesting that as the United States grows to a population of 400 million by 2050, its ethnic character will grow as well. Jenkins states that American society will shift its view of race from a black and white affair to a multicolored reality. He says that by 2050 "nearly 100 million Americans will claim Hispanic origin, making the United States of America one of the world's largest Latino societies, more populous than any actual Hispanic nation with the exception of Mexico or Brazil, with sixty percent of Hispanic Americans claiming Mexican descent."[18] How will these changes impact denominational growth in the coming years? How will these changes impact Baptist denominational growth? Jenkins contends that "Southern" populations will account for most of the denominational growth that occurs in the coming decades.[19] Given the national and global trends in population growth, who do we have in mind as the intended audience for Christian higher education in the Baptist tradition?

Since Baptist University of the Americas, its eight sister Baptist universities, and the Baptist General Convention of Texas are located deep in the southwestern part of the United States and are neighbors with Mexico, reflection on Texas is appropriate in this part of the discussion. Today, Texas already has surpassed the demographic predictions that Jenkins suggests for North America. Steve Murdock, director of the Institute for Demographic and Socioeconomic Research at the University of Texas at San Antonio, predicts that by 2050, Texas will experience a population increase from 20 million to 50 million. He further documents that 96 percent of the growth will be non-Anglo.[20] It is amazing to think that Texas will grow by 30 million people by 2050, but even more compelling is that nearly 29 million new Texans will be ethnic, with Hispanics in the clear majority. Several Texas urban centers already have majority Hispanic populations, such as San Antonio with 60 percent, El Paso with 78 percent, and Brownsville with 95 percent. Murdock predicts that university enrollments in Texas public universities will shift dramatically from the year 2000 to 2040. Anglo enrollment in public universities will shift from 61 percent in 2000 to 32 percent in 2040; African American enrollment will shift from 10 percent in 2000 to 8 percent in 2040; Hispanic enrollment will shift from 21 percent in 2000 to 45 percent in 2040; and all other ethnic groups will shift from 7 percent in 2000 to 15 percent in 2040.[21] In other words, the non-Anglo enrollment in public universities will move from 38 percent in 2000 to 68 percent in 2040. This represents a dramatic shift in university student enrollment over the next thirty-five years. I seriously doubt private Christian universities across Texas will be able to insulate themselves from an academic context where more than two of every three students are not Anglo. I pose the question again: exactly who are we thinking about when we consider making Christian higher education available to the next generation of Baptists, and in this case, Texas Baptists, given the future that Jenkins, Martinez, and Murdock describe?

Even if Murdock has overstated his case, and rather than a thirty-point differential in non-Anglo enrollment in Texas public universities by 2040, ethnic minorities grow only 12 points to a 50 percent non-Anglo enrollment, how would Christian universities in Texas function in this kind of academic context? On the other hand, if Murdock has understated his case and we shift twelve points in the other direction, we would find ourselves in an academic context where 80 percent of university students would be non-Anglo. In that scenario, how would we be prepared to provide Christian higher education to the next generation of Baptists?

Reaching the New Audience

How will Christian higher education be made available to the next generation of Baptists? The current system of college entrance exams and requirements for entry into higher education makes college admission inaccessible to many non-Anglo citizens and most Hispanic students. Hispanics are generally not oriented to the system of higher education and face social and economic challenges that prevent them from attempting to obtain a college degree. The most pronounced reason Hispanics in Texas do not enter college is that they do not finish high school. In fact, the national Hispanic high school dropout rate was 34 percent in the late 1990s, while the Texas Hispanic high school dropout rate passed the 50 percent mark, and 70 percent of all high school dropouts in the United States were either Hispanic or African American by the year 2000.[22]

While more Hispanics are enrolling in college, that number has not kept pace with the growing Hispanic population. Even so, few Hispanics finish a degree program. In 1998 the Hispanic Association of Colleges and Universities reported that only 8 percent of Hispanics nationwide held an associate of arts degree, 5.6 percent held a BA degree, 3.8 percent earned MA degrees, and only 4.5 percent earned professional or doctoral degrees. In 2000, the Census Bureau reported that 10 percent of Hispanics in the United States held a college degree, compared to 17 percent of African Americans and 28 percent of Anglo Americans.[23] Once Hispanics get to college they face financial, academic, and social hurdles that keep them from finishing their degrees.[24]

Most institutions of higher learning are not poised to provide solutions for these issues, which is one of the reasons that the South Texas Border Initiative was launched, a program that infused about $500 million into higher education in forty-one Texas counties between El Paso and Brownsville (on the Texas border), including San Antonio, Kingsville, and Corpus Christi.[25] The South Texas Border Initiative sought to make up for decades of neglect in college and university programs for a predominantly Hispanic border region in order to serve a population that is historically underrepresented in higher education. The U.S. Department of Education paints a dismal picture of educational efforts to prepare Hispanics for collegiate work. Over the past thirty years, the Department of Education can account for $10 trillion spent on educational programs, resulting in a 31 percent national dropout rate for Hispanics.[26] Edwin Hernandez and Kenneth Davis confirm poor performance of Hispanics in higher education and conclude by saying that "despite increased educational attainment during the past decades, Hispanics remain the most undereducated major segment of the U.S. population."[27] What would happen if Baptist bodies who support Christian higher education also invested significant resources to ensure that not one more of our Baptist youth, of any cultural background, dropped out of high school but instead had an opportunity to attend one of our Baptist colleges or universities?

From our earliest beginnings in Christian higher education, Baptists in America started small schools for the purpose of "improving the social and economic status of an essentially lower-class, rural constituency," according to Bill Leonard.[28] Baptists developed schools that were accessible to its constituency to provide opportunities for Christian higher education at an affordable cost. Leonard goes on to say that the Baptist "egalitarian response was a major contribution of the Baptist tradition to American higher education."[29] Texas Baptists sought to establish schools, colleges, and universities in the mid- to late 1800s and the early 1900s to ensure that their sons and daughters would have educational opportunities in the Baptist tradition.[30] The Texas Baptist educational ministry has provided opportunities for Christian higher education for generations of Baptist youth since 1845 when Baylor University was founded. For 150 years, Texas Baptists have consistently provided access to Christian higher education for its sons and daughters. Access to higher education has been a foundational aspect of forming and shaping generations of Baptists through Christian higher education. Will this kind of education be available and accessible to our sons and daughters thirty-five years from now?

Developing intervention strategies for Baptist youth who are dropping out of high school is only half of the problem Baptist and secular educational institutions will face in America over the next thirty years. The soaring numbers of ethnic students who apply and are accepted for admission will have an impact on our institutions because they will bring significantly different worldviews with them. In the same way that missionaries must contextualize their approaches to incarnate the gospel message, colleges and universities that contextualize their institutions will have greater opportunities to provide Christian higher education to the emerging generation of Baptists. This effort will require nothing less than organizational and cultural transformation of the institution itself. This kind of change will have implications for governing board strategy, executive and administrative staffing, and faculty.

Baptist colleges and universities that fail to establish cultural diversity on governing boards will find themselves isolated from their rapidly changing context and will develop policies that are inconsistent with the real needs of its emerging constituency. Baptist colleges and universities that do not employ ethnic administrators at the executive level where policy decisions are implemented will not be aware of cultural blind spots that will impede effectiveness in the new multicultural environment. Baptist colleges and universities that fail to recruit qualified faculty with ethnic backgrounds will encounter difficulty teaching students who do not share the same cultural worldview. Faculty who serve in this new environment may need to explore non-Western educational traditions to gain insight into the basic epistemological framework of non-Western worldviews.[31]

College and university trustees, executive leaders, administrators, and faculty may need to assess cross-cultural competency in order to increase effectiveness in the emerging educational landscape that will exist over the next thirty years. The emerging multicultural and multiethnic educational context in the United States will require cross-cultural competency for those in the Christian higher education enterprise.[32] While the issue of ethnic access to Christian higher education and ethnic representation on governing boards, executive and administrative staff, and faculty could be discussed within the framework of Christian ethics, I prefer to structure this conversation within the context of strategic advantage and stewardship of the Baptist higher educational resources that have been entrusted to us to advance the vision of Christian higher education in the Baptist tradition.

Can Baptist institutions of higher education meet the needs of increasingly diverse constituencies? My answer is an emphatic yes if our educational enterprise is Christ-characterized and Christ-centered reflecting a Christian worldview; if our higher education enterprise provides an atmosphere of academic freedom consistent with Baptist identity and historic Baptist distinctives, especially the doctrine of soul competency; and if this kind of Christian higher education is made available to the next generation of Baptists who will carry the light through 2040 and beyond. Christian higher education, as described by these conditional affirmations, will be a powerful force for shaping the future for the kingdom of Christ.

Shaping the Future through Christian Higher Education

Shaping the future of our nation and world through Christian higher education will become a reality to the extent that the affirmations stated above find their way into the ethos of our institutions of higher education in the near future. The potential for the Christian higher education enterprise to positively develop the social fabric of our communities, the economic structure of our population centers, the ecclesial and denominational identity we seek to preserve, and the missiological trajectory of our witness merits the attention, devotion, and investment of our denominational bodies.

The role of Christian higher education in the formation of a person in the image of Christ is an essential part of the process of discipleship. People who are not followers of Jesus Christ who become participants in Christian higher education have a tremendous opportunity to learn in a Christian environment and have opportunities to establish a personal relationship with Christ. Christians who become participants in our Baptist educational enterprise are often transformed by the educational process. Donald A. McGavran developed a concept called "redemption-lift" in his 1970 book entitled *Understanding Church Growth*. McGavran describes how the process of redemption transformed the lives of those who came into contact with the gospel and became followers of Christ in places where Christ was not known. These redeemed believers also experienced a lift through the life of their congregations who established hospitals, schools, orphanages, and a host of other ministries to meet the human needs of their members. Through redemption-lift, cycles of poverty and economic weakness were broken and people's lives were rebuilt.[33] Lives of individuals and families around the world have been transformed and have experienced redemption and lift through faith in Christ and the fellowship of his church. This concept of redemption-lift is not merely a principle or observation but has become a reality in the history of my own family. Christian higher education, as an object and mission of Baptist bodies, is a powerful tool for the transformation of individuals and families in our communities, both socially and economically.

Economic development and advancement in the United States will depend greatly on the kind of workforce we provide for our nation's businesses. The impact of the gospel on an individual and a family cannot be mistaken, nor can the impact of Christian higher education be underestimated as it relates to economic development. As Hispanics gain more education, they increase their ability to earn more money. Hispanics with a high school education earn approximately three hundred thousand dollars more in their lifetimes as opposed to their dropout counterparts. Hispanics with a BA degree earn six hundred thousand dollars more in their lifetimes over against those who do not earn a BA degree, and those with a master's degree earn $1.3 million more in their lifetimes than their counterparts who do not possess an MA degree. This translates into a greater purchasing power and greater tax revenues. Those tax revenues produce a stronger tax base and build better communities.

With the current underachievement by Hispanics in higher education and the swelling Hispanic population in the United States, our nation is headed toward reduced access to college, reduced quality of our workforce, and reduced competitiveness in the international economy.[34] Charles B. Reed agrees, citing that our country's economic success depends on the educational level of our society as a whole. He suggests that helping poor students gain access to higher education must be everyone's top priority with respect to financial aid.[35] Several key educational leaders are coming to the same conclusion. Antonio Flores, president and CEO of the Hispanic Association of Colleges and Universities, says that we are not serving our nation well by failing to educate Hispanic youth. In fact, "The harm goes well beyond the Hispanic community and goes to the heart of our economy and social well-being as a nation."[36] Davis and Hernandez argue:

> Without improved academic achievement, the Latino community will continue to be plagued by economic problems arising from unemployment, and low-skilled employment. . . . In addition to economic effects, sociopolitical consequences involve lost national income, lost tax revenue for the support of government services, increased costs for social services, increased crime, reduced political participation, reduced intergenerational mobility, and poorer levels of health.[37]

The positive economic impact of Christian higher education in the lives of individuals, families, and communities is unmistakable. Baptist bodies have profound incarnational presence in communities through Christian higher education and its corresponding economic impact. This practical investment in our communities builds credibility for our witness of the presence of Jesus Christ as Baptist people.

The potential for Christian higher education to enhance ecclesial and denominational identity is another reason for denominational bodies to vigorously support this enterprise. Leonard suggests several significant contributions of Christian higher education in the Baptist tradition: the value of shaping religious identity and denominational consciousness, social and economic opportunities for Baptist youth, and academic preparation in a Christian environment.[38] The relationship between Baptist churches and Baptist universities has been symbiotic. The churches and universities serve each other and provide for a strong fabric of ecclesial and denominational identity. Historically, Baptists have utilized theological education to shape its clergy, Christian literature to shape the theological mind of its lay membership, and Christian higher education to shape and form denominational identity for its members. Few observers of the history of Baylor and its impact on Texas Baptists would argue that Baylor has not served a crucial role in creating, developing, and sustaining religious and denominational identity. Donald Schmeltekopf refers to the formation of denominational and religious identity by Baylor's founders as a "pragmatic approach to maintaining [Baylor's] Baptist and Christian character."[39]

The role of religiously connected universities is growing in the United States. A recent study noted that religious higher education in America is on the rise. The enrollment at one hundred member institutions of the Council for Christian Colleges and Universities rose by 60 percent from 1990 to 2002, while enrollment for secular universities remained relatively flat over the same time period.[40] The postdenominational era we live in today accentuates the need for closer relationships between Baptist bodies and Baptist institutions of higher education. The case for the need for institutions that provide Christian higher education in the Baptist tradition could not be more strategic to our denominational future than at this point in our history. An educational partnership between universities and churches gives rise to the possibility of collaboration and exponential impact in global missions.

The question of missions might seem tangential to the key question of this chapter. If we were to think of missions with a twentieth-century-mindset, we might dismiss this discussion and consider the two subjects unrelated. However, if we think about missions from a twenty-first-century perspective, we might be drawn to consider carefully the connection of Baptist bodies and their affiliated institutions of higher learning. One of the major shifts of missions in the twenty-first century is that the bulk of missional outreach will be done by the ordinary rather than the ordained. Christians who pursue their vocation as a calling and prepare for those vocations in colleges or universities that provide Christian higher education, as defined in this chapter, will be poised to advance the Great Commission in ways we have not considered in the past. Ordained and credentialed clergy do not have access to parts of the world that nonordained, nonclergy Christian professionals enjoy. Ordained and credentialed clergy do not even have access to many sectors of American culture and vocational settings that nonordained and nonclergy Baptists do.

Our Baptist colleges and universities have the potential to provide an educational experience integrated with real Christian faith that will prepare students to become active agents of the Great Commission in their vocational and social settings. In this sense, graduates from our educational institutions become what Milfred Minatrea calls "missional" rather than merely "mission-minded."[41] Doctors, dentists, educators, business professionals, nurses, scientists, lawyers, engineers, ministers, and every vocational path that emerges from our Baptist colleges and universities form an essential part of our global missionary force. In this respect, then, the health and effectiveness of our institutions of higher education impact our missiological trajectory for the future.

Conclusion

I started answering the question assigned to me by outlining three conditional affirmations of Christian higher education that would make it a justifiable mission of Baptist churches and Baptist bodies. Then I followed this discussion with four potential outcomes of Christian higher education according to the definitions outlined in the first part of this essay. Baptist colleges and universities have the resources to positively enhance the work of our churches and the impact of our denominational bodies in this new millennium. Will we be willing to go the distance to maximize our effectiveness and ensure a Baptist vision for Christian higher education that will bless the generations that follow us?

I remember standing on the top of the Rock of Gibraltar several years ago looking southward toward the northern tip of the continent of Africa. On a clear day you can see the tip of North Africa across the Straits of Gibraltar. While I stood there and peered across the water, I was reminded that only twelve miles separated the place where I was standing from northernmost Africa. Twelve miles separated a culture of religious freedom from areas of religious intolerance. An hour's ride on the ferry would put me in a place where I was not free to speak openly about my faith.

Another mountaintop view provoked similar feelings, but this time only a river separated me from vast opportunities to share the Christian faith. I was standing on the top of Mount Franklin, at the foothills of the Rocky Mountains, in El Paso, Texas. From that site I could see northern Mexico, southern New Mexico, and far West Texas. The Rio Grande magically wove these parcels of desert and mountain together. Mexico seemed so close but also so far. Christian higher education that is characterized by the Christian worldview, operational in the Baptist tradition where academic freedom, discovery, inquiry, and learning are encouraged and affirmed in a context of Christian faith, and available to the upcoming generation of Baptists over the next thirty-five years, deserves the attention and the best stewardship of our Baptist denominational bodies. This kind of education will undoubtedly develop the social fabric of our communities, increase economic development for our cities, enhance denominational identity for future Baptists, and set our missiological trajectory for generations to come. The future of our Baptist educational vision seems so close, but will it prove to be too far? My deepest prayer and highest hope is that we will cross the straits and rivers with enthusiasm, intentionality, and our best resources for the sake of our children, our grandchildren, and those who have yet to experience the kingdom of God.

Chapter Ten

Can Baptist Institutions of Higher Education Meet the Needs of Youth in a Post-9/11 World?

Denton Lotz

Introduction

As general secretary of the Baptist World Alliance, I am essentially a missionary and evangelist, roaming the world and speaking encouraging words to our Baptist brothers and sisters, most of whom are suffering from inadequate education, lack of resources, and lack of economic and political freedom. So to attempt to address issues concerning the future of Baptist higher education is a daunting task. After all, a Google search calls up 6,550,000 references to Christian higher education, and 1,050,000 references to Baptist higher education.

Given such a large and complex task, where am I to begin? I took a respite from the Web and read Ecclesiastes: "The sayings of the wise are like goads, and like nails firmly fixed are the collected sayings that are given by one shepherd. Of anything beyond these, my son, beware. Of making many books there is no end, and much study is a weariness of the flesh. The end of the matter; all has been heard. Fear God, and keep his commandments; for that is the whole duty of everyone. For God will bring every deed into judgment, including every secret thing, whether good or evil."[1] Now that preacher understood academia long before anyone ever heard of a computer!

Although I agreed to the title "Post-9/11" for this essay without hestitation, I had not thought much about the events of September 11, 2001, in the context of Christian higher education. But then I read Stanley Hauerwas's article "September 11, 2001: A Pacifist Response." In this very wise reflection on the meaning of 9/11 Hauerwas says, "Our response is to continue living in a manner that witnesses to our belief that the world was not changed on

September 11, 2001. The world was changed during the celebration of a Passover in 33 A.D."[2]

For the Christian understanding of time, the day that changed the world was indeed on a cross and in an empty tomb in Jerusalem two thousand years ago, not in New York City in 2001. With Oscar Cullmann we would affirm that indeed Christ is the center of history and that Christ defines all of our understanding of reality and time. Indeed, 9/11 and the destruction of the World Trade Center will go down in history as one of those significant dates in American history like December 7, 1941, and the attack on Pearl Harbor, but it is not the definitive date for the Christian. Rather, it is in the light of *Anno Domini* that we can only try to understand 9/11.

Samuel Huntington's *The Clash of Civilizations*

Samuel Huntington's seminal book *The Clash of Civilizations* has been analyzed and critiqued many times, but I refer to it again because I believe it offers a very helpful typology for understanding the present situation in which humanity finds itself. The fact is that with the fall of communism we did not suddenly achieve what President George H. W. Bush proclaimed as "a new world order." Instead, Soviet autocratic and totalitarian power succeeded in suppressing the national aspirations of many and various groups. However, with the fall of the Berlin Wall, all of these repressed aspirations came out, and suddenly we have "tribal-type" conflicts between Armenia and Azerbaijan, Bosnia and Serbia, Chechnya and Russia. Huntington's thesis is that the twenty-first century will experience a "clash of civilizations," and what is the basis of those conflicting civilizations but religion?

Huntington's model is helpful because the clashes that we see today are indeed religious conflicts, although there are surely economic and social issues also involved. The clashes in Eastern Europe were essentially conflicts between Orthodox Christianity and Islam. What is the conflict between Israel and Palestine but two different religions? The world, it seems, is being pulled apart because of these religious conflicts: Hinduism versus Islam in India, Buddhism versus Christianity in Burma, Catholicism and Islam in the Philippines, and the like. In addition to religious wars, there are also terrible tribal conflicts such as in Rwanda between the Hutus and the Tutsis where 1 million people have been killed in a modern-day holocaust.

Students who are from these and nearby countries in these areas of conflict do not see them as academic questions to be studied, but rather as the actual experience of their daily lives. On February 22, 2002, the Baptist seminary in Kaduna, Nigeria, was burned to the ground. Although six hundred students were able to escape, five students were attacked with machetes and brutally killed. Then Nigerian Christians witnessed the rampage of Muslims who burned nineteen churches to the ground and killed one thousand people. The Muslims felt that the seminary was making inroads into converting their people, and therefore they were justified in destroying it. What was the Baptist response? All over Nigeria offerings were collected and the seminary was rebuilt. Obviously, these students had personally experienced the clash of civilizations and thus viewed it in a different way than they would have if they had only engaged in an academic study of the conflict between Muslims and Christians in Nigeria.

Why 9/11?

Students in most Christian and secular universities in the West have been asking the questions: Why this clash? Why 9/11? Shortly after the attacks on the twin towers, courses in Islam in most universities began to be packed. Enrollment in Arabic language classes increased. Students wanted to know, why? More recently, however, interest in Middle Eastern cultures has been declining, so much so that Peter Berkowitz and Michael McFaul consider such lack of interest a threat to U.S. national security: "It remains painfully true, more than three years after September 11 that even highly educated Americans know little about the Arab Middle East. And it is embarrassing how little our universities have changed to educate our nation and train experts on the wider Middle East."[3]

In the end, I believe, it is religion that must answer the existential question, "Why?" Gordon Allport, Harvard sociologist, tells the story of a hospital built by the German government in the Cameroon. The local people would come to the hospital to get a broken leg or arm set, or to be treated for some illness. But after the hospital they would go to the witch doctor. The German doctors could not understand that phenomenon. Their secular Western scientific minds could not grasp why, after going to a modern, well-equipped hospital, their patients would go to a witch doctor. Allport said that Western medicine and technology could only bind their broken limbs, but it could not answer the question, "Why?" And it was in search of the answer to the "Why?" that the patients consulted the witch doctor. And it is in search of the answer to the question, "Why?" that more students and faculty need to study Islam and the Arabic language and culture. Departments of religion should offer courses in the study of Islam as a religion, with a Christian response. Any religion that does not strive to answer the question "Why?" will inevitably become irrelevant.

The Reaction of Political and Religious Leaders to 9/11

What was the reaction of the political and religious leaders in the West to 9/11? Some saw it as the judgment of God on America. Firemen and rescue workers became the new heroes of our day. Stories of human courage under pressure were the common message for months. But church leaders did not have much to say to help soothe the nation. What solidified the American people was the leader of the United States saying, "We are at war." Commenting upon the power of this phrase, Hauerwas says that these are "Magic words necessary to reclaim the everyday. War is such a normalizing discourse. Americans know war. This is our Pearl Harbor. Life can return to normal. The way to go on in the face of September 11, 2001, is to find someone to kill."[4] This was America's initial response, and we have not yet seen the end of it. Even before Hauerwas's article, Chris Hedges, in an article entitled, "War Is a Force that Gives Meaning to Our Lives," maintains that "the communal march against an enemy generates a warm, unfamiliar bond with our neighbors, our community, our nation, wiping out unsettling undercurrents of alienation and dislocation. War in times of malaise and desperation is a potent distraction."[5] The war against Osama bin Laden in Afghanistan and the war in Iraq have become the "potent distraction." Our country had hardly recovered from Vietnam when we found ourselves again in a self-destructive course of action. The new religion in America is Americanism. The mantra is "United we stand!" . . . or at least it used to be.

Pitirim A. Sorokin, Russian émigré and later Harvard sociologist, was a prophet of his day who as early as the 1930s warned of this kind of talk, which is part of the sensate culture of generation after generation of Americans. Sorokin warns, "Every page of human history bears witness to wars undertaken in the firm conviction that they would 'end war,' 'abolish despotism,' 'make the world safe for democracy,' 'overcome injustice,' 'eliminate misery' and the like. . . . From this standpoint, the history of human progress is indeed a history of incurable human stupidity."[6]

Outrageous statements by some Christian leaders have had a negative effect upon the Christian message overseas. Calling the Prophet Muhammad a terrorist or pedophile has only inflamed the Muslim world even more. In speaking with leaders in the Middle East we have learned that headlines in the Arab newspapers tell of Baptists attacking their prophet. In communicating the Christian message we must not denigrate the leaders of other religions. Everyone loves his native country, no matter what country that might be. To understand others we must also try to understand their language, their culture, and the history of their country. A Christian higher education should provide students with the tools to better understand other cultures and thus to be better prepared to give witness to the Christ of all truth. Furthermore, Christians have a great responsibility to ensure not only that whatever we or our government say should be truthful but also that the rhetoric we use should be considered and restrained and that every message should be analyzed and critiqued on the bases of those very criteria of truth and moderation.

The Development of the Christian Response to Other Cultures: A Model for Christian Higher Education

Bishop Stephen Neill's typology describing the Christian response to other cultures and traditions during the past two hundred years of Christian missions is very helpful for Christian higher education today as we seek to relate the gospel both to our own culture and to the culture of others. Neill describes the Christian response to other cultures as a threefold development: accommodation, indigenization, and contextualization.

Accommodation

Accommodation means simply that Christian missionaries embraced the culture, art, and means of dress of the foreign culture in order to better communicate the one universal gospel to those whom the missionaries hoped to evangelize. For example, Robert de Nobili, an Italian nobleman who came to do missions in India, presented himself to the Brahmins as a nobleman, dressed as they did, and acted as a *sanyassi guru*. Many Brahmins came to Christ because of Nobili's strategy. In a like manner, Matthew Ricci in China adopted the Confucian dress and became a great Confucian scholar. The Apostle Paul, of course, relates the same approach when he says: "To the Jews I became as a Jew, in order to win Jews. To those under the law I became as one under the law . . . that I might win those under the law."[7]

Some mission agencies from the West have not moved beyond the practices of these sixteenth-century Catholic missionaries who understood the importance of dress and external trappings of religion. On the other hand, the great German missiologist Walter Freytag told of a poor elderly Indonesian woman who came at eighty years of age to be baptized wearing as many Western clothes as possible. She somehow thought that when one became a Christian one had to become a Westerner first. Missionary work indeed has been paternalistic and imperialistic when it has demanded that converts first adopt Western dress and customs before they become Christians. The early church dealt with this also. In the book of Acts there were Judaizers demanding that the Gentiles first become Jews before they could become Christians.

What is the relevance of this idea of accommodation to Christian higher education? It has great relevance to how we relate to foreign students either on our own campuses or abroad. Christian professors in the many satellite campuses sponsored by Baptist colleges and universities overseas should not try to make foreign students into Americans, but instead they should in their actions, dress, and attitude affirm the culture to which they have come and in which they teach and minister. A certain humility is required of the teacher in such an overseas setting. Christ did not come to destroy culture but to transform culture.

Indigenization

Indigenization is the process of missionaries' turning Christian leadership over to the nationals as soon as there are indigenous Christians trained and ready to assume positions of responsibility. William Carey was successful as a missionary because of his five-pronged plan: (1) the widespread preaching of the gospel by every possible means, (2) the support of preaching by the distribution of the Bible in the languages of the country, (3) the establishment of a church at the earliest possible moment, (4) a profound study of the background and thought of the non-Christian peoples, and (5) the training at the earliest possible moment of an indigenous ministry.[8] Baptist missions have been most successful where the indigenous principles of Carey have been followed. For this reason, the establishment of seminaries overseas was a successful method to guarantee leadership for the future growth of the church.

However, the abandonment of theological institutions of higher learning overseas today, I believe, is an abandonment of indigenous churches to an uneducated ministry, and an abandonment of indigenous Christian leaders who want and need theological and pastoral training that would prepare them to lead their churches and to proclaim Christ to those within their own culture. In the absence of seminaries, Baptist colleges and universities with campuses overseas must do what they can to ensure that locals and national leaders are being trained to take on the responsibilities of reaching out to Christian constituencies in their own languages. Muslims and Catholics have understood the importance of education as a means of evangelization. Baptists have lost the vision of such missions and thus will suffer the consequences in the future of an illiterate and incompetent leadership. Indigenous training seeks to raise up leaders at the grassroots level who will be capable of assuming leadership roles when the missionaries are no longer there. A good example of such preparation is that in Burma. When the American Baptist missionaries were forced to leave in 1962, the church continued to flourish under the leadership of indigenously trained teachers and professors.

Contextualization

The final stage of mission maturity in relating to other cultures is contextualization. This seems so obviously necessary, yet many modern-day mission efforts make the colossal error of not taking seriously the cultural expressions of faith. It is not enough to dress like a national, or to have an indigenous pastor. The fact is that the gospel must become incarnate in the language and culture of the people. In the United States, for example, Southern Baptists have been successful precisely because they became the embodiment of the expression of southern culture. Southern Baptist pastors and preachers contextualized the gospel through music, art, and folksy preaching so that Baptists grew like wildfire in the South. It is said that the Baptist minister went to the frontier on foot, the Methodist on horseback, the Presbyterian in a Conestoga wagon, and the Episcopalian priest in a train. Because Baptists contextualized the gospel, there are today more than fifteen different Baptist groups in the United States and their total number of baptized believers is 32 million. If one counted children and the worshiping community, there are probably more than 60 million Baptist adherents. Baptists did well in their mission to America when one considers the relative number of other Protestant denominations: 8 million United Methodists, 4 million Presbyterians, and 2.3 million Episcopalians.

If contextualization has been the strength of Southern Baptists, it has also been their weakness. The gospel not only must be contextualized in the culture, but it must also be a prophetic witness over against the errors and evils of the prevailing culture. While we were sending missionaries to "darkest Africa," we were affirming segregation at home and not allowing those same African converts into our churches in the South. Recently, I was in Tyler, Texas, where I joined my wife in celebrating the fortieth anniversary of the first Southern Baptist Journeymen group of which she was a member. I recall very well when she came back from Nigeria where she had served. Her local church in Mississippi had prayed for her while she had been in Nigeria, but the pastor and deacons made very clear to us that no Nigerians could come to our wedding unless they wore their native costumes, and certainly no African American could participate. We were asked, "Who do you think you are, trying to integrate our church?" If the gospel had been fully contextualized, Christians would have condemned racism as contrary to Scripture. Instead, culture triumphed over the gospel, and racism to this day is alive and well in America. Christian higher education needs to be a prophetic witness against a culture of neglect and rejection. Contextualization means communicating the prophetic message of Christ in such a way that the gospel is understood as a reason for hope and, at the same time, as a judgment on all of man's actions.

The beautiful book *The Peace Child* tells the story of how one missionary allowed himself to contextualize the gospel so that a whole tribe of Stone Age people came to Christ. In a Christian higher education setting it is necessary, I believe, that educators understand the culture and context of the people to whom they are being sent and among whom they are ministering.

The Implications of Missiological Principles for Christian Higher Education at Home

But what does this threefold development in the history of missions have to do with Christian higher education here at home? I believe it has a lot to do with how Christian colleges, universities, and theological seminaries ought to relate the Christian faith to their own students, born and bred in the United States. The fact is that most of the students coming to Christian colleges, even those from Christian homes, have little intellectual means to deal with the struggles they will experience when confronted with the culture and society in which they live. Bishop Neill tells of the brilliant student who came to Cambridge to study geology. When the student discovered that rock formations showed the earth was older than the Scofield Bible indicated, his faith was challenged. His fundamentalist pastor told him he had to choose between Christianity or geology. The young student said the choice was obvious, and he chose geology. The inability of students to successfully deal with these false alternatives often comes from a lack of meaningful Christian education in our churches. Christian students sometimes come to the university with a minimal knowledge of church history or theology, and we wonder why they lose their faith. I remember one Southern Baptist educator tearfully admitting to me, after his son had left the faith and had become a dropout, "I relied too much on our Sunday schools when I should have been teaching him the Biblical background, history, and the theology of our faith." But is that not precisely the problem about which Mark Noll wrote in *The Scandal of the Evangelical Mind*? As you remember, Noll begins his study with the shocking statement, "The scandal of the evangelical mind is that there is not much of an evangelical mind."[9]

The application of what we have learned from the history and methodology of missions, I believe, will help Christian higher education reclaim the Christian mind for a lost generation. Baptist colleges have generally done well in using the first two methods—accommodation and indigenization—but I believe we need to work hard on developing a Biblical faith for our students today that is contextual and prophetic. Let me state the problem in another way: We have beautiful chapels on campus; we have Baptist professors. But have we been able to contextualize the faith for incoming secular and religious students so that they comprehend the message of Christ as it affects their daily lives? Christian Smith, professor of sociology at the University of North Carolina-Chapel Hill, states the problem in this way: "Most, though not all, religious educators in this country are failing. Most young people are not being formed primarily by their religious faith traditions; rather they are being formed by other notions and ideologies. And in part this is because adults are afraid to teach. They are afraid of not looking cool when they teach real substance."[10]

Contextualization in Christian higher education should mean teaching the substance of the gospel to students in their secular American culture, which has formed them for good or bad, so that they are able to comprehend, internalize, and act upon the reality of that faith. In other words, there are many conversion experiences along life's walk with God, but certainly the Christian academic experience should provide an opportunity for a new conversion to a mature faith in Christ. Horace Bushnell's *Christian Nurture* is not enough. We need to rediscover Charles Finney's understanding of a conversion-type theology, or as P. T. Forsythe bluntly said: "We want the new song of those who stand upon the rock, taken from the fearful pit and the miry clay, with the trembling still upon them and the slime still moist. We want the devotion of men whom grace found, and scarcely saved from the jaws of death, and took from the body of hell."[11] We want not a conversion to ignorance but a conversion to the deep truths of Christ that enlighten our understanding of culture, academia, and the family. This is the call of Christ that students need to hear, a call that issues in the commitment of one's life. As Dietrich Bonhoeffer said, "When Christ calls a man, he calls him to come and die!"

The effect this lack of contextualizing the Christian faith has had on Christian students in the American secular culture is shown in their attitudes toward human sexuality. Ron Sider in *The Scandal of the Evangelical Conscience* tells the disturbing statistics from a twelve-year study of young people who participated in the very popular program, "True Love Waits." According to Sider, researchers at Columbia and Yale studied twelve thousand teenagers who took the pledge. "Sadly they found that 88 percent of these pledgers reported having sexual intercourse before marriage; just 12 percent kept their promise. The researchers also found that the rates for having sexually transmitted diseases 'were almost identical for the teenagers who took pledges and those who did not.'"[12] Even more shocking research shows that "[o]f traditional evangelicals, 13 percent say it is okay for married persons to have sex with someone other than one's spouse."[13]

Such behavior and behavioral attitudes are only another sign of how sensate culture has captured the minds of this generation, secular and Christian. The Confucian scholar Lin Yutang, who later became a Christian, summarized the culture in which we live and against which a Christian understanding of reality and truth must takes its stand. Yutang wrote, "Stravinsky laughed at harmony, Gertrude Stein destroyed grammar, E. E. Cummings destroyed punctuation, Lenin destroyed democracy, Joyce destroyed idiom, and Dali destroyed sanity. . . . Freud played a curious role in the general destruction.

He established his laboratory in the toilet and was able to analyze a number of things about man."[14] This is the world in which the gospel must be studied and proclaimed, or our students will become dropouts from the faith.

That is the bad news, but the good news Sider proclaims is that "the small circle of people with a biblical worldview demonstrate genuinely different behavior. They are nine times more likely than all others to avoid 'adult only' material on the Internet. They are four times more likely than other Christians to boycott objectionable companies and products. . . ."[15] The fact is that a Christian education makes a difference if it is communicated and embraced.

A Call for a Baptist Postgraduate Institute for Christian Higher Education

In contextualizing the Christian faith to American youth whose worldview is more determined by Hollywood than by the Bible, it is necessary for Christian colleges and universities to recruit the best and brightest and most committed Christian intellectuals to their faculties. At the funeral of Pope John Paul II it was truly amazing that tens of thousands of young people had come to celebrate the life of a spiritual leader who had called for sacrifice and moral living that go against the grain of secular morality. It was moving to see hundreds of students with banners praising the life of John Paul II.

We Baptists and evangelicals have our own gurus and saints, but it seems very clear to me that we need to recruit for our colleges a new generation of young professors of deep spirituality who have a biblical worldview, centered on Christ. We need a new generation of young professors who are countercultural and who will be models that promote a truly Christian and spiritual lifestyle. I suspect that administrators at Baptist colleges and universities are mumbling under their breath, "Yeah, right! Show me where those professors are and I'll hire them!" When interviewed about how we can reclaim secular universities for Christ, Bishop Neill said, "Hire Christian professors." Then he was asked, "But, what if there are no Christian professors?" Neill concluded, "Then you have to go out and convert them!"

Of course, this is easier said than done, but it does highlight the need for a concrete plan to develop future Christian faculty. Several years ago I proposed to Baptist educators the need for a postgraduate institute, a Christian Institute of Higher Learning, which would help train Baptist professors to teach a biblical worldview. I am not proposing a propagandist institute for orthodoxy, but an institute with the best and brightest thinkers helping young professors, especially those coming from secular universities, to gain an evangelical and biblical worldview. I suspect the greatest struggle of most college and university administrators in Christian universities is precisely this difficulty of finding qualified intellectuals with Christian commitment to fill vacant positions.

Such an institute would have to explore such issues confronting our society today as world religions and the Christian response; what constitutes a biblical worldview; Christian morality in an age of permissiveness; the core curriculum of Christian doctrine and apologetics; a conversion theology that is Christocentric and Trinitarian; the significance of the kingdom of God and Christian faith as it relates to questions of social justice, human rights, and religious freedom; and biblical ethics. Indeed, because Christian scholars believe that all truth points to Christ, they are the ones who make academia a place of freedom. Peter Gomes, preacher at Harvard Memorial Church, reminded the Harvard Divinity School faculty of this in his recent convocation address: "I believe that the well-laid Protestant Christian foundations of this School are broad enough not only to embrace Christianity as its central tradition, but also the great wealth of religious traditions which, because of that foundation, have come now to join us. If this School's future is to be worthy of its past, that future dare not compromise the essential identity of the place, without which no other identity here would be possible."[16] Moreover, it is precisely the Christian institution that provides the basis for a truly free society. Secular academia will not be able to maintain the freedom that Christ brought to the university. The Russian philosopher Nicholas Berdyaev said it very clearly: "Man without God is no longer man; that is the religious meaning of the dialectic of modern history. . . . The man who lost God gives himself up to something formless and inhuman, prostrates himself up to something before material necessity."[17]

In sum, I believe there are enough Baptist institutions in this country today to cooperate in forming and supporting such a postgraduate institute that would become a training place for reclaiming the Christian mind in the secularized world of our day. I urge you to do so—for the revival of authentic Christian higher education.

Conclusion

George Hunston Williams, in his book *Wilderness and Paradise in Christian Thought*, tells the story of the various seals of Harvard University. The seal that once read *Veritas: Pro Christus et Ecclesiae* (Truth: For Christ and the Church), after a long history of conflict, eventually came to be today's *Veritas*. I remember George Buttrick, preacher to the university, once chided Harvard professors and students on a Sunday morning: "You people think that you can dig up *veritas* in Harvard Yard! But, let me tell you, only in Jesus Christ can you find *veritas*. Christ is the truth."

To a certain extent, the struggle Christian colleges and universities will face following 9/11 will be the same conflict that the gospel has had throughout its history. What is truth? Where is truth? For the Christian, universal truth, *veritas*, is always and only found in our relationship with and appropriation of Jesus Christ. If we are ashamed to name Christ as the center of our Baptist universities, then we should not be surprised when secularism swallows up our schools. Truth without Christ is sinking sand. Baptist schools that do not promote Christ in their leaders, faculty, and students will be lost. George Marsden's study is a testimony to that fact. As a Northern Baptist, I am witness to the fact that Brown, Temple, Bates, Denison, University of Chicago, Harvard, Yale, and many smaller colleges founded on Christ as the truth became not only non-Christian but often anti-Christian when the foundation of Christ the Truth was replaced with a nebulous idea of "truth"—somehow, somewhere, someplace, but only not in the Christian faith.

Sorokin calls this inability of modern man to open his mind and heart to another reality, the reality of God, humanity's "unteachableness." Moreover, "This unteachableness manifests itself . . . in the current hope of extricating ourselves from the crisis by means of a variety of facile but shallow artifices, without any fundamental re-orientation of values, any thoroughgoing change of mentality and conduct, any personal effort to realize man's divine creative mission on earth instead of acting merely as a 'flex mechanism'. . . . The more unteachable we are," according to Sorokin, "and the less freely and willingly we choose the sole course of salvation open to us, the more inexorable will be the coercion, the more pitiless the ordeal . . . the days of wrath, of the transition." He then concludes: "Let us hope that the grace of understanding may be vouchsafed us and that we may choose, before it is too late, the right road—the road that leads not to death but to the further realization of man's unique creative mission on this planet! *Benedictus qui venit in nomine Domini*."[18]

May God give Baptist educators in the twenty-first century the courage, wisdom, and conviction to say with the greatest intellectual of biblical record, the Apostle Paul, "For I am not ashamed of the gospel; it is the power of God for salvation to everyone who has faith."[19]

Chapter Eleven

To Whom Are Baptist Colleges and Universities Accountable?

Response 1
Daniel Vestal

The Challenges to Baptist Higher Education

The challenges facing Baptist higher education at the beginning of the twenty-first century are daunting. In fact, in my darkest moments, I find myself with little hope for the future vitality or relevance of many Baptist colleges and universities. The future of Baptist schools seems cloudy and problematic because of the convergence of two forces. First, there is the continued threat from fundamentalism, particularly in the schools that have a continuing relationship with the Southern Baptist Convention. Most state conventions in the SBC are now controlled by fundamentalists and therefore represent a constituency that is indifferent, if not hostile, to the whole enterprise of Baptist higher education. Fundamentalists clearly do not really believe in education; they support only indoctrination. For this reason, they will stifle academic freedom and excellence if given the opportunity. Second, there is the challenge from the opposite direction: secularization. The list of colleges and universities that started as Christian and as Baptist and that have become secular is much too long. Increasingly the temptation for schools started for and by Baptists is first to isolate themselves from their Baptist constituency and become Christian in a generic sense with little or no loyalty to the Baptist family. Often they gradually then lose both their Baptist and Christian identity altogether. This movement toward secularization has been well documented, and the trend still continues.

Undoubtedly financial issues play a role in both of these challenges. There is only so much Baptist money to support higher education, and the competition for that money is intense. The cost of supporting Baptist educational institutions constitutes an incentive for state conventions to divest themselves of this obligation. As Baptist colleges and universities face diminished support from Baptist organizations, they must look for money from other sources, which can cause significant change in the schools' priorities and policies. Equal to the effect of limited resources on the future of Baptist higher education is that of the scarcity of courageous, creative, and competent leadership. In many institutions, administrators have been more concerned with institutional survival than with the Baptist principles of academic and religious freedom. Some Baptist college and university leaders, rather than face an uncertain institutional future, have been willing to conform to a fundamentalist agenda and have sacrificed the integrity of their leadership. Others have capitulated to an elitist and secularist pressure to pursue the values of the secular academic marketplace rather than to continue the arduous task of combining academic excellence with unapologetic Christian commitment. Others, many of whom are leaders of vision and integrity, have simply grown weary of the struggle, which doesn't exactly inspire younger Baptists to pursue Christian higher education as a career. Someone has remarked that the most difficult position of leadership within the Baptist family is that of president of a Baptist college or university.

The Effect of the Changing Baptist Landscape

The denominational context in which Baptist colleges and universities exist today is undergoing radical change. Most interpreters of North American religious life say that we are living in a postdenominational culture—that is, that Christian denominations simply don't have the power or influence over local churches that they had in the past. And they exert even less power or influence in the lives of individuals. Although I don't believe that Christian denominations will disappear in the foreseeable future, I do believe that they will face significant reconfiguration. If so, this would mean that the age we are living in is not so much a postdenominational age as it is a neodenominational age. Churches will still affiliate, network, partner, and connect with other churches, but they will do so in different ways. One fact is clear: because individual Christians and local congregations do not feel the intense loyalty to denominations that they did in the past, the funding, support, and sense of identity that resulted from denominational loyalty will continue to fade.

This means that the question "To whom are Baptist colleges and universities accountable?" must be addressed within the context of a changed and changing denominational reality. In the past, many Baptists believed their schools were agencies of the denomination, owned and operated by the denomination, and some of them were. But even when they did not legally belong to the denomination, Baptists had an almost universal *feeling* of ownership. One would regularly hear statements such as "That school is ours" or "That's a Texas Baptist school" or "That school belongs to us." Constituents of the denomination then felt both the right and responsibility to exercise the authority and obligation of ownership.

As time passed and circumstances changed, many in the denomination came to view Baptist schools not so much in terms of ownership but in terms of trusteeship. The schools were no longer considered agencies of the denomination but rather servants of the denomination, and to ensure that the schools served the denomination well, trustees were elected to provide governance and guidance. Denominational groups were perhaps somewhat humbled in having to admit that they didn't own or operate schools in a truly legal sense, but they still believed that they could make the schools accountable through the trustee system. Most Baptist colleges and universities still have all or at least a portion of their boards appointed by a denominational group, but with the current pressures of fundamentalism and secularism, this is not likely to be the way of the future.

A Partnership Model of Accountability

Given the current denominational context and the current challenges, I contend that the future of Baptist higher education depends upon a partnership model of accountability. Both the school and the denomination must voluntarily and intentionally collaborate and cooperate to serve the needs of churches, the community, and the world. They must see themselves as mutually accountable to each other and gladly embrace that accountability in fulfilling their respective roles and missions. My contention is that Baptist colleges and universities are accountable to the Baptist family that birthed them with a founding vision and then provided students and resources through the years. The Baptist faith tradition is just that—a living tradition forged out of an historical context that gives witness to the Christian faith. Individuals who embrace that tradition and confess their Christian faith out of that tradition constitute what I call a family, and it is to that family that I believe Baptist colleges and universities are accountable.

To describe Baptists as a family is to use a sociological and relational term that acknowledges that the denomination comprises many different members. First in the family are individual Christians who are Baptists through conversion and conviction. Then, of course, there are autonomous and independent churches that make up part of the family. They relate to one another in voluntary cooperation, and they form associations, conventions, fellowships, unions, and alliances, each of which is also autonomous and independent.

Also within the Baptist family are multiple organizations, institutions, and ministries, each created for benevolent, missionary, or educational purposes. All of these disparate members make up what I describe as a family, the family to whom Baptist colleges and universities are accountable. In return, the family is accountable to the schools.

When I speak of accountability, I do not speak in legal terms, although I realize that some schools are legally accountable to one part of the Baptist family. Nor do I speak in organizational and structural terms—who elects the trustees or who owns the institution. Rather, I speak of a more intangible form of accountability that I would describe as a moral, spiritual, and relational accountability, much like a child, parent, or sibling would feel accountability to one another and the ongoing legacy of a family heritage and name. Such accountability may be described by some as idealistic or unrealistic in today's world, but I would argue that if understood and practiced correctly, this is "the tie that binds" more powerfully than any legal contract.

This kind of accountability is like a covenant. It is social, spiritual, and totally voluntary. It requires mutual trust and respect, and reciprocal support, collaboration, and cooperation to achieve common goals and to maintain continued goodwill. As each member of a family is free to think and act independently, to form an individual identity, and to pursue personal goals and dreams, so are the individuals, churches, associations, and conventions that identify themselves as Baptist. And also as each member of a family feels compelled to support other family members, to protect the well-being of the family unit, and always to act with consideration for the cohesion of the family, so too should the individuals, churches, associations, and conventions that identify themselves as Baptist act for the communal good of the Baptist family. This model of accountability is not easy to maintain and nurture, as evidenced by the fact that families can be dysfunctional, but it is a model that best fits the Baptist idea of individual freedom and voluntary cooperation. It is also a model that is appropriate to meet the challenges facing Baptist higher education and the changing Baptist denominational context.

Reasons for Hope

Although I earlier offered a rather pessimistic picture of the future of Baptist higher education, let me conclude by pointing out some reasons for hope. First, Baptists have a rich heritage in Christian education. We have taken seriously the biblical admonition to love God with our minds. We have believed that higher education is a part of the Christian mission, and we have invested heavily in preparing women and men for leadership both within the church and within society. We should celebrate that heritage and let it be an encouragement for the future. To be sure, the future has its challenges, but Christian educators have always had challenges; and the courage and vision of those in the past should be an inspiration and example for us in the present.

A second reason for hope is that many of the needs that motivated Baptists to dedicate themselves to higher education are as compelling today as they were in the past. Perhaps they are even more compelling today. We are living in a postmodern, post-Christian, postdenominational culture where many people live by a very individualistic and personalized philosophy that says whatever feels good or seems good or works for the individual is thereby appropriate. Such a culture has a deep need for schools that educate young people with an unapologetic commitment to Christian faith and values. We are living in a world with growing disparity between rich and poor, a world where human suffering is overwhelming. Such a world has a deep need for schools that educate young people for the purpose of service to the human family and of the alleviation of human suffering. We are living in a world of ethnic rivalries, racial hatred, and increasing violence. Such a world has a deep need for schools that educate young people to create what Martin Luther King Jr. called "the beloved community." We are living in a world where the environment is being destroyed by neglect, indifference, and exploitation, a world where the very future of human existence is being threatened. Such a world has a deep need for schools that educate young people to care for God's good creation and to see themselves as stewards to protect and preserve it.

But past heritage and present need are not my only reasons for hope. I believe God continues to call Christians as teachers. God still calls individuals to invest themselves in higher education as a Christian vocation. Of course, they can fulfill this vocation in a non-Baptist or non-Christian college or university, but as long as some Christian scholars and teachers maintain the vision of working together for the common good in a community of learning, Baptist higher education has a future. Here, I pay tribute to teachers, who because of their sense of vocation, exercise their gifts and use their knowledge to inspire and instruct others. I pay tribute to those who, out of their sense of vocation, instill in others a love of their discipline and a love of learning. I pay tribute to those whose Christian commitment compels them to seek truth and then impart that truth to others.

A Baptist college or university is not a church, but a Baptist college or university can be an ally and partner with churches in the service of God and humanity. As two distinct kinds of institutions, they can collaborate and cooperate in the formation of character, the pursuit of wisdom, and the promotion of the common good for the human family. With mutual respect for the role each plays in a civil society, they need not be adversarial or competitive, but can collaborate as partners. At times there may be tensions and misunderstandings between the two—such is the case in any family—but with patience and persistence, their partnership can create a bright future for Baptist higher education.

To Whom Are Baptist Colleges and Universities Accountable?

Response 2

R. Kirby Godsey

I

Many people share the uneasy sense that Baptist higher education, especially in the South, has rarely been more vulnerable than it is today. Many Baptist institutions have either broken the historic ties with their denomination or they are literally selling their academic souls for far less than a "full mess of pottage." Accountability to our church constituency has increasingly been translated to mean the exercise of some form of denominational control, reflecting the earnest conviction that some supporting constituency or some ideology should become the judge of whether the institution is fulfilling its mission and teaching the truth. However, it is a tragic mistake to assume that a college or university is not being faithful to its heritage or its tradition unless it maintains an unquestioning allegiance to its church constituency or unless its programs can be viewed through a prism of an "appropriate" orthodoxy and found to be consistent and compliant. In fact, efforts to assert denominational control are myopic, and such an approach to achieving accountability is dead wrong. A university is first a university. A college is first a college. Church constituencies should exercise no control over institutions of higher education, and the notion of sacrificing educational autonomy for the sake of receiving denominational approval or funding represents fuzzy thinking and flawed commitment.

More often than not, the assurance of accountability through control by a church constituency is usually only a thinly veiled effort to impose ideological and doctrinal boundaries on the institution. Accountability means compliance. Recent developments at Louisiana College appear to be an egregious effort to assure that the institution is faithful to a narrow, doctrinaire interpretation of its educational mission. While the board of trustees certainly remains a principal interpreter of the institution's mission, the unilateral effort on the part of the board to define the college's mission in such a way as to limit inquiry or to bar certain books from the bookstore or the classroom is a classic example of ideology being allowed to become ascendant over learning. The honest search for truth is never likely to be fostered by the fear of truth.

Under the oversight of a rigid orthodoxy or parent religious body, collegiate institutions have found themselves engaging in endless twists and turns, posturing, or creating artificial façades of religiosity in order to make their activities appear to conform to arbitrary codes of accountability. Apparently, sheer hubris causes the agents of religious ideologies to presume that their responsible participation in governance should allow them to control the institution. Such a narrow interpretation of accountability leaves the objects of this control—institutions, faculty, and students—jaded and fearful of reprisals. It is no wonder that some Baptist colleges and universities have bolted from their traditional moorings, choosing a greater measure of freedom over what appear to be efforts to exercise irrational and gratuitous control.

No legitimate educational institution wants to allow itself to become captive to a philosophical or theological set of affirmations, particularly when they arrive in the form of creeds or manifestos. As a means of assuring accountability, ideological control of an institution by any agency or ideology is always a bankrupt and unreliable strategy for ensuring institutional integrity because it makes the institution subject to an authority that is both unpredictable and capricious. At any moment the standards of accountability depend upon who happens to be in power and what their prevailing interpretations of orthodoxy happen to be.

While boards of trustees can be open and conversant with such prevailing orthodoxies, those orthodoxies and their sponsoring agencies serve as only one reference point in the governance of the institution. Because boards of trustees possess wide-ranging powers and obligations, the policies governing the election of boards become an especially important issue for church-related institutions that hope to remain free of ideological control. An educational institution, by its very nature, serves many constituencies, and the highest obligation of the board is not to the constituencies who elect them, but to the constituencies they serve through their stewardship of the institution's mission and assets. The selection of trustees should never compromise this primary focus of their accountability. So while it may be entirely appropriate for the parent religious body to have a voice in electing the board, board elections are more likely to generate greater conflict and religious and political mischief if members are nominated and elected solely by the related church constituency. The board should never become captive to a single constituency, even an important one.

We need to build together more constructive and enduring processes that preserve the principle of accountability without restraining genuine freedom of inquiry. Accountability to a church constituency or to some form of orthodoxy should be, at best, secondary or even tertiary. Accountability to such a constituency or statement of orthodoxy should be akin to our accountability to our alumni or the community. That accountability is significant and should be taken seriously, but it should not determine the content of our academic programs or the priorities that guide the search for truth.

II

The question then remains: To whom and to what are we accountable? I believe that it is important and plausible to define a higher and more enduring level of accountability and responsibility than to church-related constituencies. Baptist universities and colleges are first and foremost accountable, one, to the missions they serve; two, to the people who teach and learn within them; and three, to the truth they pursue.

Assuring accountability in this context is clearly more complex than measuring the institution against an arbitrary, doctrinal standard. The imposition of orthodoxy, however defined, runs counter to the essential character of a college or university. Even when a college or university has been established by a constituency who defined themselves by clear and definite ideological boundaries, the high calling of a college or university would beckon them, I believe, to lay aside—to suspend, as it were—their ideological predilections in favor of teaching and learning unencumbered by faith commitments. Faith commitments may be one of the motivating factors in the creation of an institution, but those same commitments should not be served up as the criteria for accountability. Doing so results in a governance arrangement that is simplistic, misguided, and, on occasion, even immoral in its governance decisions.

Accountability to mission is a far more reliable, though complex, standard. The mission of colleges and universities is dynamic, organic, continually being redefined. An institutional mission should not be a set of stale, rigid formulas composed a hundred years ago and held perpetually as the underlying foundation for the institution's endeavors. The language of the mission may remain the same, but the interpretation of the mission inevitably changes, and the priorities by which the mission is brought to life are continually modified by current issues, contemporary leadership, and new interpreters. Therefore, remaining accountable to the mission is a far more complicated process than simply reading a mission statement and assessing compliance. The real work of accountability means engaging in collaborative conversations about the meaning and expectation of the institution's mission. No single body, including even the governing board, has the singular responsibility to interpret that mission. The board does indeed hold the mission in trust, and that trust even surpasses the trust over financial and physical assets; put differently, an institution's mission is its single most important asset. But the most significant dimension of the trust held by trustees is its obligation to understand that an institution's mission is greater than any single body can interpret alone. Even board members need to reach for the courage to be colleagues in the interpretation of mission. A college or university is a community of learners in which the people who teach and learn and even the beneficiaries of teaching and learning are critical voices in the interpretation of institutional mission. A board of trustees that interprets mission in an isolated, autocratic fashion would be akin to a Supreme Court that chose to interpret the Constitution without reference to the pleadings of others. Their supremacy does not lie in their capacity to be an isolated, lone interpreter of the Constitution, but rather in their responsibility to weigh the meaning of the Constitution in the light of the current issues.

The mission of a Baptist college or university, after all, should not be interpreted in such a way that the institution is diverted from being a good college or university. A good Baptist college must, first of all, be a good college. Insofar as being Baptist becomes a rubric for defending educational practices that lack rigor, discipline, and integrity, the value of our mission becomes diminished. Focusing on our mission as a means of accountability underscores that a college or university is first and foremost a place for the education and nurturing of students and a center for learning, research, and the dissemination of knowledge. Being a good Baptist university should not be an appellation that places shackles on learning.

However, being accountable to mission certainly takes into account that our mission is special and distinct. The special mission of a Baptist college or university, in contrast to a so-called secular university, relates to our historical foundations, our responsibility for moral education, our focus on the relationship between faith and learning, and our commitment to intellectual and religious freedom. It may be helpful to explore these dimensions of our special mission and how they relate to accountability.

Most Baptist colleges and universities have deep historical ties to Baptists. While both the experience of students and the life of Baptists have been profoundly enriched and even transformed by these ties, it is mutual respect and common history, not a particular set of doctrines, that should be the ties that bind. The common valuing of learning and the nurturing of the human spirit, more than money, should define the enduring meaning of these historical roots. A prudent and responsible partnership between the university and its historical church constituency does not require that an institution abandon its Baptist heritage or identity. However, the maintenance of that historic relationship requires reason, sensitivity, civility, tolerance, and respect from persons within both the university community and the historic church constituency.

But the special mission of a Baptist school clearly should not be viewed chiefly in historical terms. The history of our Baptist colleges is deeply intertwined with the history of Baptists, and being a Baptist institution can and should modify the substance of our educational endeavors. Our distinct mission means that we should educate with an awareness that what a person believes is as significant to what a person actually does in life as what that same person knows. Affirmations of faith and claims of knowledge both influence behavior. Our charge should not be to prescribe a set of beliefs to be accepted by those who study at our institutions. Rather than prescription, our commitment to the moral dimensions of education should take a different form. Our responsibility, growing out of Baptist history and character, is to set before our students an explicit concern for the moral implications of life and learning. Our aim is to help students make discriminating moral judgments and to help them gain a better understanding of the impact of religious belief upon one's life and work.

It is also our responsibility in a Baptist institution to address the relationship between faith and learning. Though a university should not wish to impose religious belief, a Baptist university should assume some responsibility for creating the kind of learning environment in which religious commitment may be examined and affirmed. The discussions of faith and the examination of personal religious convictions are legitimate subjects for inquiry and debate. Our calling is to make faith and learning partners in the journey of education and living.

In a Baptist institution, our special mission also means that the commitment to religious freedom, so basic to the Baptist way of life, serves as the foundation for intellectual freedom, which is so essential to the life of a college or university. As Baptist educators, our devotion is to free inquiry, and the open search for truth is founded not simply in our allegiance to the values of a free and democratic society. In our institutions, the values intrinsic to learning and the open search for truth have religious moorings. So, as Baptist institutions, we should be first among those who advocate free inquiry. We do not fear the search for truth wherever it leads, for all truth is God's truth.

Let us be careful about putting doctrinal boundaries on God's truth because God's truth will likely shatter all our human boundaries, leaving us to stand in the debris of our ignorance.

Accountability to mission is ultimately meant to ensure that colleges and universities do not define success by private gain but by embracing the public good. The public good includes enriching the capacity of the sponsoring denomination to make a difference in the world. For this reason, Baptist colleges are not about enriching the denomination. That would be private gain. Instead, they are about enriching the capacity of the sponsoring religious body to be a more effective, a more intelligently pious force for human redemption.

Beyond mission, we are also accountable to those who teach and learn within our institutions. Students and faculty are more important than disciplines of study or religious affirmations. Neither students nor faculty are incidental to our institution. They are together our *raison d'être*. They are present not chiefly to serve or to defend a certain religious point of view but to pursue truth. We are accountable to serve them and to create an environment where teaching and learning can occur unencumbered by social, political, or religious limitations. That principle does not discourage the presence, even a permeating presence, of a specific religious perspective, but our accountability to those who teach and learn should assure that they do not become subordinate to a particular religious perspective and that their intrinsic worth trumps religious doctrine. Affirmations of faith are not sacred; people are. Our accountability is higher and greater to the people we serve than to the doctrines we respect and affirm.

Finally, we are accountable ultimately to the truth we pursue. Our calling as Baptist educators is not to package the truth, promote the truth, or even defend the truth. Our calling is to pursue the truth. Searching for truth is the bedrock of any institution that claims to be a college or university. In the language of faith, our accountability to truth may also be viewed as our ultimate accountability to God. The search for truth may be seen, indeed, through the eyes of faith, as a searching for the face of God.

To affirm the primacy of truth in recounting our obligations of accountability may seem to be a recitation of the obvious. For purposes, however, of understanding a Baptist university, I think it is not. When Baptists or, for that matter, any religious group support an institution of higher education, they may bring to that task their own special perceptions of truth. To make adherence to those special perceptions of truth a standard of accountability reflects a flawed understanding of accountability. The search for truth should not be subordinated to any particular theological orientation.

In reality, we often claim in our religious lives a special understanding of truth mediated through revelation or through our own religious experience. Those claims to truth may be entirely appropriate when they are held as personal convictions by which we live and to which we are personally accountable. However, when we enter the sanctuary called laboratory or classroom, we are obligated, at least for the moment, to lay aside any affirmations that would require our students not to approach the world of learning openly and without prejudice.

Our perceptions and convictions of truth gained by our own faith commitments seem to pose, from time to time, a difficult problem for us in higher education. On the one hand, we do not wish to impose our religious understanding on others. On the other hand, we do not wish to hide the significance of faith in shaping our views of reality and truth. I believe that the person of faith, in the context of a Baptist institution, must be secure enough within his or her own religious convictions to affirm them as personal life-perspectives while tolerating and respecting differing views. As we teach and nurture, we should leave open the question of personal and ultimate meaning in a way that preserves the freedom and integrity of students and faculty. Each person's journey of belief or disbelief should be tenaciously respected even when it differs radically from our own view.

Our accountability to truth is not carried out by seeking to assure that no one teaches as truth some affirmation that is outside the boundaries of our own deeply held affirmations. Indeed, our accountability would more likely be fulfilled by assuring that there are people who teach and learn whose understanding of truth is radically different from our own. The notion that our institutions should be populated only by Baptists or even by Christians again misconstrues the notion of accountability. Neither Baptists nor Christians have exclusive access to truth. It is simply not the case that Baptists or Christians are the only effective stewards of teaching and research. We may do well, even in the classroom, to listen to Jews or Muslims or even nonbelievers along the way.

III

Though institutions should resist the imposition of external religious control, those same institutions should be good stewards of their relationship with a founding religious constituency. For example, one evidence of stewardship is that a strong Baptist institution seeks to include highly qualified and competent Baptists on the faculty and staff. The institution will be considerably weakened by some arbitrary rule of employment requiring that its faculty and staff must be Baptist or Christian. Diversity of viewpoint enhances the quality of learning, but diversity is not the sole good. It is also both important and reasonable that a Baptist institution be expected to include within its ranks able and competent faculty and staff who value the religious identity of the institution, who understand the Baptist heritage that gave rise to its development, and who are committed to the preservation of the values that created the institution.

A second evidence of stewardship is that a Baptist institution has a special responsibility to educate Baptist young people. Baptists have invested heavily in the development of these institutions. One means of exercising responsible stewardship of that investment is to maintain a genuine sense of responsibility to provide outstanding educational environments that are accessible to Baptist students, perhaps through scholarships that are targeted specifically for Baptists. Our schools should be places where these students can probe and press the limits of their understanding and their believing. Our schools should provide Baptist students a tolerant and sympathetic environment, while insisting on the kind of intellectual growth that will broaden students' tolerance for differing ideas and diverse religious perspectives. In itself, a Baptist university should enable these students to enrich their minds, while exploring and strengthening their religious understanding and commitment.

Finally, a responsible stewardship of our religious identity may be found in the institution's willingness to become an intellectual force in the life of Baptists. Baptists by definition are diverse. They include the educated as well as the uneducated, persons of every level of schooling, and of every cultural strata. We have indicated that one element of accountability is our commitment to engage in an unencumbered search for truth. In fulfilling that obligation, a Baptist university must transcend doctrinal disputes and eschew emotional debates that sometimes demean the integrity of honest religious beliefs. Our schools should demonstrate the essential compatibility of reason and devotion. The university can best serve the church not by becoming compliant to some particular viewpoint, but by holding high its commitment to be an intellectual influence in the life of Baptists. Our schools can serve as forces for dialogue between differing views among Baptists, reminding them that no quarter has an exclusive hold on God's truth. It follows, then, that a Baptist institution will likely maintain a tense relationship with some members of the denomination, but this is both healthy and wise.

A Baptist university can certainly be strengthened by Baptist churches; Baptist churches can clearly be strengthened by the university. But neither ought to become accountable to the other. Their mutual respect and affirmation should be strong enough to allow them to disagree and even to engage in serious debate over weighty matters, without requiring uniformity of viewpoint. Tensions have increased in the recent years by the emergence of a more monolithic theological viewpoint among some denominational forces. Rigid, intellectual monoliths, whether they be fundamentalist, liberal, evangelical, or otherwise, are contrary, I believe, to the work and purpose of a Baptist institution of higher education. They are contrary to the work of any university, but, ironically, they are particularly contrary to the work of a Baptist university because of our religious foundations. Baptist institutions should resist any efforts by any external religious body, even a founding one, to control the learning environment. The challenge for a Baptist college is to work to maintain real conversation with its religious constituency, without becoming an uncritical voice for its theological or moral position.

Baptist churches and Baptist educational institutions will be strengthened by the willingness to listen to each other without requiring control, assent, or conformity. Baptist schools should openly affirm their religious connections as being both historically and presently significant. The church constituency should openly affirm the educational institution as a place of learning committed to the canons of truth and free inquiry. The commitment to truth and the affirmation of faith can remain strong and independent only if they are free. We should work together as free institutions, free to listen and free to speak. Let the preachers preach; let the teachers teach; let the students learn.

Chapter Twelve

The University, the Church, and the Culture

Thomas E. Corts

I

The New Testament concept of being "in this world, but not of this world"[1] summarizes the dilemma of each Christian and of each Baptist institution. The church (i.e., all Christian believers), and especially evangelicals in America, have alternately "struggled with an inherent tension between . . . keeping that which they defined as sacred uncontaminated by the profane world," and "infusing the world with sanctifying influences." [2] Should Christians protect themselves from the world, or become involved in the world in order to have an impact upon it? Since the first century A.D., even under the Emperor Constantine and in the early Middle Ages, there has been an uneasy coexistence between culture and Christianity, Caesar and Christ, *paideia* and *Logos*.[3]

My thesis is as follows: First, culture is by quiet stealth compromising our Christianity, wearing down Christians' disdain for evil, urging acceptance of what we should resist, all without our awareness and with a resultant impact upon Baptist colleges and universities. Second, in our time and in the future it will take deliberate, careful, and conscientious resistance to culture's siren songs, or we shall lose our distinctiveness and be out of business, at great loss to the church and to society. Third, Christian college leadership must be single-minded and confident in purpose and commitment, because it will not likely receive strong endorsement from the society at large.

"Culture" in this essay refers to the totality of socially transmitted behavior patterns, art, science, beliefs, and all products of human work and thought, the collected wisdom and sentiment of past and present.[4] Culture is here, surrounding us and among us, like it or not. "[A] capacity for culture is in fact one of humanity's most firmly established biological traits,"[5] and in America, our culture and our Christianity have been at times friends, but more often foes.

Yet it is not an overstatement to say today that modern American culture has overwhelmed modern American Christianity.[6] The ceaseless waves of messages from movies, newspapers, TV, and the like have wrought a sea of secularism and spawned a riptide, pulling American Christians under. In the post-World War II era, prosperity came like a tidal wave, drenching the rising middle-class Christian masses in consumerist pop culture until, thoroughly soaked and sated, they resignedly washed out into the sea of cultural abyss where today we find ourselves far from shore, and totally lost.

Back in 1948, the editor of *Christian Century* wrote that three separate forces were bidding for ascendancy in the spiritual life of America: Protestantism, Roman Catholicism, and secularism.[7] Secularism has won thus far, as we look back on the fifty years from 1950 to 2000, a time of radically shifting realities. Consider what happened in that approximate time frame. Americans, even with minimal preparation, went from high school to college in record numbers. Divorce rates rose as marriage and the family came under harsh attack. Birth control made women freer. Sex was lifted from its undercover status in public conversation. Rebellion and civil disobedience became more acceptable. We confronted racial prejudice and outlawed segregation. Laws made work less offensive and less demanding. Easy credit taught us not to defer our desires, but to have it all without waiting. Clothing styles and dress codes came to lack modesty. Relentlessly catchy slogans and rhythms stuck in our brains so that we programmed ourselves to repeat advertising jingles without conscious intent. So-called urban music marked by rap lyrics filled with violent and ribald language led to the phenomenon of street vernacular's dirtiest words tumbling even from the lips of small children. Abundant, private pornography-on-demand came within personal reach via the Internet.

Holding to claimed freedoms which the founding fathers likely never would have allowed, we endured the outrageous—the truly uncouth—on TV halftime shows, on commercials, on billboards, and in other public venues, stretching the bounds of public taste.[8] We not only *tolerated* the cult of personality among "stars" of athletics, movies, TV, and public prominence, we *made* those stars, sometimes even allowing them to invent themselves, and rewarding them with obscene profits as compensation for their illicit theft of the unmerited admiration of our young. No wonder when British children were asked in a survey what they wanted to be, 95 percent replied, "To be famous."[9] There seems to be a "world mania" for celebrity.[10]

In his Massey Lectures at Harvard in the early 1990s, Gore Vidal argued that movies had become the powerful *lingua franca* of the twentieth century and that whether one visited Harvard, Oxford, or the University of Bologna, after small talk the conversation would turn to movies. He asserted that movies (including TV) have overtaken literature as the primary conductor of culture's impulses.[11]

To illustrate just how powerful indirect movie messages can be, consider the case of a popular Hollywood film, *Sideways*. According to *USA Today*, sales of pinot noir wine "soared to record heights after the movie opened in October and again after the DVD was released in April," up 44 percent over the previous year.[12] Sales increases were credited to "those sleek bottles of Pinot Noir, the soft, sexy, scene-stealing red wine that is the metaphorical Holy Grail of *Sideways'* plot."[13]

Time magazine named among the one hundred *most influential people in the world* one Simon Cowell, a mere judge on a soon-to-fade television show called *American Idol*, a modified copycat of *Ted Mack's Original Amateur Hour* from 1948.[14] The hip-hop group Outkast is on that same list. You see, ever so gradually, "what's happening" weaves its way into public awareness, into tolerability and acceptance, communicating its way into the culture. As critic Pauline Kael once wrote of television movies: "There's a kind of hopelessness about it. What does not deserve to, lasts, and so it all begins to seem like one big pile of junk."[15]

What of the church amidst all this? I wish I could say, "Thank the Lord, the church has stood firm, unmovable against the cultural trash that least admirably represents our national scene." But, sadly, I cannot. I had hoped that the billions we have spent on Sunday schools, day schools, and vacation Bible schools would produce a generation that has its values correct.[16] I would have thought the vast sums spent on television preaching might have turned the tide. I wish all the church buildings and all the churchgoing had made a consistent and measurable difference. But we are left to admit to Christians' full participation in the culture of our time: the divorce rate is about the same among those who attend church and those who do not. The 70 percent of men between the ages of eighteen and thirty-four who visit a pornography Web site at least once a month includes believers and churchgoers.[17] The ranks of the high-and-mighty, white-collar elite who have bilked us for billions include Bible-carrying, churchgoing, God-talking criminals who will escape jail only by legal sleight of hand.[18] As the Barna Organization has concluded, "People's faith does not make as much of a difference as might be expected. . . ."[19] Whatever our defenses, the cultural tsunami has just kept coming.

After so many strong statements, it is probably time for a disclaimer. While it is ever the privilege of the old to doubt the young, I am fully aware that as I describe the heritage we have bequeathed to our successors, I am confessing some of our own generational sins. Nevertheless, in the interest of full disclosure, I herewith admit to being a card-carrying member of AARP, to being granted the senior-citizen discount at a fast-food restaurant, even without confessing my age. While my intent is objectivity, you now know my perspective.

As a graduate student I first read that communication is far more than what we *say*. It also encompasses nonverbal communication, the accumulation of our consciously and subconsciously remembered experience, and the sum total of accumulated messages—our actions and behavior.[20] A subtle, subconscious patterning of understanding, conduct, and behavior results from communication, from the processing of all the messages and responses we receive and interpret, gathered into what we come to know as culture. *Sub rosa*, in ways we never recognize, these cumulative communications, woven into the warp and woof of our culture, become the ever-so-silently conveyed meanings that influence our attitudes, that plant ideas, reinforce positions, fashion our taste and sense of tolerance and propriety, and cultivate familiarity—all by stealth.[21]

So, our culture is confronting us at every moment. In some conscious ways we can be gatekeepers, using our reasoning powers, judgment, and framework of values to oppose the culture. In other ways we unwittingly allow the culture to maneuver us as thoughtlessly as a thirsty man takes a drink of water, seeing only the necessary H_20 and never considering the multitude of unnecessary elements, harmful organisms, and particulate matter subtly sneaking into his system.

We have more means of direct messaging than any other civilization in history. The cheap, easy, and almost continuous sending and receiving intensifies the direct impact of culture. For instance, our students' lives will be shaped by cell phones and e-mail and by the ease with which they can communicate anywhere, anytime. Their calling plans access the world, making it possible to talk with friends in the military on aircraft carriers thousands of miles away or with mission volunteers on other continents. In 1950, about a million overseas phone calls originated in the United States. In 2001, the number was a staggering 6.27 billion.[22] E-mail messages float in cyberspace with unimaginable ease and cheapness among the 4 billion existing Web sites, with tens of thousands of new Web sites being added daily.[23] The computer and Web site are fast becoming teenagers' favorite source for entertainment.[24] Those e-mail messages and chat rooms, for good and for ill, affect our culture, uniting friends and families, accounting for billions of dollars of sales, provoking marriage and divorce, conveying information that resolves problems and heals diseases, facilitating crime and mischief, and coordinating terrorist acts anywhere on earth. Text messaging spreads one-to-one gossip and rumor and hearsay in split seconds, as opposed to the days required for those high school "slambooks" of my generation. Thanks to Internet rovers, the capacity for names and new words to appear suddenly in everyday usage is astounding. Terms like "24/7," "text messaging," and "googling" have emerged out of cyberspace into common usage.

Politicians have known for years that name recognition is crucial.[25] That is why yard signs, billboards, and TV commercials become so important to political candidates. If a voter in the voting booth has no strong conviction, he tends to pull the lever beside the name that seems familiar, whether he knows anything about the individual or not. Similarly, as media within our culture regularly discuss sex, divorce, adultery, murder, and racial strife, we are being conditioned. These terms—as they are more frequently heard, spoken, and written—become more familiar, more acceptable, more a part of our subconsciousness, almost routine. That is true also of curses, so-called street language, and the obscenities of movies and rap music, so offensive to my generation. They have become matter-of-fact to our children and grandchildren, losing their shock value. Their frequent use blunts our capacity to be disturbed or aggrevated by them and makes them common in the same sense that brand names or political candidates' slogans become ensconced in our awareness. It is almost as if there were a conscious campaign to get society to recognize and be somewhat comfortable with extreme words, just as political operatives seek to cultivate familiarity with a candidate's name.

If it were only America at stake, our cultural transitions would be serious enough, but America influences the entire world. Even in the 1990s, the *New York Times* stated that "American popular culture has never been more dominant internationally."[26] In Damascus, Syria, the TV series *Seinfeld* airs twice daily. For many young Syrians it affords a chance to practice their English, and a window through which they see American culture. What will a young Syrian conclude about American culture on the basis of *Seinfeld*? Similarly, a Syrian teacher of English asks plaintively for help in explaining American family life to her students. She asks, "Does 'Friends' show a typical family?" Perhaps we have not considered the moral impact of the reruns being played and replayed around the world: *Baywatch*, *The Young and the Restless*, *Dallas*, and so forth. Movies and television are the windows through which the people of the Arab world view and judge American culture, which it mistakenly sees as *Christian* culture.[27]

Though the line between entertainment and news is blurred, consider that the news buffet served to us every day by the media tends never to involve the routine or the normal. It almost always relates some extreme or exceptional human behavior. News professionals admit their inclination to feature what is unusual. "Dog bites man" is not newsworthy. "Man bites dog" is. Add to that the fact that our culture influences even the choices the media make. The media's judgment about what to feature is influenced by the culture, so if the culture seems inordinately interested in sex, children, or pets, those interests are reflected in the media. When a mother is accused of murdering her children, the story leads, even if the event occurred miles away and the mother is obviously mentally ill. A basketball star is charged with rape. An adult teacher has children fathered by one of the children in her class. A teenager is kidnapped by a man who plans to make her an additional wife.[28] Prisoners suffer abuse and torment by guards at the Abu Ghraib prison in Iraq. These are all incidents that have fascinated the public and been lead stories for days on TV and in magazines and newspapers, all purporting exclusive angles.

More than fifty years ago, Robert Maynard Hutchins chaired a commission of distinguished citizens which held hearings around the country and issued a report on the media.[29] The commission deplored declining coverage of public affairs and a tendency to present news as disconnected vignettes featuring personalities and aberrant behavior of most any kind. Five decades later, the issues are still with us. Media critic Tom Rosenstiel advised, "Being exposed to the media in and of itself is not healthy."[30]

Not only does our culture embed itself in our minds and understandings without our consent, but it also has a seductive pull by making the prurient and evil seem more interesting and prevalent than the good. There would have been nothing newsworthy, if, like the average household in America, that mother had given her children lunch, seen them to soccer practice, piano lessons, and so on. The basketball star's visit to a Colorado resort would not have attracted media attention had he simply been an overnight guest. If an adult teacher taught her schoolchildren and went home to her family, why would media notice? Had the Utah kidnapper merely proposed to an Oregon teenager, it would have been rebuffed as ridiculous and would have been unreported. That prisoners are not coddled in a Baghdad prison is expected, and not the stuff of breaking news. In each of these cases, it was the evil, the wrong, that made the situation exceptional, and it was the evil that made purveyors of news confident of the public's interest.

What happens, then, when news of aberrant behavior is spread in headlines, photographs, and newsreel footage and repeated over and again on the nightly news, in our newspapers, and in newsmagazines? Because repetition is one of the great learning devices, that wrongful conduct is planted in the mind. Unintentionally, evil is being advertised with the utmost emphasis in prime media space, so that the masses cannot avoid it. Such advertising costs commercial corporations huge sums of money, yet evil is granted this prime play gratis. Evil even gets favored positioning that no ad agency in America can obtain for its client at any price—the top right-hand corner of the daily newspaper, the lead story on the 10 o'clock news, and repeat plays as emerging details enhance the story.

We are victimized by the culture through a vicious cycle. Public taste motivates the communication of stories of deviant behavior, of persons with evil intent, of the outrageous or the not-normal, and of the trivial. These stories are sent around the world with great speed and fearful repetition, serving to condition us, to make us all the more comfortable and less likely to object to evil, violence, and antisocial behavior. We informally codify these attitudes into our culture so that our tolerance for evil, violence, antisocial behavior, and obscenity are passed along to succeeding generations.

You are familiar with the classic *The Screwtape Letters*. With apologies to the memory of C. S. Lewis, I have this vision of Screwtape writing Wormwood something like the following:

> My Dear Wormwood,
>
> Congratulations are in order. I must say you are working well with clothing designers, actors and actresses, movie makers, sports stars, media outlets, and people who influence public taste. They are being more and more open and public about good old-fashioned evil and lust. We could not be getting better publicity. Our side is well-represented in the best newspapers, TV, movies, and in all the media. And we are reaching the young who have the rest of their lives before them. Every adolescent school girl is striving to be sexy and seductive. In fairly short time, we have engineered a massive increase in the permissiveness society allows. Billboards, TV, newspapers, the movies—they're all using words, scenes, and situations that used to bring scowls. Here and there one hears objections, but children have to learn that sexual expression is healthy, and they are going to know the facts of life sooner or later. It thrills me that folks don't feel all those old-fashioned constraints. Instead, every day they become more familiar with the naturalness of hatred, lying, adultery, promiscuity. As you know, we must be unrelenting in wearing down the objections of the Enemy. Greed, lust, enmity—people have to realize that these are just human realities. If you can keep it up, dear Nephew, evil will be better known than Coca-Cola, people will no longer mouth all that religious stuff, unhappiness will be long-lasting, and we will have achieved success.
>
> Your affectionate uncle,
>
> SCREWTAPE[31]

Not one of us chose this culture whose unintended consequences dull a Christian sense of right and wrong. Yet it is the culture in which we do our work and live our lives and the culture in which our institutions will falter or prosper. It is the culture of the people we serve, the people of the church, and the people of the society at large.[32]

Perhaps it happened as the social authority of the church and of Christians seemed to wane. We simply sought and found ways to compromise and appease the culture rather than to resist it. The general public, especially in the South, delights in *talking* about Christian faith and even buying books about it.[33] In 2002, *Publishers Weekly* noted that for the first time in history, the best-selling nonfiction book and the best-selling fiction book were both from Christian publishers.[34] Pressed to bridge the gap between our Christian beliefs and our increasingly secular culture, maybe accommodation and compromise were vain attempts to keep from losing and to retain our importance.

Some could argue that when we did not accommodate or compromise, Christians tilted at windmills; for example, we became embroiled in politics—endorsing particular candidates—and campaigned against stem cell research and for monuments to the Ten Commandments. People my age remember ardent arguments over the use of modern translations of the Scriptures, whether young boys and girls should swim together at church outings, whether ballroom dancing was appropriate, whether Christians should go to movies, and whether we should burn Elvis Presley records.

Yet Christians in many ways mimicked the secular culture. One scholar asserts that concessions intended to make Christ more palatable to an increasingly secular public may have secularized and "commodified" Christianity in order to keep numbers in our churches and Christian books in the market, to keep at least some level of the society's focus on our faith.[35] We even have our own system of Christian-celebrity speakers, entertainers, musicians, and authors who imitate their secular counterparts though their message and audience may be Christian. Indeed, we might ask: "[H]ow did a culture that fifty years ago was nervous about make-up, Hollywood movies, and rock-and-roll make such an about-face and embrace worldliness? How did evangelicals become such prolific producers and consumers of popular culture?"[36] In the opinion of one observer, "The issue is not that evangelical Christians are tainted by interaction with secular culture, but rather that the boundary between 'secular' and 'evangelical' has become ever more permeable as evangelical media have grown over the past twenty years."[37]

II

Culture, the silent language, threatens every Baptist college and university and every university leader. When most of our institutions were founded, it was common to link higher education to religious purposes. We could be proud of the fact that even many state universities sprang directly from or out of familiarity with evangelical colleges. Many state university charters originally had something in them about building character and about God-given truth. In the 1890s almost every state university required chapel, and many required Sunday church attendance. Identification with a local church was common, and state university presidents were often ministers. (For example, most presidents of the University of Alabama, from its founding in 1820 until 1900, were ordained ministers, mostly Baptist, including Basil Manly.) But as colleges and universities became more sophisticated, as Darwinism rose in importance, as higher criticism of the Scriptures became more commonly known, the culture began to shift and so did the willingness to be identified with Christianity and with the church.

According to George Marsden, the result was that "[b]y the 1920s, the evangelical Protestantism of the old-time colleges had been effectively excluded from leading university classrooms."[38] As Marsden has so well demonstrated in his book, *The Soul of the American University*, it was bighearted, open, thoughtful individuals who dropped much of the religious influence of our colleges out of a desire to be tolerant, to grant freedom. In their desire to allow freedom of choice and not to make faith compulsory (as if it *could* be), in their desire to be inclusive of all views and to be pluralistic, they lost their individual religious perspectives.[39] Specific events hastened the transformation, but the culture was wearing down society's tolerance for church colleges or for Christian influence in state colleges. Among specific influences, we could cite the new rationalism of the later nineteenth century, the Scopes trial and the stress over evolution, the rise of the scientific age, the celebration of youth immediately after World War II and the subsequent rebellion and defiance of youth in the 1960s, the national anger over Vietnam, the permissiveness produced by the Woodstock generation, and the institutional requirements imposed by federal aid. Well-intentioned, powerful influences slanted our culture from a position that was totally accepting and expecting of heavy religious influence to a posture of almost disdain for religious concepts within the higher educational community. Indeed, there seemed to develop almost an inverse index: the more intentionally religious an institution was, the less academically strong it was and the less respect it tended to garner in academic circles.

Yet, one has the feeling that ours is a world in transition about religion. After September 11, 2001, and with the war in Iraq, Islam has made the world more conscious of religion than it has been in a long time. In the academic realm, even Stanley Fish has written that "it is one thing to take religion as an object of study and another to take religion seriously. To take religion seriously would be to regard it not as a phenomenon to be analyzed at arm's length, but as a candidate for the truth."[40]

But the reality is that our culture is still working against the believing evangelical Christian. Many individuals in our society would defend our right to believe whatever we desire, including all the tenets dearest to the evangelical heart, but the culture leans against our evangelical colleges and universities. Consider a few practical ways in which our culture opposes, rather than embraces, our institutions.

First, our society does not warm to people who take their religion seriously, any religion. It is simply not cool to be too much concerned about matters of deep conviction that can so readily distinguish one person from another. Consider the treatment of religion in the movies, TV, and the print media. They are all a bit reluctant to make religion an important subject. When ABC employed Peggy Wehmeyer, she was the only correspondent of a national news network whose attention was devoted to religion. In a financial decision, ABC terminated her contract in 2001, and for all the money spent on news gathering, not a single major TV network now has a religion correspondent.[41] The big daily newspapers, if they have a religion section at all, confine it to an emphasis once per week, and they might not have even that, were it not for the prospect of attracting significant church advertising.

A perfect illustration has been the flap over Mel Gibson's movie *The Passion of the Christ*. First, we endured the inflated charges that the film, heavily reliant upon the New Testament, was anti-Semitic. Later, there was amazement at the film's box office success, but no one knew quite what to say about it. Generally, the media found certain extremes to report and then fell back on a roster of quotations from people who were impressed by the film's success and from people who were shocked and surprised by its success. The media seemed to consider the public's response to the film to be newsworthy itself, but they did not know how to fit such a powerful message about Jesus into their generalist approach.

We have to admit that a civilization that prides itself on pluralism and diversity might see it as undemocratic or inconsiderate to make exclusive claims for one religion, especially evangelical Christianity. Our society likes soft, friendly, nonspecific, and cozy words about religion, such as "values," "faith," and "virtues," but it is uncomfortable with confessional religion, belief with genuine conviction, and the clear assertion of one religion over another. *Touched by an Angel* is about as hard-core religious as the networks can abide.

Thus, if our society declines to respect and exalt Jesus, why should we be surprised if that society does not sanction and condone *our* devotion to Jesus? If we confess that Jesus Christ is Lord of ourselves and of our institutions, we cannot expect society to appreciate that confession or to respect and esteem us for it. After three decades as president of a Baptist college, I conclude that there are many people—even many *Christian* people—who are reluctant to endorse our institutions because they are uneasy about preferring one religion over another, embarrassed about being too public about Jesus Christ, and apologetic about the possibility of authentic academic quality and intellectual prowess in an avowedly Christian setting. The more explicitly Christian our institutions are, the less appealing we seem to be to the broad public.[42]

Another way culture works against Christian higher education is in attitudes toward size. Our Christian institutions are smaller than state and other private universities (that is, private institutions without professed ties to the Christian faith or a strong Christian emphasis), but society sees significance in numbers. It assumes that no university would actually *choose* to be small. Even in church circles—perhaps because of our devotion to the concept of church growth (what church would not want to grow?)—we expect that every institution aims to enlarge itself. Ask a newspaper editor which is more important, a city of 15,000 or a city of 1,500? Which has greater significance, a business with gross sales of $150 million or $50 million? Which would you rather have move to your city, a plant employing 1,500 persons or one employing 150? Our culture values big numbers: if a little is good, more is better.

The above-mentioned prejudices support another cultural practice that opposes us: publicity and recognition. We are fortunate that many of our institutions are cited in *U.S. News & World Reports'* rankings. But we know that other rankings have looked askance at universities with required chapel and required religion courses. We all know certain accrediting and recognition agencies that still believe that Christian standards interfere with quality academics. And most of us have faced foundation executives who are eager to have their foundations' names listed among supporters of big-name universities but skeptical about whether there is anything to be gained by providing grants to our institutions.

And, of course, there is athletics. Each of us lives in a state that has a flagship state or private university with big-time athletic power. People who claim to be deeply committed Christians, in the vise-grip of our culture, find major athletic events such as football games prime spots for doing business, for making the social scene, for contact with old friends. I cannot explain the hold these university sports have on alumni and even non-alumni, yet there is obviously great media appeal in all mass events, large arenas and stadiums filled with cheering fans who pay multi-thousand-dollar sums for the privilege of buying a ticket. In a culture that fixes on mass performances and mass events, the crowd of ten thousand who attend a Baptist college football game holds no special appeal. And consider the money involved. In 1993, Nike paid the University of North Carolina-Chapel Hill $11 million for five-year exclusive rights to put its Nike swoosh on the UNC uniforms, shoes, and coaches' jackets.[43] That is a rich and powerful backdrop against which Baptist colleges must compete for students and for financial support.

After all the above discouraging facts, I wish I could assure you that you will, at least, find affirmation among the people of our Baptist churches. Unfortunately, that is not the case. Our own Baptist people have a hard time granting their own Baptist colleges and universities the respect they deserve. In a reversal of long-standing demographics, over the last few years the major state university in most regions, including regions that are heavily Baptist, has become more attractive to prospective students, even among high-income families, than a Christian college or university.[44]

The mass culture tends to be influenced by the name game. The more prevalent a name, the stronger the brand, and the more attractive the product, just as with politicians and name recognition. When a student tells his friends he is thinking about one of our institutions, he is not likely to get reinforcement from peers, family, or even guidance counselors.

At various times in our histories, certain pastors and denominational leaders have enjoyed the role of policeman, finding more joy in discovering some infraction or shortcoming on our campuses than in celebrating any accomplishment. As one pastor said, it is easier to recommend a state university that is cheaper and where parents have no religious expectations than to endorse a Baptist university that costs more and where people are unrealistic in what they expect.

Truth be told, I dare say most of our close churchgoing friends believe that each Baptist college president would in a flash drop the reins of the institution presently held and dash to be president or provost at our nearest state university. More than a decade ago, I was contacted by a headhunter who wanted my name in the pool of candidates for the presidency of a distinguished institution, well-endowed, with no crises. Hardly thinking about it, I said, "I'm afraid I'm not your man. You know, I would not know how to give a cocktail party, and my conscience wouldn't allow it if I knew how." He seemed surprised, but we talked about that and he assured me that was not a requirement. I told him that for a person with my values and beliefs I was probably where I ought to be. Though gracious and respectful, he was mystified, disbelieving, as though thinking, *Surely he doesn't realize what he's rejecting.* (I should also say that he never called me again!) Most of us are where we are out of deep personal conviction, a conviction that is incomprehensible to many.

III

What shall we do? First, we need to work harder to make our own constituents aware of what our institutions are and proud of what we offer. We still have in our own areas too many devout Baptists who have never been on our campuses, met our students and professors, or considered what makes our institutions distinctive. All the public relations efforts we aim at the general public might first be aimed at Baptists.

Second, we ought to review our mission statements with a hard eye on the special difference our institutions profess, and if we profess it, ask ourselves if that difference is slogan or reality. We need particularity—product differentiation—to show how we are unlike the marketplace. Many mission statements are so cliché-ridden they almost smell like mothballs. We highlight a few pious phrases to pacify the sponsoring denomination, phrases such as "Christian context," "Christian environment," or "Christian atmosphere." Next, we generally appease the faculty, paying homage to the scholarly and academic side, saying something about "academic excellence" despite difficulty citing anything about our institutions that truly excels. Our institutions should not be suffering identity crises. We should know who we are and whose we are, and be secure in that identity. We cannot expect great institutions to spring from mediocre or fanciful intentions. Mission statements need to be articulated to trustees, to prospective faculty, to all personnel, and to students. Peter Drucker said, "The first task of the leader is to make sure that everybody sees the mission, hears it, lives it. If you lose sight of your mission, you begin to stumble and it shows very, very fast."[45] Surely, one way to resist the fiery darts of our culture is to know and to have agreed upon what our identity *is* and what we *intend* to be.

I once visited a college as a consultant. It was in trouble with its primary accreditor. It was running a significant deficit. It was being accused by federal authorities of some serious financial lapses. It had poorly qualified personnel teaching even graduate courses. Yet all the blather of the mission statement was about "Christian" and "excellence," "finest," and "best." When confronted, the president told me, "Well, that's what we're aiming for."

Associating our institutions with the God of the universe, we need to be certain that we are working to be exceptional institutions. Truthfulness is required. Shabbiness, whether in academics, the physical campus, treatment of individuals, or administrative practices, is not worthy of our Lord. Where we are uncomfortable about weaknesses, we should move to correct them. Where claims are overstated, we should change them. And we should have the courage *not* to participate in practices that compromise our integrity, such as excessive tuition discounting.

Well, with a sigh, the reader might ask, "Do you have any *other* words of encouragement?" A number of years ago, I was in a small group of Christian college and parachurch organizational presidents meeting with Martin Marty, the well-known church historian. Marty asked where in our society could we expect to find encouragement to faith among the young. Someone answered, of course, the church, but Marty pointed out that the church has young people for such a short time, only a few hours a week at best, and then only for a couple of years. He next asked if the media—newspapers, magazines, and TV—could promote faith development. After a litany of such possibilities, all of which were rejected, he concluded that the Christian college may be the last, best hope for promoting the development of a vibrant personal faith that is strong enough to last. That is a noble purpose. Let us hold to it and not shrink from claiming it.

As one now coming to the end of his career, I have two other points of counsel for our mental health. First, we must seize the high ground and remind ourselves that there is solid, reasonable justification for our Baptist colleges and universities. "Civilization is doomed unless the hearts and minds of men can be changed, and unless we can bring about a moral, intellectual and spiritual reformation."[46] That was not spoken by Billy Graham but by Robert Maynard Hutchins—in 1947. Who has the greatest chance at that sort of reformation if not Baptist colleges? According to surveys, back in the 1950s there was no correlation between a college education and religious belief. By the 1970s, the college-educated were far less likely than others in this country to attend religious services or hold Christian views.[47] Shall we give over the educated, the people who have the capacity to love God with their capacious minds, shall we surrender them to the culture?

Second, we need to make our peace with the reality that our institutions are not like all others; they have a higher and holier calling, no matter the bias of the culture. We must be sufficiently confident in the One for Whom we work that when the recognition and respect bestowed on other institutions does not come to us in a culture like ours, we do not despair. While our institutions need all the friends we can get, our priority is not popularity within the secular culture. "When the trumpet of the Lord shall sound, and Time shall be no more," we will account for our stewardship only to the Lord our God.

Part Four

Conclusion

Chapter Thirteen

The Future of Baptist Higher Education: Secular or Religious?

Martin E. Marty

The Problem of the Future

The idealist philosopher Michael Oakeshott has provided me with a framework for understanding how knowledge is usually grasped through different academic disciplines. What he has to say suggests a problem for me as a historian who usually focuses on the past but who wishes in this case to talk about the future. Oakeshott speaks of experience as a "whole," yet because we cannot grasp it whole, we find ourselves dealing with "arrests in experience." He calls these "modes." Each mode develops and relies on a particular language appropriate for that mode, and the language of one mode is not translatable to or valid for the other modes.

Each mode has a crucial differentia that distinguishes it from other modes. For science, the differentia is measurement. Scientists work *sub specie quantitatis*. In this book, the social scientific chapter(s) operate in this mode. They measure how many schools have made certain adaptations, how many students believe this or that. Unlike scientists, poets—none of whom are represented here, perhaps to our loss!—work *sub specie imaginationis*. The crucial differentia for the poetic mode being the imagination, poets do not have to test and measure, and they probably are most "poetic" when they do not. Third is the historical mode. Unlike either scientists or poets, historians write *sub specie praeteritorum*, in the light of the awareness of and reckoning with the past. Historians as historians really have nothing to say until after something has happened, after something has left a trace. Let me add one more mode that is relevant to our collective purpose in this book; the practical mode, which includes religion, ethics, and the like, finds its articulators busy attempting to alter the world, working as they do *sub specie voluntatis* and *sub specie moris*, in the light and context of the human will and the moral order.

Oakeshott suggests that any attempt to cross from one mode to another—that is, to employ the language or criteria of one mode to work in another—is *ignorantio elenchi*, a category mistake. It is obviously a mistake to try to do science in a poetic mode. When Basil Fawlty's motor car falters and stops, he is making a category mistake when he tears a twig or branch from a roadside tree and beats on the hood. The social scientist, working in the scientific mode that demands testing and measurement, can inform us that, say, 90 percent of American Catholic women of child-bearing age blithely practice some sort of artificial birth control, the "natural" method having rendered them unblithe. They will confess this violation of church teachings to a bored priest who simply yawns, exacts no acts of penance, and goes on to more important works of ministry. Were we to tell the pope that social science tells us 90 percent of American Catholic women ignore Catholic teaching on birth control so he had better think about changing the magisterial teaching against it, we can imagine his reaction: "That's a very sad statistic, but it has nothing to do with the truth of our teaching." He is working *sub specie voluntatis* and *moris*, and he will try to change the world by putting church teachings into practice.

Now, back to my dilemma as a scholar working in the historical mode: as an historian I have nothing, nothing at all to say about the future. I can learn from the stories the historians like Bill Leonard tell in this book. I can shift to the practical mode and reflect about what the will and the moral sphere might do with the insights gained from these stories. But in the historical mode I cannot predict or foretell. After September 11, 2001, we might speculate in terror that terrorists could succeed in dirty-bombing or water-polluting or otherwise destroying every Baptist university in sight, leaving no foreseeable future for Baptist higher education. Or we might speculate, with only slightly more credibility, that a few thousand newly minted Baptist millionaires could follow the example of the Baptist saints who have gone before by endowing our Baptist educational institutions and thereby helping to ensure their future.

With only untested notions about the future of Baptist higher education, the historian used to examining the past cannot picture in any kind of detail what Baptist colleges and universities will look like tomorrow or what the terms "secular" and "religious" and "Baptist" might mean. So we gather collegially and, working in our various modes, throw what light we can on the question of the future of Baptist higher education, as I am charged to do in this synthetic chapter.

The Secular and the Religious

Two words or concepts that are woven through these chapters, "secular" and "religious," demand attention. We use these terms sometimes with conceptual propriety but often quite casually and with varying intentions. Let me wander naively onto the landscape created by these chapters. Here we are playing phenomenologist. Edmund Husserl has us picture the phenomenologist as an explorer who is coming upon a landscape that to her—let's see the explorer as a she—is unknown, uncharted, unmapped. She sees an island. From offshore she can tell from the visual outline of the island if it is the home of a volcanic mountain. Other details are hidden, and she must warily chart a path through the terrain. She must be extremely attentive and note what might otherwise go overlooked. We need to approach the terrain of Baptist higher education with the same care and attentiveness. (I once assisted a senior pastor in a large parish, who advised, "Marty, write down everything you see the first six weeks; you'll never see anything again after that.")

The Baptist educators, visionaries, and chroniclers in this book, and the non-Baptists invited in, deal variously with the secular. The word "secular" comes from *saeculum*, and in one of its meanings refers to the rather neutral idea of something that deals with this age, this empirical world in our time and place. But if we bring Christian interpretation to the word, sometimes the meaning takes on negative connotations. However, in the biblical tradition such a realm—that is, the empirical world—should be regarded positively. God created this *saeculum* and pronounced it good. The secular world represents the raw material for culture, for human artifaction, and to turn one's back on it would be to disqualify one's self from any meaningful role in higher education and perhaps would, in fact, qualify one to be a heretic.

However, theologically the secular can also mean something in conflict with the sphere of God's activity. The historian comes on the human scene and says that something has happened to the *saeculum*. The historian may blame Adam's fall, employ the doctrine of original sin, agree with the cartoonist that "people are no damn good," or just show an alertness born of experience and inquiry. Often on these pages the reader will find authors speaking of the secular as something into which one falls, the slippery slope on which we are all sliding. Inevitably. All of them have the wisdom and grace to recognize boons that come with alterations in the *saeculum* and that produce positive features of the secular order. It is hard to overlook the great gifts that have come to higher culture and education through institutions named Yale, Harvard, and all the slid-down-the-slippery-slope schools. Still, these writers all agree that there has also been loss and that in various ways the secular represents a threat to religious, Christian, Baptist higher education. And they are not wrong in that assessment. In fact, with the slippery slope and the historical record in mind, one could well follow Franz Kafka's advice: "In the fight between you and the world, back the world."

The alternative to this meaning of "secular" is the religious. I certainly could not be expected to settle controversies over the definition of the religious. Volumes if not libraries have been devoted to that subject. As one of eight editors of the massive *Encyclopedia of Religion*, I define religion as the kind of stuff you write about if it belongs in a book with that title. In general, in these pages, "religion" as it applies to higher education is used to mean the obverse of the coin on whose other side is "secular." Here "religious" refers to everything from an ecclesiastical reference to what "binds" people, just as the etymology of the word would suggest. While every author here knows of the downside of religion—"the killer that heals and the healer that kills"—in the present context religion usually is seen as a good thing, something that Baptist and other Christian institutions of higher learning should set about retrieving, guarding, warranting, and projecting.

But is "secular" versus "religious" the most effective way to analyze and address our subject? I would argue that my own assigned topic would better read: "A secular *and* religious future." In many writings in which I have been called to review the history of the complex and much debated "secularization theory," I have defended a concept that I have rather inelegantly called "religio-secular," a nonsanctioned word to lexicographers, but a reality in our quotidian lives and our higher educational vocations. The religious and the secular are so entangled, so dynamically inter-webbed that they are inseparable. We make do with this construct.

Thus, if the secular represents the sphere in which we are to ascertain and follow our vocations, equip ourselves for our professions, embark on careers, maybe find jobs and then go to work—my pentad of practical outcomes of higher education—we are very secular. Even that minority of students in Baptist schools who study pre-theology and go on into theological and ministerial professions are deeply involved in the secular world. In the newspaper supplements devoted to educational topics we more often see banner advertisements for what our schools can do for a student's *career*, than for his or her *calling* or vocation. We may think that a calling is more important than a career, and, at our best, we may demonstrably contribute to our students' desire to pursue vocation, but any educator who cannot help students develop professional skills and career opportunities will himself have a short career and may as well embark on some other profession.

Two all-embracing institutions make up our religio-secular world: the nation-state and the market. The Christian needs to bring critical eyes, sound judgment, and a healthy sense of suspicion to the "powers that be," whether rulers by divine right or popular consent. Paul in Romans 13 and someone in a Petrine epistle say nice things about the earthly higher powers being ordained by God, but that's not the final word about what the Christian's relationship to the secular world ought to be. In the Gospels Jesus takes care of this by calling Herod "that fox" and by pointing to the godlike image of Caesar on the coin that Jews were not supposed to carry and telling them they should "render" him and it back to the state. Can anyone honestly suggest that any Baptist or other Christian-based institution of higher education is ready as an institution basically to question the nation-state part of the *saeculum*?

Baptist heroes invoked on these pages, including the quasi-Baptist hero (and my personal hero in his bizarre and challenging sort of way) Roger Williams, would not seek or gain or hold tenure at one of today's Baptist schools. They would not likely be candidates for advancement or development officer.

As I read Leonard's essay, I found myself in much sympathy, since for years I have tended to live near where he does in the zone of Baptist studies. But I wrote on the margin, "What has Roger Williams done for you [meaning Baptists at large, not Leonard up close] lately?" Where is the hearing for Baptist dissent, a theme for which Leonard speaks so clearly?

Several essays on these pages celebrate the fact that Baptists and perhaps historic Baptist educators among them stressed "soul liberty" and "separation of church and state." But today, when Baptists run or try to strongly influence the executive and legislative branches of government and aspire for a trifecta by seeking to control the judiciary, are there any traces of historic Baptist teaching on the separation of church and state surviving in what the public perceives about Baptists? Question policies associated with the concept of "patriotism" and "nationalism" and you will not have to worry about "the future of Baptist higher education." There won't be any.

The case is the same with the other reality, the market. Left and right, Republican and Democrat, elitist or populist, critic or affirmer, we are all enveloped in the market world, inescapably. After the implosion of communism with the tearing of the Iron Curtain and the fall of the Berlin Wall, there is only one real survivor within the surviving countries—including China—and that is the market. (Cuba and North Korea are the two main nonmarket countries, but we are not sure they will ultimately turn out to be survivors.) We live in an epoch wherein the market, sometimes code-named "free market" or "free enterprise" or "capitalism" or "mixed economy," frames our endeavors. It governs our career choices, curricula, and expression in our universities. It is amusing, ironic, and confusing to hear professors who cling to tenure and who have a TIAA-CREF or other pension plan sounding radical as if they could and would transcend the rules of the game and the ethos of the market. The market is the air we breathe, the unseen guest at table conversations.

Of course, good things come of it. And I do not have the imagination to conceive of any alternative to it. However, I do not agree with those who proclaim that the market way is the only economic organization and practice envisioned and prescribed by biblical, theological, and historical Christian norms. If it were, one would have to ask what God was doing and how believers were serving God before late-medieval Catholics, John Calvin and then the Puritans, and then Adam Smith and David Ricardo "invented" it.

Now, note well: While the nation-state is religio-secular by any definition, whether we speak of "civil religion" or "public religion" or "national religion," the market, which may appear religio-secular in many manifestations as when born-again CEOs testify to the gospel or Catholic political scientists relate their endeavors to Christian interpretations of natural law, is usually secular, frankly secular. Dollars and pounds do not have denominational significations. Wall Street does not know or care whether my stocks are earned Methodistically or Baptistically, and my broker does not examine the theological balance sheet of the firms into which my pension account went. (Story: Being a naif in respect to the market, and not having met my excellent broker until after decades of nothing but phone contact, I did get across to him that we should not invest in any firm that is *essentially* a polluter or *essentially* a munitions-maker, only to have him phone one day urging me to invest in a particular huge brewery. I all but shouted, "No, they're almost fascists!" I had read about the company's racist policies and political commitments that alarmed me. "Oh, OK then, no fascists either!") I exaggerate. There are funds that do scrutinize firms in the light of perceived biblical norms of justice and ethical practice, but they constitute an almost infinitesimally small share of the market. If you really want religious practice that makes demands on the market, go to Islam, where *shari'a* forbids the taking of interest.

One has to notice that in a Christian context the god of the market is Mammon, and that the gospel portraits of Jesus find him more worried about what Mammon will do to the soul and spirit than almost any other force. "You cannot serve God and Mammon," yet reflexively we tend to.

So nation-state and market are secular, but they are the arena in which Christian learning and vocation occur. In some other context I could be celebrating dimensions of national and market life that are positive, that are better than any known alternatives, that are full of opportunity, and all of these dimensions should inspire us as we plan curricula and campus life. I have only tried to show that the secular is inescapable in the religious, Christian, Baptist higher educational world, and that the religio-secular world, perceived dialectically, is a world of promise. What does that mean for our project and our projection?

Remembering and Forgetting Slippery Secular Slopes

Though, as I have said, the religio-secular world, perceived dialectically, is a world of promise, secularism is nevertheless a spectre haunting us. It is a spectre of secularism as a force that has had, is now having, and is supposed to have in the future a damaging if not nearly annihilating effect on Baptist and other Christian-related higher education. Any numbers of essays here make explicit reference to the work of scholars such as James Burtchaell, Robert Benne, and most effective of all, George Marsden. In the main, their chronicling strikes me as being accurate, and we can acknowledge their scholarship and their achievement. It is the use that some make of their findings and that some are tempted to make of them that should lead to the suggestion that always to begin with the kind of accounting they provide may limit the imagination. There is no doubt at all that with the possible exception of an often-neglected chapel, major private universities progressively marginalized religious concerns on their campuses. One bit of doggerel had it:

> It's nice to have Old Trinity
> To remind us of divinity.

Eventually even the few reminders fade away and finally disappear. Replacing the religious dimension of the institutions, in these interpretations, is a combination of militant secularism, casual and indifferent secularity, and a set of preoccupations that do not transcend the boundaries of the secular. The observations of this process of secularization of educational institutions in the past have led to the identification of forces that seem to be leading to secularization in today's at least reminiscently, tangentially, marginally, tenuously related Baptist-and-other-Christian higher education. The prime metaphor has been the "slippery slope," and the prophesy is clear: we will all hit bottom some day, without much hope of climbing out of the secular pit.

The counsel that follows these observations varies in character. The subtitle for this part of my chapter could have read "Lamentations and Jeremiah"—"Lamentations" because the books in which these themes appear lament the passing of something that was different, other, generally good, and to be cherished, and "Jeremiah" because, in the model of American colonial preaching, the jeremiad became a cultural form of expressing judgment and woe. The authors to whom I am referring, however, do not stop with writing modern lamentations and jeremiads. They move beyond the expressions of woe to offer little glimmers of Christian reminiscence for what Karl Rahner calls "selective retrieval." Others, writing in the mode of Alasdair MacIntyre in *After Virtue*, argue that we are entering a new Dark Age, in which the meanings of Christian and natural law are too remote, too inaccessible, to be retrieved directly. So these writers counsel us to do the next best creative thing, which is what the Benedictines and their kin did: build equivalents of monasteries and keep the lights on and the books available. That is not an insane policy, so far as it goes.

It is also appropriate, however, to follow up the affirmation of this scholarship of secularization by asking some pointed historical questions. Were the Harvards and Yales and all the other examples of secularized institutions such great bearers of Christian meaning when they were in their prime, or have we created a fictional model of these institutions as we imagine them in the past? If one reads close-up, first-hand accounts of student immorality, faculty prejudice, cultural hegemony, the miserliness of church support, and the narrow boundaries of most such schools, one might find in these accounts reasons enough for the theological affirmation of liberation from much of what went on at these early faith-based institutions. I happen to cherish those religious pasts, but I certainly do not romanticize them.

Similarly, while there were Everest-high piles of reasons for the secular move—arrogance, secularist blindness, unreflective prejudices against Christianity, Oedipal strikings at the Rev. Daddy or just plain Daddy—there were also causes for secularization that had little to do with any of the above. There simply were not enough Congregationalists surviving to people the complexifying Ivy League schools. Should they have starved and closed, or adapted to pluralist change? The same is true for Baptist-oriented schools today. To the issue of decreasing pools of students add the practical adjustments some schools have seen fit to make. On the principle that one should never attribute to malice what should be attributed to lethargy or low imagination or accommodation, one notes that the agenda for universities changed in a world marked with words ending in "–ation": industrialization, modernization, immigration, and the like, or ending in "–ism" such as nationalism and capitalism. Could the old containers have held all these new needs and intentions?

The essay by Larry Lyon on religious identity, academic reputation, and secularization states the historical case in detail and, I believe, accurately. The question he raises of whether or not being religious constitutes a "handicap" for educational institutions points to certain prime aspects of our culture. There is no point in ducking Lyon's dose of realism. Yet I also wonder whether the university as it existed before being thus handicapped was as useful to Christian purposes or as rich in human learning as many of the nostalgic readings suggest. James P. Wind wrote a dissertation on how Baptist William Rainey Harper repeatedly outlined what a Christian influence in a modern secular and democratic universe might do. Wind wanted to track down the traces of Harper's influence in the born-to-be-heterogeneous new faculty at the University of Chicago in the 1890s. Wind wanted to find in the minutes of faculty discussions some criticisms of Rabbi Emil Hirsch or of the post-Congregationalist pragmatist John Dewey. He never found one line in any faculty record of a pro or con reference to the whole venture.

Go further back a century. For years I had read of the great influence of President Timothy Dwight on Yale College and revivals there around 1800. For my dissertation it was important for me to check his great four-volume systematic theology, published in 1817–18, said to be key to his Christian witness and construction. The University of Chicago copy had traveled to Germany, was part of the Hengstenberg collection that Harper bought and brought back to stock and seed the University of Chicago library. In olden days one could see who had previously checked out the book, and I found that decades before I consulted the volumes, students such as Perry Miller and Henry Steele Commager had taken out the books. Leather-bound, gilt-edged, the very format cried out "Important! Determinative! Classic!"

But I found that after the first few pages the rest of the pages were uncut, the lines never read. I learned that the chapters were originally lectures imposed on the sleepy two or three hundred irreverent—they tell us—half-infidel (in their adolescent braggadocious testing of the professorial waters) students at six a.m. It occurred to me to ask: Did *anyone* ever hear the words? Did *anyone* other than Dwight or the typesetter ever read them? Yet they were considered important and influential because of what several writers call "hegemony." Given the realities of these early institutions, it may not have taken the move to national universities to see that a behavioral and intellectual secularization was occurring.

Richard Franklin's brief but packed chapter on who our students will be over the next decade and beyond might be describing a cohort who have more in common with Yale students of 1800 than they do with the mythic picture we have of students who were in the church-based but secularizing colleges before modern national universities came to prevail. Students, as Franklin and others suggest, come in delicious varieties, and they often confound those who feel certain they understand what characterizes a semipermanent stereotypical student—especially in matters religious. Who would have foreseen the growth of religious studies from near-zero programs in the 1930s to a thousand programs in tax-supported colleges and universities in the 2000s? Not that religious studies at public universities has as large an impact on a student's Christian formation as church-related colleges can achieve, but the growth of such studies at public institutions does suggest that there are spiritual strivings and curiosity about religion at such schools that indicate a religio-secular context rather than pure secularism.

As I drive down the highways and see the billboards advertising Christian-based and church-related colleges and universities, I often see small letters indicating a certain denominational affiliation or a certain heritage. The words in big letters advertise the three new campuses, the two new business schools, the values of engineering education, and the like. The competition in a market economy is of a sort that schools cannot be satisfied with turning out nothing but clerics and clerically minded laity, as many of these schools once did. And it is possible to give Christian interpretations to the engineering, dentistry, and accounting majors and professions without finding it necessary to religiocify them all. Nor can one legitimately say that the schools should concentrate on liberal arts, social sciences, and humanities and forego professional programs in order to keep the Christian note. Indeed, every survey I have seen shows a more favorable attitude toward religion in natural science departments than in comparative literature or sociology or anthropology departments, no matter that religious issues are often a part of their subject matter.

The authors in this book are most creative when, having paid respect to the slippery-slope theory, they move on to seek slopes without slippery surfaces, or slippery surfaces that don't slope, and then ask, "Even so, what then?" Dr. Lewis Thomas points out that we never say we learn through trial and triumph. We say "through trial and error," though we do not learn from error; we learn instead from "what then?" the question that comes after we realize we have made an error. Insofar as the perceived slide into secularity was an error, some of our authors are now in the "even so, what then?" stage.

Baptists, Baptist Churches, Baptist Conflict, Baptist Schism

Conferences on a Catholic (post-Burtchaell), other-Protestant (post-Benne), or (regnant in this field) Calvinist-Reformed-Kuyperian models would analyze much the same problems and envisioned similar solutions as in this Baptist-related inquiry. There are many oblique or passing references to what these other traditions, such as the Lutheran version which informs my outlook, have to offer. While study of these other traditions and some acquaintance with those individuals who have articulated and embodied those traditions would enhance the present inquiry, at the moment we are charged to deal with the not-insignificant Baptist, sometimes southern Baptist or Southern Baptist orbs.

These essays are refreshingly open about the data of change, impressively earnest about relating to it positively, often imaginatively involved in envisioning alternatives about the Baptist future. I would need to put both terms in the plural: Baptists and futures. Had there been no conflict in the Southern Baptist Convention, I am confident that books such as this would have been produced to deal with other aspects of the cultural crisis. It may be seen as ill grace for a non-Baptist to overstate the case, but a few statements of cases are called for.

The fundamental change necessitating and inspiring self-scrutiny and new charting has to do with what the crisis in the Southern Baptist Convention did to occasion lamentation, panic, or creative moving on. It was a contradiction to combine the idea of "university" with the "censoring-by-board" operations that led to so much tribulation and so many trials for faculties, administrations, and conscientious students. As we watched the acquisition of power by the Convention, by some state conventions, and by some convention-controlled boards, and their insistence on effecting purges along party lines, and as we came to see how Convention headquarters, in the person of the sequence of elected presidents from one party, used appointment and excommunicative powers, it became clear that these tribulations and trials had to occur (and test me on this—I am ready to stand corrected); the pope and the Vatican, even in a quarter century of caution and control, did not have nearly as much power over personnel and professorial status or to make unilateral decisions as did Convention headquarters. So it became a conviction of many who are represented here that the survival of Baptist universities—in more than name—meant a distancing and even exile from the Convention. Now many of these essays are in an "even so, what then?" mode. And we hear numerous proposals.

It is in this larger context that R. Kirby Godsey's reflection from the front lines on the "accountability" question addresses issues so clearly. Yes, to whom are the Baptists and universities accountable? I don't read here any pleas for mere and pure autonomy, solipsism, isolation, and certainly not for irresponsibility. But those who want to promote accountability are necessarily busy these days, and they may not finally come to agreement. Godsey's urging for accountability to mission goes a long way to set a framework for future discussions. Similarly, Daniel Vestal faces the accountability question and references Baptist familiality, a concept which, when not associated primarily with family quarrels, does provide a rich metaphor for what "kin" in academe and church life did or can or could mean as another element in the discussion. It won't satisfy the inquisitors or enforcers, but it has good historic warrant.

What has to impress the outsider is the passion so many writers here display for Baptists when they were Baptists; when, in Paul Tillich's terms, theonomy was the marker, not the *heteronomy* ("other law") that came forward. The change does evoke questions, however. As I read some authors here, the issue is that if Baptists need to restate their beliefs now, the accent should be more on "This We Believe" and "This Is Who We Are" than on "This You Gotta Believe or Get Out or We'll Get You Out." There is faith here that the

Baptist distinctives, now in some quarters blurred or replaced, can make it better on their own than when assent is coerced, or at least when attempts at coercion prevail.

The conflict issues aside, however, there is still an urgent and informing agenda. One thing that has to strike the non-Baptist reader is the internal pluralism of the Baptist tradition. Invoke continental Anabaptism, as a few here do, and pose that against British Baptist expressions; move to the United States and note general versus particular, Calvinist versus Arminian, North versus South, Landmark versus Other, Baptist denomination versus Baptist denomination, and you have touched on a half dozen of myriad variations. The alphabetical listings in the Yellow Pages suggest a few more. Then traverse the regions, the alma mater traditions, the disciplines, the ethos of various campuses, and you will find it hard to discover the base for a clear Baptist identity. Everything in the Baptist tradition calls for plurals, as in *identities*. In the face of this pluralism, Baptist higher educators have found themselves under pressure from Baptist hierarchs and constituencies to find a single model. In the Southern Baptist Convention and in some state conventions the one that won out is a kind of Reformed Homogenizing Fundamentalism, which was anything but Baptist in origin, but is attractive to Baptists who are in retreat from a world and a set of churches where pluralism, modernity, diversity, ambiguity, paradox, and contradiction abound and threaten.

Over against that Fundamentalist set of fundamentals, William E. Hull spells out Baptist distinctives with both a definitional sense and a catholic spirit. If only those distinctives prevailed today, we would not find these authors having to ask as many questions as they do. His concept of a "shared vision of what it means to be Baptist" would go far.

Similarly, David P. Gushee offers something of a vision and an identity even as he reports honestly on the struggle to find it. He uses the phrase "the normative intellectual vision and theology," something that would be hard to find and defend, on the evidence of the chapters in this book. But he spells out helpfully many of the elements of a non-normative but strong vision. I found myself withholding consent from his implication that the broad-based "evangelical" complex eschews the mainstream culture. On some terms, yes: on some subjects. I do not have to be very ornery, however, to claim that when one looks at who runs the government today; who sets the highest premium on business and market and success, even within the norms of practical church life; who is most nationalistic and overall most militant about American international aims, this evangelical complex can be most counted on by "the powers that be" and is less ready to distance itself and criticize than are other religious complexes. Historically, Baptists have been typed as dissenters. Yet under the multi-ring tent that is American life today, while no one runs all the show, Baptists and evangelicals run many of the shows in many of the rings.

One call in particular that Gushee makes has its attractions—his call for agreement that Baptist identity, while it is very, very important, is not *too* mportant and that general and central classic Christianity should be the norm. Gushee argues the case for this rather eloquently, though he does not follow up with an analysis of the problems that come with the claim. The Vincent of Lerins rule about holding to what has always and everywhere been believed goes a long way to describing the outlines of a charter. I find it attractive, though recognizing that the Great Tradition is always necessarily mediated by the littler traditions. So in an institution of higher learning one cannot hurry past these differences. James D. G. Dunn in *Unity and Diversity in the New Testament* suggests that all of the earliest Christian expressions witness to the reality that "the human Jesus is the exalted Lord." Yet Dunn finds that within the New Testament and then certainly in the sub-Apostolic era, sincere and pious articulators disagreed on polity, baptism, the Lord's Supper, and more—and that just for starters. After twenty centuries there is a vast amount of diversity under the leaky Baptist tents. Universities will explore these issues, but, our authors suggest, cannot accept someone's definition of them or another's effort at enforcement.

Descript, Not Nondescript Higher Education

My references to the bewildering and inspiring diversities of disciplines, intentions, vocations, regions, and Christian affirmations enhoused in Baptisthood are not a call for de-Baptistizing the universities. For a long time I have been trying to get a word into a future *Oxford English Dictionary on Historical Principles*. One now finds "nondescript," as meaning "neither here nor there." I yearn for the word "descript," which would mean here, there, this particular place and phenomenon. What is clear in these essays is that the description in the past depended upon accidents of cultural isolation, response to definition by the other (including the other Christian), isolation, and, after the period of dissent, hegemony. The Christian university from the thirteenth to the eighteenth centuries depended upon its tie to Christian polities that assured the prevalence if not the monopoly of one expression. Unless theonomists and theocrats prevail in the United States (and a historian on historical grounds cannot predict outcomes), even a creed as politically reinforced as those of Catholics or current Southern Baptists (or, regionally, Latter-Day Saints—there are no other candidates) is not going to provide a single clear foundation or unifying principle for our higher educational alternatives.

The Husserlian explorer who wants to be attentive and take notes is likely to observe a vast array of responses to and initiatives within the Baptist-and-university project in the future. Do others share my assumption, based on evidence in the arguments presented here, that Baptists operating free of the state, in soul liberty, with informed conscience, and conscientious Christian minds are going to find and agree on a sufficiently capacious approach that would deserve the definite article and adjective "the Baptist" distinctive? Here, in higher education, a decent respect for the inquiries of many scholars, pastors, students, and supporters would call for "friendliness to the mission" of Baptist-related and informed higher education, and then to see a hundred flowers grow.

Penultimately, let me return to a theme hinted at when I was criticizing the near-determinism of the "slippery slope" theory. The theory does not do enough justice to surprise and counter-trends in history. The history of the Christian church, including in its educational endeavors, is not monochromatic or mono-dimensional or mono-anything. There have been dark ages and ages of Enlightenment, declensions and revivals; there was post-Enlightenment as there is now post-modernity. Now is not the time to use postmodern uncertainties as the openers and wedges to assault the secular or to turn even a little bit triumphalist about the new focus on Christian concerns. Historical change such as the Islamization of much of Europe can abort efforts to quicken Western European Christianity—but it may also prod Christians to engage in *resourcefulness*, *retrieval*, and some *renewal*.

In much of the larger Christian world, there are colleges and universities that were founded by Christians as missions and that had slipped on slopes or attached themselves to postcolonial movements as debilitating as colonialist endeavors. Yet many of them are now finding new footings and, with low resources, are bringing refreshment to Christian higher education concerns. These might ultimately also refresh the North American world. Meanwhile, in the furies of religious renewal in parts of North America, for all the repressive and imperial instincts one observes, there are also in Christian-based colleges and universities new apologias and educational mission-extensions. I found refreshing Pastor James Denison's front-line analysis of the arguments against seeing higher education as being integral to the movement of evangelization and renewal. While I am less sure than he that there is *the* biblical worldview, there are many forms of biblical witness that can inspire and are inspiring many sorts of Christians not to let modernity, postmodernity, or any of the other "-ities" of our era have the last word. There is in Denison's writing not a hint of simplistic optimism or triumphalism-in-waiting, but there are indications of what hope might look like.

Similarly, Albert Reyes checks in with words about justifiable mission in Baptist churches and bodies. His essay, reflecting his background in other cultures—Hispanic/Latino—and an at-homeness in Anglo culture, is a bold affirmation of Baptist mission in higher education. He accompanies this affirmation with three questions about "What do you mean by? . . ." that are not all that different from the questions others ask on these pages. But they do show what cultural contexts and more-than-national aspirations do to color questions and responses. In his pages there is more pastoral-intellectual contextualization that suggests promise.

In sum, the "descript" Baptist can help provide an identity to a college or university and an educational enterprise but, however inclusive the scope of the word "Baptist," its interpreters are too diverse to be easily confined into conformities. And we will be better off if these varieties show up. If an argument, which demands that I defend something that I know in order to defeat the Other, is guided by the answer, then a conversation is guided by the question. No one says, "I sure won that conversation." Not that argument never has its place. There are undoubtedly times when faculties, boards, student associations, and others have to argue and vote or take some other form of decisive action. However, most of what is talked about in Baptist and other Christian higher education circles does not have to be resolved by an argument where one wins and one loses. There are too many niches, canyons, crevasses, peaks, depressions in the landscape of learning and in the deeps of Baptist and other Christian expression to lose faith in the encounter with the secular or to yearn for a religious absolute. Access to the religio-secular world is so enticing and promising that one hopes Baptists will deal with it in such a way that there will be Baptist future*s*, marked by reverence for the past but not by nostalgia for it. And that confident Christian expression, voiced in humble and inquiring tones and with multiple approaches, can help make this rich heritage available to students and to the culture at large for generations to come.

Chapter Fourteen

Can the Secular Be Sanctified?

Curtis W. Freeman

Southern Baptists were the first Free Church movement to create a civilization: it's called the South.[1] To be sure, Baptists flourished in other geographical regions, but their majority presence in the South earned them the status of a *de facto* established church.[2] This is indeed ironic for a people whose heritage and story is one of dissent and liberty, but history often writes the greatest ironies.[3] In the beginning it never occurred to our Baptist forebears in the Old South that they needed to establish colleges and universities in order to enlarge their constituency, but in time they grew to see the value of education. By the mid-nineteenth century Baptists and other evangelicals became quite successful at their ventures into higher education. They realized that a literate, and perhaps even an educated, ministry and laity were crucial to maintaining and expanding their social influence in upwardly mobile communities like Richmond, Virginia, and Nashville, Tennessee.[4]

The search for "wider fields of usefulness" was not the only motive of Baptists and other southern evangelicals for founding institutions of higher learning.[5] As noted historian of the South Donald Mathews suggests:

> Evangelicals built colleges to increase educational opportunities, improve the quality of their common life, and enhance their own prestige, but they had a strictly ideological motive as well. They wanted to make sure that the college education received by their children was shaped by Evangelical assumptions and goals. Fearful of a non- or anti-Christian ethos, which, along with an aristocratic bias, seemed to pervade state universities, Evangelicals were relieved when they could find ways to control their own colleges, in which their world view, far from being critically scrutinized, was acclaimed.

Yet the founders of these denominational colleges also believed that they had something special to contribute. Education may make students smart, but only Christian education can make them good. The assumption behind Christian higher education was then a reciprocal relationship between the colleges and the culture: "If education could 'elevate' Evangelicals, they in turn could discipline education, putting it at the service of the Evangelical surge to tame and convert society."[6]

Secularization As Decline

Although Baptist colleges and universities underwent significant changes throughout the nineteenth and twentieth centuries, a remarkable number of them survived into the twenty-first century. Many of these schools remain close to their founding visions as small liberal arts colleges, while others have embarked on a path toward becoming major research universities. Determining how faith and learning can remain related in these different settings will be as different as each institution. The last several decades have proven that the religio-cultural synthesis which once held Baptists in the South together has now all but disintegrated. There is good reason to believe that this breakdown of the Baptist hegemony in the South can in fact be traced to the loss of the true symbols of our faith—fried chicken and sweet tea.

That the forces of secularization have had their effect is evident not only in the broader culture, but, as Larry Lyon suggests, even more so in higher education, which has become an "extreme exemplar" of secularization, the influences of which even Christian colleges and universities have not successfully escaped. Citing the theoretical work of sociological studies, Lyon explains that secularization "promised declining importance of religion in social life, diminished strength for religious organizations, and waning religious commitment among individuals."[7] This description of secularization fits broadly into the *declension theory* that is exemplified in James Tunstead Burtchaell's tome *The Dying of the Light*. As the thesis goes, because only rarely was the Christian character of American church-related colleges vitally resident in academics, it consequently became attached to notions of piety and morality, which in time were degraded by the intellectual embrace of liberalism and rationalism. As the title of the book suggests, the story within the stories of Christian higher education is one of the dying of the light of faith.[8] Indeed, the very conference from which this collection of essays was originally presented invoked Burtchaell's version of the declension theory, as the description states:

> Although this phenomenon of secularization and transformation of educational mission reaches back into Baptist history, with prominent examples

> being Brown University and the University of Chicago, in the last twenty-five years, the "light" has been extinguished in a growing number of venerable Baptist institutions in the South. The University of Richmond, Wake Forest University, Stetson University, Furman University, and Meredith College serve as ready examples.[9]

Lyon has also completed another study which asks whether Baylor University will go the way of Wake Forest, with the assumption that Wake has declined from its founding as a religious school to become a secular university. The study has evoked not a little disagreement about whether Wake Forest's light has been extinguished and, if so, whether the light might be rekindled.[10]

Although some may wish to challenge the secularization thesis and, perhaps more specifically, the declension theory which the "dying of the light" metaphor implies, from an historical vantage point it seems fairly clear: As Baptist colleges and universities "come of age" and embrace the full range of academic disciplines, they will also be subjected to secularizing forces that create a struggle for the soul of the institution. In important ways this is unavoidable, especially for those who aspire to be tier-one schools. There are only so many Baptist astrophysicists who are doing research on the state of plasma at the moment of the big bang, and a Baptist school may have to hire a non-Baptist in a pinch. And there are a limited number of national merit scholars in Myrtle, Mississippi, so the search for the brightest students may take recruiters elsewhere. But make no mistake about it: changing the composition of the faculty and students makes a difference in the ecology of an institution.

Given the prevalence of the declension theory, it is not surprising that many Christian educators view secularization as an evil to be combated, as a recent article in *Christianity Today* illustrates. The author states:

> Our recessive conservative genes have conditioned us to see this phenomenon as the inevitable process of secularization in higher education. In the conservative analysis, Christian colleges and universities are all perched atop a slippery slope. One moment of relaxed vigilance—one twitch or stumble in a secular direction—and down slides the college into the tar pits of apostasy. The only thing left of its former faith would be a stately chapel building—a fossilized artifact of the college's Christian past. The process started with Harvard—once the pride of Puritanism—and has since claimed almost every once-Christian college.[11]

The assumption is that Baptist colleges stand as a fortress against the anti-Christian ethos that surrounds them and which must be ever vigilantly countered by a Christian worldview. In his chapter on "The University, the Church, and the Culture,"[12] Thomas Corts laments the loss of the vision of an earlier generation of Christian education which understood the purview of its mission as including the responsibility "to tame and convert society."[13] He repeatedly stresses that Baptist schools are being overwhelmed by the sea of secularization that is not neutral toward the faith. In what might well be described as an evangelical jeremiad, Corts persuasively describes how secular culture is subverting the mission of Christian higher education. Surely he is right that it is not enough to mouth clichés like "academic excellence" and "Christian context," which have all but lost their meaning. But one is left to wonder whether it is genuine hope or wishful thinking that leads him to say that Christian colleges that seek "a higher and holier calling" are "the last best hope for promoting the development of a vibrant personal faith that is strong enough to last."

Nevertheless, it seems fair to say that the threat of secularity has created a heightened sense of urgency to be vigilant. It is tempting to point to the Fundamentalist movement of recent years as an aberration, but, in fact, Baptist schools have made a practice of forcefully resisting the secularization of the academy, often by presidential fiat. Nowhere is this more entertainingly or truthfully demonstrated than in Clyde Edgerton's satirical novel *Killer Diller*, where the Sears twins, President Ted and Provost Ned, as *in loco parentis*, seek to preserve the God-fearing, free-enterprise affirming, Bible-believing Baptist heritage of Ballard University and save students "from wayward and sinful trends brought on by the modern world."[14] Agents of the university do their best to insulate students from the worldliness of "ugly words and un-Christian situations" only to discover too late that the world subtly accommodates to the ways of religion.[15]

The hero of the story is a young man named Wesley Benfield, a recovering car thief and con artist, who seeks protection under the Ballard bubble where his struggle to come to terms with his sexuality collides with Old Testament polygamy and the Song of Solomon. One day President Ted tells Wesley:

> "Don't ever abandon that book," he says, nodding toward the Bible. "It's true cover to cover. Cover to cover or nothing, I say. And it's being attacked from all quarters. We've even got *Baptists* now denying its literal truth. So, son, you're important to us. You're helping the Ballard family fight the secularization of Christian higher education—through your example. And, by the way, I hope someone has mentioned that we'd like for you to give a little testimony at the LinkComm Christmas luncheon—about what Jesus means to you, what Ballard, the Ballard family means to you."[16]

When it comes time for the Christmas luncheon, Wesley and his gospel band entertain the guests. President Sears introduces him as "a shining example of what Christ can mean to one who has been in trouble." He characterizes Wesley as "A fine student. A bright student. A Christian student."[17] Just as planned, Wesley stands up before the audience with television cameras rolling and radio microphones open. He begins to preach a sermon on creation. After summarizing the creation account from Genesis 1, Wesley continues:

> Now friends, that's the first version; and the second version is a little different. The second version comes in the Bible right after the first version and it says that God created man before the animals—instead of after. Did you know, friend, that there were two versions? I didn't. What these two versions agree on is that God done it all. What it disagrees on is in what order. This teaches us not to sweat the small stuff. This teaches us that if you believe every word in the Bible is absolutely true like some kind of steel trap, then you believe both of those versions are absolutely true, and if you believe that then you ain't using the brain God gave you and you should be making mud pies or something like that—keeping everything in neat little piles. Because on the earth God made, you can't have two different things happen at the same time with the same people. That's a truth in the universe.[18]

After his sermon, Wesley leaves the scandalized audience behind and escapes outside where his band members and girlfriend are waiting in a van to whisk him off to Myrtle Beach, South Carolina.

The decline of faith in American universities of the sort Ballard University was determined to resist is surely symptomatic of the overall secularization of Western culture.[19] Yet President Sears is not alone in questioning the value of Christian colleges that do not exist as an alternative to the moral relativism of secularity. For example, when Charles Colson suggested that "the collapse of Enron exposes the glaring failure of the academy," more than a few readers clucked their tongues in disbelief.[20] Colson pounded the secularization theme hard, contending that America is reaping the whirlwind sown by universities that for decades have systematically assaulted ethics and truth. He has a point. That Bernie Ebbers, the founder of WorldCom, is a Baptist and a graduate of a Baptist college should be cause for concern, but we should also not lose sight of the fact that Donald Rumsfeld, the principal architect of the war on terrorism, is a graduate of Harvard. If each of these cases is representative, the first indicates the failure of Christian higher education to foster the sort of moral character that equips people to choose wisely and live justly. But the second case is more problematical. Though a secular institution like Harvard is not interested in fostering Christian values, when the alternatives to secular institutions are places like Terwilliger College, the fictional *alma mater* of Elmer Gantry, which upheld "a standard of scholarship equal to the best high schools," then secularization does not look so bad.[21] What Edgerton's fictional description of Ballard University illustrates so well is what many, but perhaps not enough, observers have discovered in the real world of Baptist higher education: Secularization is far more subtle than it appears. So if the exaggerated and reductionistic account of secularization proposed by the declension theory has been overplayed, is there an alternative theory?

Secularization as Disestablishment

George Marsden has proposed a *disestablishment theory*, which in a more nuanced way explains "the transformation from an era when organized Christianity and explicitly Christian ideals had a major role in the leading institutions of higher education to an era when they have almost none."[22] Marsden's disestablishment theory comes with less of a ready-made explanation of how the secularization process works than the declension theory, yet it shares with declensionists the sense of loss about the secularization of Christian higher education. To illustrate, Marsden quotes the founding bylaws of Duke University, which state that its aims were "to assert a faith in the eternal union of knowledge and religion set forth in the teachings and character of Jesus Christ, the Son of God."[23] The substance and spirit of this founding aim was distilled into the motto *eruditio et religio*. The words, of course, are Latin and when translated mean "knowledge and religion," but there can be no missing that, ironically, "*et*" is also Southern for "ate." It suggests that in light of Duke's history the motto may also be read "knowledge ate religion," thus indicating the union between knowledge and religion was not as eternal as the university founders thought, which is precisely Marsden's point.[24]

A recent fictional example of disestablishment of religion in the university is in Tom Wolfe's novel *I Am Charlotte Simmons*, which describes undergraduate campus life at Dupont University, an elite but sports-obsessed school where moral decadence masquerades as higher education.[25] The premise of the novel is a postmodern coming-of-age tale about a young woman from western North Carolina who loses her identity in college and finally rediscovers who she is in a moment of Cartesian self-understanding. Wolfe's description of campus life at Dupont, which observant readers notice bears more than a passing resemblance to Duke, is a carnal carnival where students crave sex and alcohol, love to party, and use lots of four-letter words. Academic life fares no better. Professors are poorly dressed put-ons, administrators are indecisive bureaucrats, athletic coaches are pandering capitalists, and the commencement speaker is a hypocritical moralist.[26]

Wolfe's tawdry tome offers a grotesque vision of secularization, which may tell us more about the author's own imagination than it does about life on contemporary college campuses, but as in most stories there is an element of truth. If the disestablishment of religion at Duke enabled it to ascend to the level of a premier research university, it was not without costs. The originating vision of a higher education as the initiation of the young into the wisdom of the past has been all but lost. The result is a generation that has been abandoned to their own resources because their elders have nothing of value to pass on.[27] Yet it is precisely at this point that the university needs the continuing witness of the church and the gospel story it seeks to tell. As Richard Franklin and Albert Reyes wonderfully illustrate, the Baptist stake in higher education will be even more severely challenged in the future by the Millennial student population and changing ethnic demographics.[28]

It is important to note, however, that the sort of disestablishment described by Marsden is not far removed from the conviction of the freedom of the church that Baptists historically have maintained. This bedrock belief has a variety of permutations but is most often invoked as "the separation of church and state." As a basic belief, it is less a theory of the state and more a theology of the church. Although it has implications about the state and its policies, the principal concern is about the church and its practices. This conviction was forged in the crucible of revolutionary England and colonial America, which had established churches. In these contexts Baptists learned to advocate for the church to be disestablished from the state.[29] Positively stated, this meant that the church needed no foundation or power other than the gospel. To contend that the church is free by virtue of her relation with Christ and should be disestablished from the powers that be is in fact to argue for a kind of secularization of the state.

It is not surprising, then, that *The Secular City*, which remains one of the most important books on secularization, was written by Baptist theologian Harvey Cox. Unlike the death-of-God theologians who celebrated secularity, Cox urged readers to come to terms with the inevitable secularizing processes of modernity so that the church might continue to have a witness. Drawing from Bonhoeffer's vision of a "religionless Christianity" in a "world come of age," Cox predicted that secularization would eventually marginalize religion. He cautioned, "Secularization rolls on, and if we are to understand and communicate with our present age we must learn to love it in its unremitting secularity."[30] Cox found out that secularization may not be a slippery slope but it is a slippery subject. When he revisited the theme twenty years later in *Religion in the Secular City*, he discovered that religion sometimes proves amazingly resistant to secularity.[31] Yet the concern of Cox, like his Baptist forebears, was not to underwrite secularization, but to call for faithful witness to the gospel in an age when the church has become disestablished from the state and the powers that be.

None of the authors in this collection celebrates the sort of secularization of Baptist universities that leads to the dying of the light where religion is relegated to a mere historical reminder that is architecturally engraved and where faith is studied as just another object with the tools of the social sciences.[32] But neither does any of them recommend that Baptist colleges and universities delineate the religious and academic in two discrete spheres: a spiritual realm that is extracurricular and a secular one that is resident in the curriculum. "Quality academics in a Christian environment" may be a mantra repeated by many Baptist and other Christian institutions of higher learning, but it is not the model endorsed by anyone in this volume. The authors recognize that the two-spheres model not only leads to substandard education, but it also separates questions of faith from the academic life of the university. If religion has any role at all in the secular university, it is at the margins of the academy. All of the authors in various ways seek to come to terms with the "uneasy partnership" of the college and the church after the ecclesial parent becomes disestablished from its academic child.[33]

William Hull indicates the need for Baptist colleges and universities to develop a guiding vision that grows out of the "denominational DNA" of Baptist principles, which include responsible dissent, revolutionary democracy, and relational discipleship. Based on the pattern of dissent by a disestablished church, Hull suggests that Baptist schools would be better served "not to *integrate*, but to *interrogate* the curriculum with the Christian faith." This proposal, which is surely worth exploring, may be more difficult than a *prima facie* consideration suggests given the fissiparous state of contemporary Baptist life. Still, Hull is on to a very important point. Perhaps consensus about the faith is not necessary for conversations about it. Given that all too often religious questions must be checked at the door, one has to wonder how Baptist schools might be different if students were allowed and, indeed, encouraged to give voice to questions that arise from their faith in the classroom. Just such an openness, as Hull suggests, is a distinctly Baptist way.[34]

David Dockery gestures in the direction of a consensus theology of Baptist higher education which has "Christ at its center, the church as its focus, and the influencing of culture as a key element of its vision." Such a theology, he believes, is "congruent with the Trinitarian and Christological consensus of the early church." While no doubt many Baptists share the orthodox aim of this vision, it is more accurate to admit that because Baptists have tended toward a Unitarianism of the First or Second Person, such a theology would require a Trinitarian revision of the faith.[35] Dockery contends that the resulting theologically informed approach to Baptist higher education begs for "a comprehensive understanding of all areas of life and thought."[36] James McClendon argues along similar lines that theology is essential to the university because it "is by definition the discovery, understanding, and transformation of the convictions of a convictional community, including the discovery and critical revision of their [i.e., the convictions'] relation to one another *and to whatever else there is.*"[37] McClendon's definition gives substance to the aim expressed in Dockery's title, which suggests a need to provide a theology "of" as well as "for" Baptist higher education by attending to the conviction set of Baptists and offering critical revision of those convictions in light of the research and teaching of the university.

It seems more plausible that the sort of project Dockery has in mind is less like the critically reflective intellectual program sketched out by McClendon and more like the one envisioned by David Gushee. In his chapter Gushee commends the importance of being "critically aware of the particularities of Baptist identity" rooted in a distinct confessional tradition, but he recommends that Baptist schools would be well served by adopting "as a starting point the normative theological identity . . . classic, orthodox, ecumenical Christianity" as represented in such ancient confessions as the Apostles' Creed. Gushee notes that the seventeenth-century Baptist confession, the Orthodox Creed, recommends that the ancient ecumenical creeds of the church "ought thoroughly to be received, and believed."[38] Those who explore Gushee's proposal would do well to ask whether the notion of these creedal statements as "the theological boundary-setter," which he acknowledges "would *not* be big enough to include modernist or in some cases post-modernist revisions of classic Christian theology," adequately preserves and protects the liberty of conscience that Baptists have always linked to the affirmation of confessions of faith.[39]

Several of the chapters take up the question of retaining Baptist identity in the university. Hull urges readers to "remember the Baptist story" that begins with John Smyth in Puritan England, moves to Roger Williams in colonial America, and concludes with John Leland in revolutionary Virginia.[40] It is a familiar and often repeated narrative, although no direct historical link can be established between any of these figures to suggest that they stand in the same continuum of history. Beginning his chapter with a quotation from William Whitsitt, who exposed the secessionist theory of Baptist origins as lacking historical evidence, Bill Leonard urges against hegemonic appeals to any sort of grand Baptist myth of monogenetic origins. Instead he offers a more complex and polygenetic account of Baptist identity which acknowledges such competing traditions as pro-education Rhode Island and anti-education Black Rock, both of which lay claim to *the* Baptist approach to higher education. Leonard makes it clear that his preference is for the minority voice of the General Baptist tradition, which understood the freedom of conscience within the voluntaristic theology of Arminianism, and that he is suspicious of the Particular (or Regular) Baptist emphasis on divine sovereignty, in which Christian liberty is construed in terms of the conviction that Christ is Lord of the conscience. Yet his account of the liberty of conscience and the freedom of dissent is in the end thoroughly historicized, which makes extracting these principles of Baptist identity messy work.[41]

Secularization as Dialectical

So far two very different theories of secularization have been presented: One that regards secularization as a negative process to be resisted and a second that takes it as a neutral consequence of modernity to be embraced. Both of these options have points in their favor, but neither offers a satisfactory account for Baptist schools. As Leonard succinctly puts the issue: "Many believe that the primary, perhaps the only, choices lie between blatant secularization of the college campus and the explicit Christianization (if not Baptistification) of a school's educational ethos."[42] Conversely, Gushee exposes the soft underbelly of the Baptist endorsement of secularization in the university as essentially neutral. He echoes Marsden's thesis that secularization can be seen in the shift from "established belief" to "disestablished belief" to "established nonbelief" at schools like Harvard, Princeton, Yale, Stanford, and Chicago.[43] Borrowing on Martin Marty's question, I would propose a third option that conceives of the future of Baptist higher education as secular *and* religious, but making such a case will require another account of secularization.[44]

The earliest generations of Christians viewed the dominant social order to be under the control of rebellious powers that resisted the rule of Jesus Christ. They believed that history was moving inexorably toward a great apocalyptic end in which Jesus would triumphantly return as rightful Lord to establish an earthly kingdom that would endure for a thousand years.[45] This early chiliastic eschatology was displaced in the fourth century beginning with Emperor Constantine, whose celebrated conversion to Christianity gave favored status to the church, and later with Emperor Theodosius, who made Catholic Christianity the official religion of the empire.[46]

Whereas the apocalyptic eschatology of earlier Christians viewed the empire as a symbol of demonic power, the realized eschatology of fourth-century church leaders like Eusebius and Ambrose celebrated the Christianization of the empire as a fulfillment of biblical prophecy. They believed that the era of Christian emperors inaugurated a new age, which they described as *tempora christiana* (i.e., Christian times). In his edict of Thessalonica issued on February 28, 380, Theodosius proclaimed:

> It is Our will that all peoples who are ruled by the administration of Our clemency shall practice that religion which the divine Peter the Apostle transmitted to the Romans, as the religion which he introduced makes clear even unto this day. . . . That is, according to the apostolic discipline and evangelical doctrine, we shall believe in the single Deity of the Father,

> the Son, and the Holy Spirit, under the concept of equal majesty and of the Holy Trinity. We command that those persons who follow this rule shall embrace the name of Catholic Christians. The rest, however, whom We adjudge demented and insane, shall sustain the infamy of heretical dogmas, their meeting places shall not receive the name of churches, and they shall be smitten first by divine vengeance and secondly by the retribution of Our own initiative, which We shall assume in accordance with divine judgment.[47]

Theodosius attempted to systematically eliminate all rivals to Catholic Christianity through political means, yet despite his efforts to Christianize civilization, things took a much different direction.

On August 24, 410, an invading army led by Alaric the Goth sacked Rome. Although the empire did not collapse for another sixty years, the invasion foreshadowed the ending of an age for Roman Christianity. When news of the sack of Rome reached Jerome in Bethlehem, he confessed to being so shocked that he forgot his own name and was unable to speak.[48] Christians like Jerome, for whom Rome was the embodiment of Christendom, found it impossible to imagine life beyond a Christianized empire. Pagan leaders seized the opportunity to argue that the sack of Rome was the judgment of the old gods for which the Christians were to blame.

Writing from far-off North Africa, Augustine seemed to see what his contemporaries did not. He suggested that the Gothic invasion was neither a sign of the coming apocalypse nor the end of the Christian era. Rather, Augustine detected the hand of divine providence in these events. He envisioned not one *saeculum* but two. One was temporal, and the other was eternal. Each age had its own city, but within the temporal age the two cities were mingled together like wheat and tares. The city of God exists in the present age, but its citizens live as exiles. It is on pilgrimage "in this world" (*in hoc saeculo*), but its citizens journey by faith "to another world" (*ad alterum saeculum*).[49] This pilgrimage is a spiritual journey, as Augustine explained:

> The true Sion, the true Jerusalem . . . hath given us birth, she is the Church of the saints, she hath nourished us, she, who is in part a pilgrim, in part abiding in the heavens. In the part which abideth in heaven is the bliss of angels, in the part which wandereth in this world is the hope of the righteous. . . . Let those then who, being in this life, groan, and long for their country, run by love, not by bodily feet; let them seek not ships but wings, let them lay hold on the two wings of love. What are the two wings of love? The love of God, and our neighbour.[50]

Soaring on the wings of love, the church travels homeward. The journey manifests the hidden design of providence and displays the mysterious presence of grace. The citizens of the earthly city have forgotten that they, though rebellious, are still creatures of the Living God, but the church exists to sacralize the secular age.

The third sense is an understanding of religion that is integral to the academic life of the university. Here I am thinking about a project like the one envisioned by John Henry Newman in *The Idea of a University* where theology serves to examine the deep convictions of culture and history.[51] Theology for Newman was not merely a field of knowledge, but a condition for it. In such an endeavor, a church-related university repays the debt to its parent (the church body) through teaching and research that lead to human flourishing by forming minds that are able to conceive of the good, the beautiful, and the true. Theology serves this purpose by pointing to what Bonhoeffer called "the natural" which even "after the Fall is directed towards the coming of Christ" and away from "the unnatural" which "closes its doors against the coming of Christ."[52] The principle heresy of the modern university was to dethrone theology as the queen of the academic disciplines and to replace it with some version of anthropology, blinded by a loss of its eschatological vision. Consequently, when our best efforts now fail us, we have nowhere to turn but to ourselves. Betrayed by our own failure we are left alone to ponder the empty mysteries of anthropodicy.[53]

The Christian witness in modern Baptist universities coming of age might do well to follow the example of Augustine's two-city typology. Secularization is neither the devil's work nor the end of history. As the Apostle Paul declared, "Jerusalem above is free, and she is our mother."[54] So only by faith can we trace the vectors of the city of God in pilgrimage. The question at issue within the reflections of these essays, then, is not whether religion can survive in the future at Baptist universities, but whether Baptists can foster an academic life in the university that at the same time is informed and enriched by a flourishing faith. Here universities need more than a mere historical reminder of their church parent. They need the full range of witnesses from the living family of God's pilgrim people within the chapel walls and lecture halls. When the gaze is properly on the eschatological horizon, those within the university community can imagine the kind of teaching and research that might lead to human flourishing by forming minds that are able to conceive of the good, the beautiful, and the true.

One of the most interesting and well-attended events at the university where I teach happened at a conference about faith and science. It did not occur because the president, who is a Presbyterian layman, asked the faculty to discuss Calvin's *Institutes*. Nor was it a response to the university trustees who established a center for creation research and required all students of Biology 101 to read a book on intelligent design. It happened when two members of the appointment, promotion, and tenure committee (one from the divinity school and the other from the biology department) became friends and decided to talk with their colleagues about jointly sponsoring a lecture by a biologist who had written a book entitled *Finding Darwin's God.*[55]

Even more surprising, take a guess where the book's author, Kenneth Miller, is a highly regarded professor of biology. Remember Brown University, the ex-Baptist school that slid down the slippery slope of secularization? Perhaps it is no accident that Miller is also a practicing Roman Catholic for whom sacramental worship and natural theology provide rich resources connecting faith and science, but who would have expected this book from Brown? So maybe God still has some surprises for us. Let's hope so. The truth is that this sort of event is not all that uncommon at our university as there are similar conferences, conversations, and courses jointly sponsored by the divinity school and the schools of law, medicine, public policy, environment, and so forth. It stimulates the conversation across the campus and through the curriculum, but it does so in ways that are integral to academic life.

Another important and overlooked way that the Christian witness to the university is sustained is by a free and faithful chapel. There is as little value in a campus pulpit that is merely an extension of the university public relations office as there is for sermons that simply accommodate the gospel to the reigning intellectual elitisms of the academy. William Willimon, the former dean of Duke University Chapel and current United Methodist bishop, once told me that he regularly received reports from trustees, alumni, donors, faculty, and students who were upset about a sermon. "What do you tell them?" I asked. Without hesitation, he shot back his well-rehearsed line: "I tell them I'm not going to apologize for Jesus." The university desperately needs such a truthful witness.

In his review of Wolfe's novel, Willimon recounts a conversation with the author, who asked about the statues at the entrance to Duke Chapel, one of which was Savonarola, the friar of Florence who was burned at the stake. As he walked away, Wolfe muttered, "Only the church would pull a stunt like that." Later it occurred to Willimon how right that was. A crazy monk is the first one to welcome students to the chapel, as if to say, "Don't let investment banking lead you to hell! Don't sell out to the Republicans! We're going to have a bonfire of the vanities after service today. Throw all that trash on the fire!" Willimon concludes, "The university . . . badly needs a church with enough guts to pull a stunt like that."[56] Can Baptists pull something like this off? The jury is still out, but there is reason for hope, and God knows we need it.

Notes

Chapter 1

1. H. Leon McBeth, *The Baptist Heritage* (Nashville: Broadman Press, 1987), 235.
2. Most Baptist churches in America at this time were connected to regional societies or associations, some of which were state conventions. From this connection, congregations gathered in the Triennial Convention of Baptists to join in common cause for missions and other endeavors, such as higher education. In 1845 the southern states separated from the Triennial Convention to form the Southern Baptist Convention.
3. *Encyclopedia of Southern Baptists* (Nashville: Broadman Press, 1958), 1:389–90.
4. Quoted in David B. Potts, *Baptist Colleges in the Development of American Society: 1812–1861* (New York: Garland Publishing, 1988), 13.
5. Ibid., 23.
6. Ibid., 27.
7. Ibid., 28.
8. See James Tunstead Burtchaell, *The Dying of the Light: The Disengagement of Colleges and Universities from their Christian Churches* (Grand Rapids: Eerdmans, 1998), 393.
9. Ibid., 398.
10. William Cathcart, ed., *The Baptist Encyclopaedia* (Philadelphia: Louis H. Everts, 1881), 2:1190.
11. Ibid., 2:1199.
12. McBeth, *Baptist Heritage*, 444.
13. William Henry Brackney, *The Baptists* (New York: Greenwood Press, 1988), 17.
14. From the first constitution of the South Carolina Baptist State Convention, quoted by William J. McGlothlin, *Baptist Beginnings in Education: A History of Furman University* (Nashville: Sunday School Board, 1926), 50.
15. Burtchaell, *Dying of the Light*, 358.

16. Quoted in McBeth, *Baptist Heritage*, 442.
17. Sources on Baptist identity are numerous and include William H. Brackney, ed., *Baptist Life and Thought: 1600–1980* (Valley Forge: Judson Press, 1983); Henry Cook, *What Baptists Stand For* (London: Carey Kingsgate, 1958); Paul S. Fiddes, *Tracks and Traces: Baptist Identity in Church and Theology* (Carlisle, UK: Paternoster, 2003); Curtis W. Freeman, James Wm. McClendon Jr., and C. Rosalee Velloso da Silva, eds., *Baptist Roots: A Reader in the Theology of a Christian People* (Valley Forge: Judson Press, 1999); Timothy George and David S. Dockery, eds., *Theologians of the Baptist Tradition* (Nashville: Broadman & Holman, 2001); Winthrop S. Hudson, *Baptists in Transition: Individualism and Christian Responsibility* (Valley Forge: Judson Press, 1979); Erroll Hulse, *An Introduction to the Baptists* (Haywards Heath, UK: Carey Publications, 1976); Charles A. Jenkens, *Baptist Doctrines* (St. Louis: C. R. Barns, 1892); McBeth, *Baptist Heritage*; and Walter B. Shurden, *The Baptist Identity: Four Fragile Freedoms* (Macon, GA: Smyth & Helwys, 1993).
18. It is important to note here the distinction for Baptists between "confessions" and "creeds." Confessions affirm what one believes, whereas creeds prescribe what one must believe. This distinction has historically been important to Baptists because of their view that only Scripture has absolute authority. No confession or creed can be placed above Scripture.
19. John A. Broadus, *Baptist Confessions, Covenants, and Catechisms* (Nashville: Broadman & Holman, 1996), 56–93.
20. McBeth, *Baptist Heritage*, 241.
21. William L. Lumpkin, *Baptist Confessions of Faith* (Valley Forge: Judson Press, 1959), 360.
22. Broadus, *Baptist Confessions, Covenants, and Catechisms*, 132–33.
23. McBeth, *Baptist Heritage*, 677–79. Also see Brackney, *Baptists*, 235–36. The New Hampshire Confession of 1833 was appealing to many Baptists because of its "high" view of Scripture. Article one reads, "We believe the Holy Bible was written by men divinely inspired, and is a perfect treasure of heavenly instruction; that it has God for its author, salvation for its end, and truth, without any mixture of error, for its matter." See Broadus, *Baptist Confessions, Covenants, and Catechisms*, 131.
24. See Lumpkin, *Baptist Confessions of Faith*, 393.
25. Virtually all Baptist confessions begin with either a statement about Scripture or about the Godhead. Our list acknowledges this pattern, but we believe it makes sense to place Scripture as an introduction since it is seen as the basis for all doctrines that follow. Moreover, the Trinitarian language of the first doctrine is consistent with several Baptist confessions: the Orthodox Creed of 1679 speaks "Of the Holy Trinity"; the Philadelphia Confession of 1742 devotes chapter 2 to "Of God and of the Holy Trinity"; the New Hampshire Confession of 1833 addresses "Of the True God" as "revealed under the personal and relative distinctions of the Father, the Son, and the Holy Spirit"; and both the 1925 and the 1963 Baptist Faith and Message have sections dealing at length with the Godhead, the eternal God who has revealed "Himself to us as Father, Son,

and Holy Spirit." This prevalence of Trinitarian language in Baptist confessions of faith does not necessarily mean that all Baptists are in fact Trinitarian. Some have claimed that Baptists subscribe to a "Unitarianism of the Second Person," for example. This is a debated question among some Baptist interpreters, but is beyond the purview of this chapter. For further discussion on this issue, see Curtis W. Freeman, "God in Three Persons: Baptist Unitarianism and the Trinity," to be published in *Perspectives in Religious Studies,* Spring 2006.

26. This is the language of the Philadelphia Confession of 1742. See Broadus, *Baptist Confessions, Covenants, and Catechisms*, 60.
27. Lumpkin, *Baptist Confessions of Faith*, 394.
28. Broadus, *Baptist Confessions, Covenants, and Catechisms*, 132.
29. Ibid., 62.
30. Ibid., 394–95.
31. Ibid., 272–73.
32. McBeth, *Baptist Heritage*, 75–76.
33. Lumpkin, *Baptist Confessions of Faith*, 396.
34. Ibid., 396.
35. Broadus, *Baptist Confessions, Covenants, and Catechisms*, 90.
36. Ibid., 133.
37. Lumpkin, *Baptist Confessions of Faith*, 400.
38. Broadus, *Baptist Confessions, Covenants, and Catechisms*, 83.
39. Lumpkin, *Baptist Confessions of Faith*, 399.
40. Ibid., 397.
41. Ibid., 392–93.
42. McBeth, *Baptist Heritage*, 68.
43. E. Y. Mullins, *The Axioms of Religion* (Philadelphia: Judson Press, 1908), 53–54.
44. It is important to emphasize here that Baptists historically have seen the principle of regenerate church membership—believer's baptism—as the starting point for religious liberty. One doesn't become a Christian without a voluntary response to God's initiating grace. This implied capacity for salvation was expressed by Mullins as "the competency of the soul in religion." What is often omitted by Baptist interpreters is Mullins's additional wording, "a competency under God, not a competency in the sense of human self-sufficiency" (see Mullins, ibid., 53). This omission tends to produce an Enlightenment view of freedom of religion within the Baptist context today—that is, a belief in the autonomy of each individual Baptist to decide in whatever way one wishes in all matters of the faith. While we certainly affirm freedom of religion as a basic human right within the political order, it is not the same teaching as "the competency of the soul in religion . . . under God." For Baptists and all Christians, the believer does not stand alone. In the first place, he or she is never "independent of the Scriptures" (ibid., 53), but in addition, he or she is always also a member of a local congregation and the larger Body of Christ.
45. See C. Stephen Evans, "The Christian University and the Connectedness of Knowledge," in *The Baptist and Christian Character of Baylor*, ed. Donald D.

Schmeltekopf and Dianna Vitanza with Bradley J. B. Toben (Waco, TX: Baylor University, 2003), 30–33.

46. Ibid., 32.

Chapter 2

1. I am thinking primarily of Baptist colleges and universities in the South and Southwest, regardless of whether they retain a formal relationship to their state Baptist conventions. For this paper, my emphasis is on the teaching function of such schools in relation to undergraduate students, not on scholarly research and not on graduate or professional education.
2. George M. Marsden, *The Soul of the American University: From Protestant Establishment to Established Nonbelief* (New York: Oxford University Press, 1994); Philip Gleason, *Contending with Modernity* (New York: Oxford University Press, 1995); Douglas Sloan, *Faith and Knowledge: Mainline Protestantism and American Higher Education* (Louisville: Westminster John Knox, 1994); James Tunstaed Burtchaell, *Dying of the Light*; Robert Benne, *Quality with Soul: How Six Premier Colleges and Universities Keep Faith with their Religious Traditions* (Grand Rapids: Eerdmans, 2001).
3. Objections to these supposedly "whiny" "declension narratives" are articulated forcefully in the recent book edited by Douglas Jacobsen and Rhonda Hustedt Jacobsen, *Scholarship and Christian Faith: Enlarging the Conversation* (New York: Oxford University Press, 2004).
4. Various versions of this statement have been quoted in various places. One is in a PBS interview with Michael Beschloss, located at http://www.pbs.org/newshour/conversation/july-dec02/beschloss_11-14.html, accessed March 29, 2005.
5. This is a theme throughout Marsden, *Soul of the American University*, but is especially strong in ch. 19: see 365–66.
6. Bill Readings, *The University in Ruins* (Cambridge, Mass.: Harvard University Press, 1997). Perhaps the most devastating recent treatment is novelistic: Tom Wolfe, *I Am Charlotte Simmons* (New York: Farrar, Straus, & Giroux, 2004). See the important book by Naomi Schaefer Riley, *God on the Quad: How Religious Colleges and the Missionary Generation Are Changing America* (New York: St. Martin's, 2005).
7. Burtchaell, *Dying of the Light*; see esp. 771.
8. An important recent book emerging from this slice of the higher education landscape is Stephen R. Haynes, ed., *Professing in the Postmodern Academy* (Waco, TX: Baylor University Press, 2002).
9. Benne, *Quality with Soul*, 49.
10. Stanley Fish speaks of the irrepressible, unliberal religiosity of many secular university students in his "One University under God?" *Chronicle of Higher Education* online, January 7, 2005, accessed at http://chronicle.com.
11. Wheaton College President Duane Litfin proposes the terms "umbrella" and "systemic," rather than "critical-mass" and "orthodox," to describe the same

basic options. See his *Conceiving the Christian College* (Grand Rapids: Eerdmans, 2004), ch. 2.

12. David K. Naugle, *Worldview: The History of a Concept* (Grand Rapids: Eerdmans, 2002), the authoritative treatment of the concept clearly shows that its history and use extend far beyond the confines of the Dutch Reformed model I discuss in this section.
13. Ronald A. Wells, ed., *Keeping Faith: Embracing the Tensions in Christian Higher Education* (Grand Rapids: Eerdmans, 1996). The account offered here of the vision of Calvin College is indebted to Benne, *Quality with Soul.*
14. James D. Bratt, ed., *Abraham Kuyper: A Centennial Reader* (Grand Rapids: Eerdmans, 1998).
15. It remains the central theme of many of the most recent books on the subject of religion in higher education: see Douglas V. Henry and Bob R. Agee, eds., *Faithful Learning and the Christian Scholarly Vocation* (Grand Rapids: Eerdmans, 2003); David Claerbaut, *Faith and Learning on the Edge: A Bold New Look at Religion in Higher Education* (Grand Rapids: Zondervan, 2004); and Harry Lee Poe, *Christianity in the Academy: Teaching at the Intersection of Faith and Learning* (Grand Rapids: Baker Books, 2004).
16. Arthur Holmes, *The Idea of a Christian College* (Grand Rapids: Eerdmans, 1975). See Benne, *Quality with Soul,* 104–6.
17. See David S. Dockery and David P. Gushee, *The Future of Christian Higher Education* (Nashville: Broadman & Holman, 1999); David S. Dockery and Gregory Alan Thornbury, eds., *Shaping a Christian Worldview* (Nashville: Broadman & Holman, 2002).
18. See the lectures collected in Arthur L. Walker Jr., *Integrating Faith and Academic Discipline: Selected H. I. Hester Lectures* (Nashville: SBC Education Commission, 1992).
19. Jacobsen and Jacobsen, *Scholarship and Christian Faith.*
20. Crystal Downing, "Imbricating Faith and Learning: The Architectonics of Christian Faith," in ibid., 33–44.
21. Ibid., 24–29.
22. This concept is addressed helpfully by Mikeal Parsons, "Building the Faculty at a Christian University: The Significant Contribution Model," in Donald D. Schmeltekopf et al., *Baptist and Christian Character of Baylor,* 67–68.
23. Dennis Hollinger, *Head, Heart, and Hands* (Downers Grove, IL: InterVarsity, 2005).
24. Bratt and Wells, "Piety and Progress: A History of Calvin College," in *Keeping Faith,* 40–42.
25. Ibid., 43, quoting Wolterstorff.
26. Nicholas P. Wolterstorff, *Educating for Life,* ed. Gloria Goris Stronks and Clarence W. Joldersma (Grand Rapids: Baker Books, 2002). Compare his *Educating for Shalom: Essays on Christian Higher Education* (Grand Rapids: Eerdmans, 2004).
27. Tony Campolo, "The Radical Christian College," in Walker, *Integrating Faith and Academic Discipline,* 146–54.

28. The most prominent current example is Jim Wallis, *God's Politics* (San Francisco: HarperSanFrancisco, 2005).
29. David S. Dockery, "The Great Commandment as a Paradigm for Christian Higher Education," in Dockery and Gushee, *The Future of Christian Higher Education*, ch. 1. Intercultural competence goals have been integrated into the Union 2010 strategic plan. I chair the university's Intercultural Competence Committee.
30. Burtchaell, *Dying of the Light*, 780.
31. Wolterstorff, "The Standing of the Work of our Hands," a 1995 lecture found in Wells, *Keeping Faith*, 133–51. The quote is from 150.
32. Benne, *Quality with Soul*, 112–13.
33. Mark Schwehn, *Exiles from Eden: Religion and the Academic Vocation in America* (New York: Oxford University Press, 1993).
34. On Newman, see his classic, *The Idea of a University* (New Haven: Yale University Press, 1996), and Frederick Aquino, "The Craft of Teaching: The Relevance of Newman for Theological Education," *Christian Higher Education* 2 (September 2003): 269–84.
35. Dietrich Bonhoeffer, *Life Together* (New York: Harper & Row, 1954).
36. For a work emphasizing colleges and universities as transmitters of particular ecclesial traditions, see Richard T. Hughes and William B. Adrian, *Models for Christian Higher Education: Strategies for Success in the Twenty-First Century* (Grand Rapids: Eerdmans, 2003).
37. John Paul II, *Ex Corde Ecclesiae*, 7.
38. Benne, *Quality with Soul*, 125–26.
39. Richard G. Malloy, "The Truly Catholic University," *America* 191, no. 10 (October 11, 2004), accessible online at http://www.americanmagazine.org. This case is also made powerfully from the Baptist side by Samford University president Tom Corts in his "The University, the Church, and the Culture," *The Educator* (first quarter, 2005), accessible online at http://www.baptistschools.org.
40. Michael L. Budde and John Wright, *Conflicting Allegiances: The Church-Based University in a Liberal Democratic Society* (Grand Rapids: Brazos, 2004).
41. I am grateful for Douglas Henry's paper, "Can Baptist Theology Sustain the Life of the Mind? The Quest for a Vital Baptist Academy," especially its reflection on tradition, following Alasdair MacIntyre and applying his key insights to the Baptist academy. Manuscript viewed in draft form, November 2004.
42. Douglas V. Henry, "Why We Can't Wait—Freedom, the Protestant Free Church, and *Gaudium et Spes*." Unpublished manuscript presented at "The Call to Justice" conference, Vatican City, March 2005.
43. Mark A. Noll, "Christian Higher Education and Southern Baptists: Hopeless or Hopeful?" *The Educator* (first quarter 2004), 5.
44. The following is drawn from Burtchaell, *Dying of the Light*, 436–39. My summaries are italicized.
45. Henry, "Why We Can't Wait"; Beaty, "Protestant Free Church Christians and *Gaudium et Spes*: An Historical and Philosophical Perspective"; Scott Moore,

"Not the *Free* Church in the Modern World? Response to Objections." All unpublished manuscripts presented at "The Call to Justice" conference, Vatican City, March 2005.

46. Moore, "Not the *Free* Church," 6–7.
47. Beaty, "Protestant Free Church Christians," 21n4.
48. Henry, "Why We Can't Wait," 4. He then develops a rich account of liberty in "Can Baptist Theology Sustain the Life of the Mind?"
49. Ibid., 3.
50. Duane Litfin, following others, describes such a school as an "ecumenically orthodox Christian university" or EOCU. See Liftin, *Conceiving the Christian College*, ch. 11.
51. Institutional embodiments of this trend include the Evangelicals and Catholics Together process, renewal movements in the mainline denominations, the publication strategy of Brazos Books and InterVarsity Press, and such journals as *Pro Ecclesia*, *Touchstone*, and *First Things*.
52. William Hull worries that Union University's turn to evangelicalism puts us at risk of developing too narrow or "tightly drawn" confessional boundaries, but this can be prevented by a turn to the classic creeds rather than modern formulations. See "Where Are the Baptists in the Higher Education Dialogue," in John M. Dunaway, ed., *Gladly Learn and Gladly Teach* (Macon, GA: Mercer University Press, 2005). James Leo Garrett has persuasively shown that while "Baptists have consistently affirmed that the canonical Scriptures are always superior to and more authoritative than any or all postbiblical tradition," Baptist theology has been broadly shaped by classic Christian orthodoxy. The Orthodox Creed of General Baptists (1678) included the texts of three major historic creeds, and the 1905 inaugural meeting of the Baptist World Alliance included the recitation of the Apostles' Creed at the direction of the president, Alexander Maclaren. See Garrett, "The Roots of Baptist Beliefs," accessed online at www.baptist2baptist.net/Issues/BaptistPolity/rootofbaptistbeliefs.asp.
53. Of course, this does raise the question of who decides whether or not someone or some idea falls within or outside the creedal tent. The Catholic Church has an answer to this: the magisterium and its cascading levels of authoritative interpreters of the faith, down to the local level. Free-church Protestants, including Baptists, lack such a hierarchical structure, by design. Leaders of any Baptist university who seek to establish some kind of doctrinal parameters must face this question.
54. Douglas Henry, "Can Baptist Theology Sustain the Life of the Mind?," 6.

Chapter 3

1. William E. Hull, "Where Are the Baptists in the Higher Education Dialogue?," *Gladly Learn, Gladly Teach*, ed. John Mason Dunaway (Macon, GA: Mercer University Press, 2005).
2. Marsden, *Soul of the American University*; Mark Noll, *The Scandal of the Evangelical Mind* (Grand Rapids: Eerdmans, 1994); Burtchaell, *Dying of the Light*. For a Baptist perspective on the secularization thesis, see William H. Brackney,

"Secularization of the Academy: A Baptist Typology," *Westminster Studies in Education* 24, no. 2 (2001): 111–28; "Secularization of the Academy: A New Challenge to Baptist Historians," *Baptist History & Heritage* 39, no. 1 (2004): 59–79.

3. For a brief survey of conflicts that convulsed Southern Baptist higher education in the second half of the twentieth century, see William E. Hull, *Southern Baptist Higher Education: Retrospect and Prospect* (Birmingham: Samford University, 2001), 1–15.
4. Benne, *Quality with Soul,* 67.
5. On ways in which the Southern Baptist Convention controversy of 1979–1991 dramatized the cruciality of congregational support for denominational enterprises, see Arthur Emery Farnsley II, *Southern Baptist Politics: Authority and Power in the Restructuring of an American Denomination* (University Park: Pennsylvania State University Press, 1994). For a summary and update, see his "People Power: How Majorities Rule Denominations," *Christian Century*, October 5, 2004, 34–39.
6. E. Glenn Hinson, "A Word From . . . ," *Review & Expositor* 101, no. 2 (2004): 168. The entire quote is italicized for emphasis in the original. Further on this concern of Hinson, especially his rejection of efforts to describe our Baptist identity as "evangelical," see the entire article just cited (167–70) plus the following: "Why Baptist Colleges?" *The Southern Baptist Educator* (May–June 1972): 3–4; "A Rationale for Baptist Higher Education," *Search* 4, no. 1 (1973): 11–21; "Baptists and Evangelicals: What Is the Difference?" *Baptist History and Heritage* 16, no. 2 (1981): 20–32; James Leo Garrett Jr., E. Glenn Hinson, and James E. Tull, *Are Southern Baptists "Evangelicals"?* (Macon, GA: Mercer University Press, 1983), 129–83, 209–14; E. Glenn Hinson, "The Educational Task of Baptist Teachers of Religion on the Edge of a New Millennium," *Perspectives in Religious Studies* 22, no. 3 (1995): 227–37; "A Word from . . . Introduction to the Centennial Issue," *Review & Expositor* 101, no. 1 (2004): 13–16; "Forming Baptist Identity(ies) in American Higher Education," *Perspectives in Religious Studies* (forthcoming).
7. Carol Holcomb, "Integration of Faith and Learning: Musings of a Baptist Historian," unpublished manuscript, 4.
8. With courtesy yet candor, Mark Noll has reminded us that Baptists have never really hammered out a comprehensive philosophy of education, partly because our best-known thinkers have been pastor-theologians and seminary teachers concerned primarily with conversion and church life. See Mark A. Noll, "Is There a *Baptist* Theology in the House? A Review Essay," *Perspectives in Religious Studies* 28, no. 3 (2001): 285–90; Noll, "Christian Higher Education and Southern Baptists," 5–6.
9. On the early history of religious dissent in the British Isles, see Michael R. Watts, *The Dissenters: From the Reformation to the French Revolution* (Oxford: Clarendon, 1978). On the development of the Free Church tradition in England with special reference to the Baptists, see Ernest A. Payne, *Free Churchmen, Unrepentant and Repentant and Other Papers* (London: Carey Kingsgate, 1965).

10. For a detailed study, see the two-volume work of William G. McLoughlin, *New England Dissent, 1630–1833: The Baptists and the Separation of Church and State* (Cambridge, Mass.: Harvard University Press, 1971). For a more popular summary, see McLoughlin's *Soul Liberty: The Baptists' Struggle in New England, 1630–1833* (Hanover, NH: University Press of New England, 1991), esp. 1–12, 289–303.
11. Nathan O. Hatch, *The Democratization of American Christianity* (New Haven: Yale University Press, 1989), 162–89. On John Leland, see 93–101. On growth: "Baptist membership multiplied tenfold in the three decades after the Revolution; the number of churches increased from five hundred to over twenty-five hundred" (3).
12. On this understanding of iconoclasm, see Gabriel Vahanian, *Wait without Idols* (New York: George Braziller, 1964), 21–30.
13. For a brief but insightful introduction to the contemporary context, see Martin E. Marty, "Baptistification Takes Over," *Christianity Today*, September 2, 1983, 33–36.
14. For a recent inventory of global Baptist life, see Denton Lotz, "Who and Where in the World Are the Baptists?," *Baptist History and Heritage* 40, no. 1 (2005): 8–22.
15. On the centrality of agency to the American metanarrative, see James E. Block, *A Nation of Agents: The American Path to a Modern Self and Society* (Cambridge, Mass.: Belknap, 2002).
16. McLoughlin, *Soul Liberty*, 2.
17. On a continuing tradition of Baptist dissent see David Stricklin, *A Genealogy of Dissent: Southern Baptist Protest in the Twentieth Century* (Lexington: University Press of Kentucky, 1999). For a popular summary, see Edwin S. Gaustad, "U.S. Baptists and Modernity: Great Dissenters, Lousy Conformists," *Baptist History & Heritage* 36, no. 1, 2 (2001): 101–12.
18. On "the hazards of conformity and the importance of dissent" (vi), see Cass R. Sunstein, *Why Societies Need Dissent* (Cambridge, Mass.: Harvard University Press, 2003).
19. Cited in Rollo May, *The Courage to Create* (New York: W. W. Norton, 1975), 60.
20. The literature has been enormous and continuous since Allan Bloom's *The Closing of the American Mind* (New York: Simon & Schuster, 1987) launched a national debate over what is often called "political correctness." For a sample of fairly shrill polemic, see the books of Charles J. Sykes, *ProfScam: Professors and the Demise of Higher Education* (Washington, D.C.: Regnery Gateway, 1988); and *Hollow Men: Politics and Corruption in Higher Education* (Washington, D.C.: Regnery Gateway, 1990). For more mediating efforts, see Gerald Graff, *Beyond the Culture Wars: How Teaching the Conflicts Can Revitalize American Education* (New York: W. W. Norton, 1992); and Russell Jacoby, *Dogmatic Wisdom: How the Culture Wars Divert Education and Distract America* (New York: Doubleday, 1994). For a summary of the concerns of Graff and Jacoby, see Russell Jacoby, "Intellectuals and their Discontents," *The Hedgehog Review* 2, no. 3 (2000): 46

and Gerald Graff, "Two Cheers for the Argument Culture, *The Hedgehog Review* 2, no. 3 (2000): 53, 64–66.

21. On the broader cultural challenge in contemporary American life, see Lewis H. Lapham, *Gag Rule: On the Suppression of Dissent and the Stifling of Democracy* (New York: Penguin, 2004).
22. Lawrence H. Summers, "Why Universities Endure: On the Authority of Ideas," *Harvard Magazine*, November–December 2004, 72.
23. For a brief overview of the history, assumptions, and limitations of this approach, with particular attention to the work of Arthur Holmes and Nicholas Wolterstorff, see Jacobsen and Jacobsen, *Scholarship and Christian Faith*, 15–31.
24. It is helpful to study both the definitions and examples of all cognate words related to "integrate" in J. A. Simpson and E. S. C. Weiner, eds., *The Oxford English Dictionary*, 2nd ed. (Oxford: Clarendon, 1989), 7:1063–66.
25. In Scripture there are many variations in worldview between the two testaments, such as between Ecclesiastes and Ephesians. Or in the same testament, as between Ezra-Nehemiah and Ruth-Jonah. Or even in the same genre, as between the rationalism of Matthew, the empiricism of Mark, the traditionalism of Luke, and the mysticism of John. Biblical theologians have searched for a unifying theme, such as "covenant" or "kingdom of God" or *Heilsgeschichte,* but none of them is adequate to cover the rich diversity in which the faith is expressed. In church history we note not only the major perspectival differences between Eastern Orthodoxy and Roman Catholicism but how, even in the West, what was first expressed in a Jewish worldview was subsequently adapted to neo-Platonic, Aristotelian, existentialist, enlightenment, and scientific/critical conceptual patterns.
26. For example, many of the disciplines are experimenting with significantly altered worldviews because of the "paradigm shift" from modernism to postmodernism, and it is not surprising that "integrationists" differ over how to handle these changes. For commentary, see Riley, *God on the Quad,* 226–31. In addition to the literature cited there, see Dan R. Stiver, "Baptists: Modern or Postmodern?" *Review & Expositor* 100, no. 4 (2003): 521–52; A. J. Conyers, "Can Postmodernism Be Used as a Template for Christian Theology?" *Christian Scholars Review* 33, no. 3 (2004): 293–309.
27. For an extended example of how a somewhat reluctant Baptist questions the academy in a profoundly baptistic way, see Wendell Berry, *Life Is a Miracle: An Essay against Modern Superstition* (Washington: Counterpoint, 2000), esp. 55–89, 129–42.
28. The acceptance of Christianity by Constantine is usually dated to his visionary conversion of October 28, 312, followed by an edict of toleration issued at Milan in the following year. This alliance between church and state provided enormous benefits for "adherents of the catholic faith" but prescribed harsh punishments for "heretics and schismatics."
29. On an eschatological understanding of higher education which comes, appropriately enough, out of Messiah College with Mennonite roots in the Anabaptist tradition, see the introductory essay of Rodney J. Sawatsky, "Prologue: The Virtue

of Scholarly Hope," in Jacobsen and Jacobsen, *Scholarship and Christian Faith*, 3–14.

30. For an apt description of this mood, see Hatch, *Democratization of American Christianity*, 184–89.
31. On the crucial contribution of Roger Williams and the Baptists to the concept of the sacredness of conscience in relation to governmental noninterference, see Robert N. Bellah, "Is There a Common American Culture?" *Journal of the American Academy of Religion* 66, no. 3 (1998): 615–25. On the subsequent judicial struggle to protect freedom of conscience, see Phillip E. Hammond, *With Liberty for All: Freedom of Religion in the United States* (Louisville: Westminster John Knox, 1998).
32. William R. Hutchison, *Religious Pluralism in America: The Contentious History of a Founding Ideal* (New Haven: Yale University Press, 2003), distinguishes three stages in the development of pluralism: toleration, inclusion, and participation (6–7). Inherent in the Baptist ideal is the third stage, a mandate "to share responsibility for the forming and implementing of the society's agenda" (7).
33. William Bullein Johnson, *The Gospel Developed through the Government and Order of the Churches of Jesus Christ* (Richmond, VA: H. K. Ellyson, 1846), 17. Italics in the original.
34. Samuel P. Huntington, "The Clash of Civilizations," *Foreign Affairs* 72, no. 3 (1993): 22–49; subsequently expanded into a book, *The Clash of Civilizations and the Remaking of World Order* (New York: Simon & Schuster, 1996). On the discussion generated, with a response by Huntington, see *The Clash of Civilizations? The Debate. A Foreign Affairs Reader* (New York: Foreign Affairs, 1993). On the author's academic career, which undergirds this seminal work, see Robert D. Kaplan, "Looking the World in the Eye," *The Atlantic Monthly*, December 2001, 68–82.
35. Andrew Sullivan, "This *Is* a Religious War," *The New York Times Magazine*, October 7, 2001, 53.
36. This is an enormously challenging agenda for trilateral conversations between Jews, Christians, and Muslims because monotheism, depending on how it is understood, can be either a powerfully unifying or a powerfully alienating force in competing religions. On a typology of "elective" versus "metaphysical" monotheism, see Martin S. Jaffee, "One God, One Revelation, One People: On the Symbolic Structure of Elective Monotheism," *Journal of the American Academy of Religion* 69, no. 4 (2001): 763–75. For a disturbing treatment of monotheism and identity politics, see Regina M. Schwartz, *The Curse of Cain: The Violent Legacy of Monotheism* (Chicago: University of Chicago Press, 1997).
37. See especially Emil Brunner, *The Misunderstanding of the Church* (Philadelphia: Westminster, 1953), a statement all the more important because it originated in a European context with its long history of established churches. For a further refinement of Brunner's thought along Baptist lines, see his *The Doctrine of the Church, Faith, and the Consummation*, vol. 3, *Dogmatics* (London: Lutterworth, 1962), 133.

38. The political philosopher Michael Walzer has traced the earliest forms of that political radicalism that gave rise to the modern democratic state back to the English Calvinism of the Puritan movement, an important antecedent of the Baptists. See his *The Revolution of the Saints: A Study in the Origins of Radical Politics* (Cambridge, Mass.: Harvard University Press, 1965).
39. Brunner, *Doctrine of the Church*, 80.
40. Best known among the many working in this field are Roger Finke and Rodney Stark. See their *The Churching of America, 1776–1990: Winners and Losers in Our Religious Economy* (New Brunswick, NJ: Rutgers University Press, 1992), and *Acts of Faith: Explaining the Human Side of Religion* (Berkeley: University of California Press, 2000).
41. Cited by Frederick Rudolph, *The American College and University: A History* (Athens: University of Georgia Press, 1990), 12, from Walter C. Bronson, *The History of Brown University 1764–1914*, 1.
42. For a detailed study of this process, see Julie A. Reuben, *The Making of the Modern University: Intellectual Transformation and the Marginalization of Morality* (Chicago: University of Chicago Press, 1996).
43. Corts, "The University, the Church, and the Culture," see ch. 12 of this book.
44. Tom Wolfe, *The Bonfire of the Vanities* (New York: Farrar, Straus & Giroux, 1990); *A Man in Full* (New York: Farrar, Straus, & Giroux, 1998).
45. Wolfe, *I Am Charlotte Simmons.*
46. Cited from an interview by Mary Ann Glendon, "Off at College," *First Things*, February 2005, 41.
47. For an insightful analysis of the problem together with a historical survey of mainline Protestant efforts to address it, see Sloan, *Faith and Knowledge*.
48. See especially Parker J. Palmer, *To Know As We Are Known: A Spirituality of Education* (San Francisco: Harper & Row, 1983); *The Courage to Teach: Exploring the Inner Landscape of a Teacher's Life* (San Francisco: Jossey-Bass, 1998); *A Hidden Wholeness: The Journey toward an Undivided Life* (San Francisco: Jossey-Bass, 2004). Although Palmer is not a Baptist, his highly developed Quaker sensibilities give him a deep affinity for the Baptist understanding of community.
49. Stanley Fish, "One University, Under God?" *Chronicle of Higher Education*, January 7, 2005, C4.

Chapter 4

1. Bill Leonard, *Baptist Ways: A History* (Valley Forge: Judson Press, 2003), 15.
2. Donald G. Mathews, *Religion in the Old South* (Chicago: University of Chicago Press, 1977), 88.
3. H. Leon McBeth, *Sourcebook for Baptist Heritage* (Nashville: Broadman, 1990), 238.
4. Ibid.; see also Leonard, *Baptist Ways*, 173–74.
5. Bill J. Leonard, *God's Last and Only Hope: The Fragmentation of the Southern Baptist Convention* (Grand Rapids: Eerdmans, 1990).

6. Bill J. Leonard, "A Crumbling Empire: Is there a Baptist Future in the South?" in Corrie E. Norman and Don S. Armentrout, eds., *Religion in the Contemporary South* (Knoxville: University of Tennessee Press, 2005), 75–88.
7. For these discussions, see Nancy Tatom Ammerman, *Baptist Battles: Social Change and Conflict in the Southern Baptist Convention* (New Brunswick, NJ: Rutgers University Press, 1990); David T. Morgan, *The New Crusades, the New Holy Land: Conflict in the Southern Baptist Convention, 1969–1991* (Tuscaloosa: University of Alabama Press, 1996); and Leonard, *God's Last and Only Hope*.
8. William Lindsey and Mark Silk, *Religion and Public Life in the Southern Crossroads: Showdown States* (New York: Altamira Press, 2005), and Charles Reagan Wilson and Mark Silk, *Religion and Public Life in the South: In the Evangelical Mode* (New York: Altamira Press, 2005).
9. Much of the material in this section of the chapter was presented first at a conference on Baptists and higher education sponsored by Samford University in London, England, in August 2004.
10. Daniel Featley, *The Dippers Dipt, or, the Anabaptists Duck'd and Plung'd over Head and Eares, at a Disputation at Southward* (London: Nicholas Bourne & Richard Royston, 1646), 36.
11. Ibid.
12. Isaac Backus, *Church History of New England, from 1620 to 1804* (Philadelphia: American Baptist Publication Society, 1844), 43.
13. Isaac Backus, *A History of New England, with Particular Reference to the Baptists*, 2nd ed. (1871; reprint, 2 vols. in 1, New York: Arno Press, 1969), 1:75.
14. Leonard Busher, *Religions Peace: or, A Plea for Liberty of Conscience* (1616; republished in Edward B. Underhill, ed., *Tracts on Liberty of Conscience and Persecution, 1614–1661* [London: T. Haddon, 1846]), 17.
16. Ibid., 22.
17. Ibid., 30; see also Leonard, *Baptist Ways*, and B. R. White, "Early Baptist Arguments for Religious Freedom: Their Overlooked Agenda," *Baptist History and Heritage* 24 (1989): 6–7.
18. Thomas Helwys, *The Mystery of Iniquity*, cited in W. T. Whitley, *A History of British Baptists*, rev. ed. (London: Kingsgate Press, 1932), 33.
19. Lumpkin, *Baptist Confessions of Faith*, 140.
20. Thomas Helwys, *A Short Declaration of the Mystery of Iniquity*, Richard Groves, ed. (Macon, GA: Mercer University Press, 1998), xxxii.
21. Lumpkin, *Baptist Confessions of Faith*, 232.
22. Ibid., 233.
23. Ibid., 279.
24. Ibid., 279–80.
25. Ibid., 296.
26. Ibid., 331–32.
27. Leonard, *Baptist Ways*, 6.
28. Lumpkin, *Baptist Confessions of Faith*, 316.
29. Fiddes, *Tracks and Traces*, 6.

30. Ibid., 119.
31. Ibid., 120.
32. This is evident in some of the pronouncements of the group promoting a Baptist "Manifesto" and in the activities of the Southern Baptist Convention in demanding a particular kind of conformity to the denomination's confession of faith.
33. Roger Williams, *The Bloudy Tenent of Persecution for the Cause of Conscience Discussed*, A. C. Underhill, ed. (1644; reprint, London: Hanserd Knollys Society, 1848), 109.
34. Ibid., 112–13.
35. H. Shelton Smith, Robert Handy, and Loefferts Loescher, *American Christianity* (New York: Charles Scribner's, 1960), 1:167, citing John Clarke, "Ill Newes from New England."
36. Ibid., 1:168.
37. O. K. Armstrong and Marjorie Armstrong, *The Baptists in America* (Garden City, NJ: Doubleday, 1979), 71.
38. Edwin S. Gaustad, *Baptist Piety: The Last Will and Testament of Obadiah Holmes* (Valley Forge: Judson Press, 1994), 40.
39. Richard T. Hughes and William B. Adrian, eds., *Models for Christian Higher Education* (Grand Rapids: Eerdmans, 1997), 1.
40. Ibid., 1–2.
41. Ibid., 6–7.
42. Ibid., 7.
43. Article XII, "Education," *Baptist Faith and Message*, 1925, in McBeth, *A Sourcebook for Baptist Heritage*, 514–15.
44. Ibid.
45. Will D. Campbell, *The Stem of Jesse* (Macon, GA: Mercer University Press, 1990), 38.
46. Ibid., 40, 76.
47. Fiddes, *Tracts and Traces*, 5.
48. Ibid., 6.
49. Lumpkin, *Baptist Confessions of Faith*, 149. This segment is actually the conclusion appended to the formal confession.

Chapter 5

1. William E. Hull, "Southern Baptist Higher Education: Retrospect and Prospect." Unpublished Hester Lecture given at the annual meeting of the Association of Southern Baptist Colleges and Schools, 1996.
2. See Friederich Schleiermacher, *On Religion: Speeches to its Cultured Despisers*, trans. John Oman (1799; New York: Harper & Row, 1965).
3. See Charles Hodge, *Systematic Theology*, vol. 1 (repr., Grand Rapids: Eerdmans, 1975).
4. See Schmeltekopf, et al., *Baptist and Christian Character of Baylor.*
5. George, "The Future of Baptist Theology," 1–10.
6. Noll, "Is There a Baptist Theology in the House?" 285–90.

7. See Leonard, *Baptist Ways*; also see R. Stanton Norman, *The Baptist Way* (Nashville: Broadman & Holman, 2005).
8. See 1994 Annual of the Southern Baptist Convention.
9. McBeth, *Baptist Heritage*, 68.
10. See C. S. Lewis, *The Great Divorce* (New York: Macmillan, 1946).
11. See Robert L. Saucy, "Doing Theology for the Church," in *The Necessity of Systematic Theology*, ed. John Jefferson Davis (Grand Rapids: Baker, 1978), 61–74.
12. Miroslav Volf, "Theology for a Way of Life," in *Practicing Theology: Beliefs and Practices in the Christian Life*, ed. Miroslav Volf and Dorothy Bass (Grand Rapids: Eerdmans, 2002), 245–63.
13. See John Hannah, *Our Legacy* (Colorado Springs: NavPress, 2001).
14. See Jaroslav Pelikan, *The Vindication of Tradition* (New Haven: Yale University Press, 1986), 54–56; also see Pelikan, *The Christian Tradition*, 5 vols. (Chicago: University of Chicago Press, 1989).
15. T. S. Eliot, *Christianity and Culture* (New York: Harcourt Brace, 1940).
16. In this regard we can learn from the helpful guide offered by J. I. Packer and Thomas C. Oden, *One Faith* (Downers Grove, IL: InterVarsity, 2004).
17. See Hull, "Southern Baptist Higher Education."

Chapter 6

1. Neil Howe and William Strauss, *Generations: The History of America's Future, 1584 to 2069* (New York: Morrow, 1991); *13th Gen: Abort, Retry, Ignore, Fail?* (New York: Vintage Books, 1993); *Millennials Rising: The Next Great Generation* (New York: Vintage Books, 2000).
2. Howe and Strauss, *Generations*, 60.
3. Ibid., 64.
4. Neil Howe and William Strauss, *Millennials Go to College: Strategies for a New Generation on Campus* (Great Falls, VA: American Association of Collegiate Registrars and LifeCourse Associates, 2003).
5. See Robert Debard, "Millennials Coming to College," in *Serving the Millennial Generation: New Directions for Student Services*, ed. Mike Coomes and Robert DeBard (San Francisco: Jossey Bass, 2004), 33.
6. Ibid., 12.
7. Howe and Strauss, *Millennials Go to College*.
8. Harris Poll #12, "A 21st Century Juxtaposition: Grandma, Grandpa and High Technology," February 1998; retrieved February 5, 2005, from http://www.harrisinteractive.com/harris_poll/printerfriend/index.asp?PID=207.
9. Howe and Strauss, *Millennials Go to College*, 51–52.
10. Roger Casey, "Millennials: The New College Generation," *Rollins Alumni Record*, Spring 2004, 14.
11. Ibid., 15.
12. Diana Oblinger, "Understanding the New Students," *EDUCAUSE Review* 38, no. 4 (July/August 2003): 37–47.
13. Linda Sax, "Our Incoming Students: What Are They Like?" *About Campus* 8, no. 3 (2003): 15–20.

14. Quoted in Rebecca Costello, "Millennials Thriving," in *The Colgate Scene*, January 2005; retrieved February 25, 2005, from http://www4.colgate.edu/scene/jan2005/millennials.html.
15. Don Tapscott, *Growing Up Digital: The Rise of the Net Generation* (New York: McGraw-Hill, 1998).
16. Brian O'Reilly, "Meet the Future," *Fortune,* July 2000, 1; retrieved December 2004 from http://www.youthinelligence.com/company/yiarticle_print.asp?yiArticleID=20.
17. Ibid., 1.
18. Northwestern Mutual Financial Network, "Millennium Generation Studies: The Fifth Study," 2004; retrieved December 13, 2004, from http://www.nmfn.com/contentassets/pdfs/study.pdf.
19. Kenneth Judd, "Understand Millennial Generation To Manage Them Successfully," December, 2000; retrieved December 13, 2004, from http://www.digitu.com/enews/012millennials.html (online monthly newsletter).
20. O'Reilly, "Meet the Future," 1.
21. Northwestern Mutual Financial Network, "Millennium Generation Studies."
22. Riley, *God on the Quad*, 175–76.
23. George Barna, *Real Teens* (Ventura, CA: Regal Books, 2001).
24. Richard Cimino and Don Lattin, *Shopping for Faith: American Religion in the New Millennium* (San Francisco: Jossey Bass, 1998), 38.
25. Barna Group, Ltd., *Teens Change Their Tune Regarding Self and Church*, 2002; retrieved January 12, 2005, from http://www.barna.org/FlexPage.aspx?Page=BarnaUpdate&BarnaUpdateID=111.
26. Barna, *Real Teens,* 38.
27. Robert Webber, "How Will the Millennials Worship?" *Reformed Worship* 59 (March 2001): 2–3; retrieved February 25, 2005, from http://www.emergingchurch.org/files/How_Will_the_Millennials_Worship.htm.
28. Howe and Strauss, *Millennials Go to College*, 32.

Chapter 7

1. Beth McMurtrie, "Future of Religious Colleges Is Bright, Say Scholars and Officials," *Chronicle of Higher Education,* October 20, 2000, A41.
2. George Marsden, "Religious Scholars in the Academy: Anachronism or Leaven?" a paper delivered at "The Future of Religious Colleges," a conference held by the Taubman Center for State and Local Government and the Center for American Political Studies, Harvard University, October 6–7, 2000.
3. Christopher Jencks and David Riesman, *The Academic Revolution* (New York: Doubleday, 1968).
4. Ibid., 329.
5. David Riesman, *Constraint and Variety in American Higher Education* (Garden City, NJ: Doubleday, 1958).
6. McMurtrie, "Future of Religious Colleges," 20.
7. Marsden, "Religious Scholars in the Academy."

8. Hughes and Adrian, *Models for Christian Higher Education*, 445.
9. Benne, *Quality with Soul*, 95.
10. Marsden, *Soul of the American University.*
11. Bruce Keith, "The Institutional Context of Departmental Prestige in American Higher Education," *American Educational Research Journal* 36, no. 3 (1997): 415.
12. Burtchaell, *Dying of the Light.*
13. Marsden, *Soul of the American University*, 280.
14. Burtchaell, *Dying of the Light*, xi.
15. Merrimon Cuninggim, *Uneasy Partners: The College and the Church* (Nashville: Abingdon Press, 1994).
16. Michael J. Buckley, *The Catholic University as Promise and Project: Reflections in a Jesuit Idiom* (Washington, D.C.: Georgetown University Press, 1998).
17. Mark R. Schwehn, "A Christian University: Defining the Difference," *First Things*, May 1999, 25–31.
18. Thomas Reese, ed., "Keeping Colleges Catholic," *America*, April 9, 1998, 13.

Chapter 8

1. See Burtchaell, *Dying of the Light*, 823–24.
2. C. Stephen Evans, "The Christian University and the Connectedness of Knowledge," in Schmeltekopf, et al., *The Baptist and Christian Character of Baylor*, 38.
3. The following survey follows my earlier treatment of postmodernism in historical context, "Shaking the Foundations: The Shift in Scriptural Authority in the Postmodern World," *Review and Expositor* 95 (1998): 545–58.
4. In his letter to the Smyrnaeans, Ignatius wrote, "Let the laity be subject to the deacons; the deacons to the presbyters; the presbyters to the bishop; the bishop to Christ, even as He is to the Father" (ch. ix). Later he claimed, "Nor is there any one in the Church greater than the bishop, who ministers as a priest to God for the salvation of the whole world."
5. Williston Walker, professor of ecclesiastical history at Yale. states "By the sixth decade of the second century monarchical bishops had become well-nigh universal" (*A History of the Christian Church*, 3rd ed. [New York: Charles Scribner's, 1970], 42).
6. In *Against Heresies* 3:3:2, Irenaeus made his position clear, speaking of "that tradition derived from the apostles, of the very great, the very ancient, and universally known Church founded and organized at Rome by the two most glorious apostles, Peter and Paul; as also the faith preached to men, which comes down to our time by means of the successions of the bishops." He then added, "It is a matter of necessity that every Church should agree with this Church, on account of its preeminent authority."
7. *De unitate ecclesiasticum,* ch. 6. For an excellent discussion of the "clergy" in the patristic era, see A. Di Berardino, "Clergy, Clerics," in *Encyclopedia of the Early Church*, trans. Adrian Walford (New York: Oxford University Press, 1992), 1:181–83.
8. *The First Epistle of Clement* 12 (*Ante-Nicene Fathers* 1:8).

9. Justin, *Dialogue with Trypho* 42 (*Ante-Nicene Fathers* 1:215–16).
10. Clement of Alexandria, *The Instructor* 2:4 (*Ante-Nicene Fathers* 2:248).
11. *Origen's Commentary on John* (*Ante-Nicene Fathers* 10:396–99).
12. John P. Newport and William Cannon, *Why Christians Fight Over the Bible* (Nashville: Nelson, 1974), 163–64.
13. Martin Luther, *Luther's Works*, ed. Helmut T. Lehmann (Philadelphia: Fortress, 1967), 37:76.
14. *Letters of Martin Luther*, ed. and trans. Margaret A. Currie (London: Macmillan & Co., Ltd., 1908), 93; *Table Talk*, ed. and trans. Theodore G. Tappert (Philadelphia: Fortress, 1967), 346–47.
15. John Calvin, *Institutes*, ed. John T. McNeill, trans. Ford Lewis Battles, *The Library of Christian Classics* 20 (Philadelphia: Westminster, 1960), 1.6.1, 1.7.2
16. Quoted in Shurden, *Baptist Identity*, 18.
17. Ibid.
18. Herschel H. Hobbs, *The Baptist Faith and Message*, rev. ed. (Nashville: Convention Press, 1996), vi–vii.
19. Quoted in Shurden, *Baptist Identity*, 15–16.
20. Ibid., 16.
21. Pope John Paul II, *Prayers and Devotions: 365 Daily Meditations*, ed. Bishop Peter Canisius Johannes van Lierde, trans. Firman O'Sullivan (New York: Viking, 1994), 148–49.
22. Alan Wolfe, *The Transformation of American Religion: How We Actually Live Our Faith* (New York: Free Press, 2003), 205.
23. See *Discourse on Method*, trans. Donald A. Cress (Indianapolis: Hackett, 1980), part 4, 17–21.
24. Locke's central claim: "All ideas come from sensation or reflection," our senses or the operation of our minds on them (*Essay Concerning Human Understanding* 2.1.2).
25. See *An Enquiry Concerning Human Understanding* (La Salle, IL: Open Court, 1967), 49, 84.
26. See *Prolegomena to Any Future Metaphysics* (Indianapolis: The Library of Liberal Arts, 1950 [1783] 5–12).
27. See *Groundwork of the Metaphysics of Morals*, trans. H. J. Paton (New York: Harper Torchbooks, 1964), 126–27.
28. Sources for the following survey include Stanley Grenz, *A Primer on Postmodernism* (Grand Rapids: Eerdmans, 1986); Millard J. Erickson, *Truth or Consequences: The Promise and Perils of Postmodernism* (Downers Grove, IL: InterVarsity, 2001); Erickson, *The Postmodern World: Discerning the Times and the Spirit of Our Age* (Wheaton, IL: Crossway, 2002); Erickson, *Postmodernizing the Faith: Evangelical Responses to the Challenge of Postmodernism* (Grand Rapids: Baker Books, 1998); Roger Lundin, *The Culture of Interpretation: Christian Faith and the Postmodern World* (Grand Rapids: Eerdmans, 1993); Dennis McCallum, ed., *The Death of Truth* (Minneapolis: Bethany House, 1996); Timothy R. Phillips and Dennis L. Okholm, eds., *Christian Apologetics in the Postmodern World* (Downers Grove, IL:

InterVarsity, 1995); and Gene Edward Veith Jr., *Postmodern Times: A Christian Guide to Contemporary Thought and Culture* (Wheaton, IL: Crossway, 1994).

29. This description of Nietzsche comes from Grenz, *Primer on Postmodernism*, 88.
30. See Friedrich Nietzsche, *The Genealogy of Morals*, trans. F. Golffing (Garden City, NY: Doubleday, 1956), 255; and *Beyond Good and Evil*, trans. M. Cowan (Chicago: Henry Regnery, 1955), 100–101.
31. Nietzsche, *Genealogy of Morals*, 209–10; *Beyond Good and Evil*, 18–19; cf. Grenz's *Primer on Postmodernism*, 97.
32. Friedrich Schleiermacher, *The Christian Faith*, ed. H. R. Mackintosh and J. S. Stewart (Edinburgh: T&T Clark, 1976), 131. For more on Schleiermacher's seminal hermeneutical contributions, see Anthony C. Thiselton, *New Horizons in Hermeneutics: The Theory and Practice of Transforming Biblical Reading* (Grand Rapids: Zondervan, 1992), 204–36.
33. See Grenz's description, *Primer on Postmodernism*, 99–103.
34. Hans-Georg Gadamer, *Philosophical Hermeneutics*, ed. and trans. David E. Linge (Berkeley: University of California Press, 1976), xix.
35. Ludwig Wittgenstein, *Philosophical Investigations*, vol. 1.65, in *Great Books of the Western World*, 2nd ed., ed. Mortimer J. Adler (Chicago: Encyclopaedia Britannica, Inc., 1990), 55:333.
36. See Daniel and Aline Patte, *Structural Exegesis: From Theory to Practice* (Philadelphia: Fortress, 1978).
37. See Hans-Georg Gadamer, *Truth and Method* (New York: Crossroad, 1984), 261.
38. Foucault's most important writings include *The Order of Things: An Archaeology of the Human Sciences* (New York: Random House-Pantheon, 1971); *The Archaeology of Knowledge and the Discourse on Language*, trans. A. M. Sheridan Smith (New York: Pantheon, 1972); and *Power/Knowledge: Selected Interviews and Other Writings, 1972–1977*, ed. Colin Gordon (New York: Pantheon, 1980).
39. Derrida's major works include *Of Grammatology*, trans. Gayatri Chakravorty Spivak (Baltimore: The Johns Hopkins University Press, 1976); *Writing and Difference*, trans. Alan Bass (Chicago: University of Chicago Press, 1978); *Positions*, trans. Alan Bass (Chicago: University of Chicago Press, 1981); and *Margins of Philosophy*, trans. Alan Bass (Chicago: University of Chicago Press, 1982).
40. Rorty's major work is *Philosophy and the Mirror of Nature* (Princeton: Princeton University Press, 1979). His own summary of his pragmatic philosophy is "Pragmatism, Relativism, and Irrationalism," in *The Consequences of Pragmatism* (Minneapolis: University of Minnesota Press, 1982).
41. Os Guinness, "This Too Shall Pass Away," in *Unriddling Our Times: Reflections on the Gathering Cultural Crisis*, ed. Os Guinness (Grand Rapids: Baker Books, 1999), 118–19.
42. George M. Marsden, *The Outrageous Idea of Christian Scholarship* (New York: Oxford University Press, 1997), 100.
43. David F. Wells, *God in the Wasteland: The Reality of Truth in a World of Fading Dreams* (Grand Rapids: Eerdmans, 1994), 145–46.

44. Richard T. Hughes, *How Christian Faith Can Sustain the Life of the Mind* (Grand Rapids: Eerdmans, 2001), 44.

Chapter 9

1. For a detailed account of my Baptist heritage and identity, see Albert L. Reyes, "Unification to Integration: A Brief History of the Hispanic Baptist Convention of Texas," *Baptist History and Heritage Journal: The Baptist Community* 40 (2005): 44–55.
2. Lee Harvey and Peter T. Knight, *Transforming Higher Education* (Bristol, Pa.: Open University Press, 1996), 7.
3. Ibid., 11.
4. Ibid., 8–9.
5. Noll, *Scandal of the Evangelical Mind*, 22.
6. Marsden, *Outrageous Idea of Christian Scholarship*, 6.
7. Bill Leonard, "What Can the Baptist Tradition Contribute to Christian Higher Education?" in Hughes and Adrian, *Models for Christian Higher Education*, 367–68.
8. Richard T. Hughes, "Christian Faith and the Life of the Mind," in Henry and Agee, *Faithful Learning and the Christian Scholarly Vocation*, 3–4.
9. C. Stephen Evans, "The Calling of the Christian Scholar-Teacher," in Henry and Agee, *Faithful Learning and the Christian Scholarly Vocation*, 40–41.
10. Matt. 22:36-37, *New International Version of the Bible* (Nashville: Broadman & Holman, 1996), 874.
11. Noll, *Scandal of the Evangelical Mind*, 6.
12. Hughes, "Christian Faith and the Life of the Mind," 4.
13. Ibid., 20–21.
14. Ibid., 21–24.
15. Phillip Jenkins, *The Next Christendom: The Coming of Global Christianity* (Oxford: Oxford University Press, 2002), 2–3.
16. Haya El Nasser, "Thirty-Nine Million Make Hispanics Largest Minority Group," *U.S.A. Today,* www.usatoday.com/news/nation/census/2003-06-18-Census_x. htm.
17. Juan F. Martinez, "The Future of Hispanic Ministry," a presentation at the 2004 Rollins Lectures at Learning Resources Center, Baptist University of the Americas, San Antonio, Texas, March 2, 2004.
18. Jenkins, *Next Christendom*, 100.
19. Ibid., 101.
20. Paul Burka, "Power," *Texas Monthly*, February 2005, 98–113.
21. Steve Murdock, "The Population of Texas: Historical Patterns and Future Trends Affecting Education," a report produced by the Institute of Demographic and Socioeconomic Research at the University of Texas at San Antonio, http://txsdc.utsa.edu, n.d., 60–62.
22. Alejandra G. Rodriguez, "The Hispanic Dilemma: What Are We Doing About It?" www.newhorizons.org/strategies/multicultural/rodriguez.htm., 2002.

23. Scott Williams, "A College Lockout?" *Hispanic Business*, October 2002, 30.
24. Ibid.
25. Matt Flores, "Schools of Hard Knocks," *San Antonio Express and News*, February 23, 2003, 1A.
26. Brent Gilmore, "No Child Left Behind: Hispanic Task Force Overview," The U.S. Department of Education, Office of English Language Acquisition, July 11, 2003.
27. Kenneth Davis and Edwin I. Hernandez, *Reconstructing the Sacred Tower: Challenge and Promise of Latino/a Theological Education* (Scranton, Pa.: University of Scranton Press, 2003), 11.
28. Leonard, "What Can the Baptist Tradition Contribute to Christian Higher Education?," 377.
29. Ibid.
30. Jerry F. Dawson, *Teaching Them: A Sesquicentennial Celebration of Texas Baptist Education* (Dallas: Baptist General Convention of Texas, 1996), 53.
31. Timothy Reagan, *Non-Western Educational Traditions: Alternative Approaches to Educational Thought and Practice* (Mahwah, NJ: Lawrence Earlbaum Associates, Publishers, 2000), 7.
32. For a broader discussion of cross-cultural competency, see Albert L. Reyes, "America's Bible Belt Doesn't Fit Anymore," *Review and Expositor* (Summer 2004): 383.
33. Donald A. McGavran, *Understanding Church Growth*, 3rd ed. (Grand Rapids: Eerdmans, 1970), 210–12.
34. William C. Symonds, "Colleges in Crisis," *BusinessWeek*, April 28, 2003, 75.
35. Charles B. Reed, "Student Financial Aid Where It Is Needed the Most," *Association of Governing Boards*, July/August 2002.
36. Williams, "A College Lockout?," 34.
37. Davis and Hernandez, *Reconstructing the Sacred Tower*, 13.
38. Leonard, "What Can the Baptist Tradition Contribute to Christian Higher Education?," 381–82.
39. Schmeltekopf, "A Christian University in the Baptist Tradition," 6–7.
40. Riley, *God on the Quad*, 7.
41. Milfred Minatrea, *Shaped by God's Heart: The Passion and Practices of Missional Churches* (San Francisco: Jossey-Bass, 2004), 10–11.

Chapter 10

1. Eccles. 12:11-14.
2. Stanley Hauerwas, *Performing the Faith: Bonhoeffer and the Practice of Nonviolence* (Grand Rapids: Brazos Press, 2004), 209.
3. Peter Berkowitz and Michael McFaul, "Studying Islam, Strengthening the Nation," *Washington Post*, April 12, 2005, A21.
4. Hauerwas, *Performing the Faith*, 202.
5. Ibid.

6. Pitirim A. Sorokin, *The Crisis of Our Age* (Oxford: Oneworld, 1992), 263f.
7. 1 Cor. 9:20.
8. Neill, *History of Christian Missions*, 263.
9. Noll, *The Scandal of the Evangelical Mind* (Grand Rapids: Eerdmans, 1994), 3.
10. Interview by Michael Cromartie, "What American Teenagers Believe: A Conversation with Christian Smith," in *Books and Culture*, January/February 2005, 11
11. P. T. Forsythe in *Minister's Prayer Book*, ed. John W. Doberstein (Philadelphia: Fortress, 1959), 196.
12. Ron Sider, "The Scandal of the Evangelical Conscience," in *Books and Culture*, January/February 2005, 39.
13. Ibid.
14. Lin Yutang, *From Pagan to Christian* (Cleveland: World Publishing, 1959), 182–83.
15. Sider, "The Scandal," 42.
16. Peter Gomes, "The Backward Glance and the Forward Look," *Harvard Divinity Bulletin* 32, no. 4 (2004): 12.
17. Nicholas Berdyaev, in *A Diary of Readings*, ed. John Baillie (London: Oxford University Press, 1955), 242.
18. Sorokin, *Crisis of Our Age*, 264.
19. Rom. 1:16.

Chapter 12

1. See, for example, John 17:16-18; 1 Cor. 5:10; Col. 2:8, 20.
2. Candy Gunther Brown, *The Word in the World* (Chapel Hill: University of North Carolina Press, 2004), 6.
3. "In Christ, therefore, they [Christians] claimed to possess a principle of understanding superior to anything existing in the classical world. By this claim they were prepared to stand or fall." Charles Norris Cochrane, *Christianity and Culture* (New York: Oxford University Press, 1957), vi. "This is not a struggle to be settled by mere blows, as though the contending forces were nothing more than masses in motion. Nor is it a mere battle of abstract ideas, to be conducted in the rarefied atmosphere of the academies. What it demands is a united effort of hand and heart and head, in order to expose the fictitious character of secular valuations and to vindicate the reality of Christian claims" (516).
4. Definitions of "culture" are many and varied. Taking some concepts from Edward T. Hall, *The Silent Language* (Greenwich, CT: Fawcett Publications, 1959), we can consider key elements: "Culture is communication and communication is culture." "Culture is not one thing, but many." "Culture is concerned more with messages than it is with networks and control systems." "There is no experience independent of culture against which culture can be measured." "Cultural indeterminacy and cultural relativity are not easy concepts. . . . They mean more than what is good by one set of standards may be bad by some other" (169–70).
5. Nanelle R. Barash and David P. Barash, "Biology, Culture, and Persistent Literary Dystopias," *The Chronicle of Higher Education*, December 3, 2004, B10.

6. Nathan Hatch, historian of American Christianity, states that "plausible arguments can be made that, at all levels of American society, the juggernaut of secularism rolls on, pressing religious belief into smaller, less consequential territory." Hatch, *Democratization of American Christianity*, 211.
7. Quoted in Marsden, *Soul of the American University*, 401.
8. Advertisements on broadcast television discuss "lifestyle" pharmaceutical products in language that must be endlessly curious to children and young people, but the culture seems unconcerned.
9. "Babylon's Burning," *The Times* [of London] *Magazine*, October 9, 1993, 13.
10. Ibid.
11. Gore Vidal, *Screening History* (Cambridge, Mass.: Harvard University Press, 1992).
12. "Pinots from Heaven," *USA Today*, August 10, 2005, D1.
13. Ibid.
14. "The 100 Most Influential People," *Time*, April 26, 2004.
15. Quoted in "Babylon's Burning," 10.
16. Of course, Christian colleges and universities could be mentioned as having benefited from church support. I believe it likely that, while the influence of the Christian college has been qualitative rather than quantitative, we could find that strong leadership in the church, overwhelmed as it may be by the culture, has still come from the ranks of Christian colleges and universities.
17. Jonathan A. Knee, "Is That Really Legal?" *The New York Times*, May 2, 2004.
18. The churchmanship of Kenneth Lay, former CEO of Enron, son of a Baptist minister, and trustee of Houston's First United Methodist Church, has been extensively profiled. Richard Scrushy, former chairman and CEO of HealthSouth, and his wife have been photographed carrying a Bible into the courtroom and have been regular attenders at Mountaintop Church in Birmingham, Alabama. They also host and sponsor a devotional television program. Greg Garrison, "HealthSouth executive, accused of fraud, heard sermons on ethics," *Religious News Service*, May 30, 2003.
19. www.barna.org.
20. Hall, *Silent Language*, 31.
21. Hall said, "the ultimate purpose of this book . . . is to reveal the broad extent to which culture controls our lives" (*Silent Language*, 38).
22. John Steele Gordon, "The Fifty Biggest Changes in the Last 50 Years," *American Heritage* (June/July 2004): 23.
23. Ibid., 24.
24. One site, subservientchicken.com, was an interactive view of a person in a chicken suit who responded to the viewer's computer commands (a subtle ad for Burger King). The ad agency that created the site said it had received more than 215 million hits, with the average visitor remaining at the site for seven minutes. Rob Walker, "Poultry-Geist: If We're so Sick of Marketing, Why are We Watching This Chicken?" *The New York Times Magazine*, May 23, 2004, 18.

25. An excellent manual that supports the value of name recognition and "branding" is available online at http://texaspolitics.laits.utexas.edu. Particularly, see section 9.2, "Advertising."
26. "The New Colossus: American Culture as Power Export," *The New York Times*, January 30, 1994, Section B1.
27. *Changing Minds, Winning Peace: A New Strategic Direction for U.S. Public Diplomacy in the Arab and Muslim World*, report of the Advisory Group on Public Diplomacy in the Arab and Muslim World, Washington, D.C., 2003, 21.
28. The cases of Andrea Yates, Kobe Bryant, Mary Kay LeTourneau and Vili Fualaau, and Elizabeth Smart received extensive and repetitive coverage in daily newspapers, newsmagazines, and TV.
29. *A Free and Responsible Press*, ed. Robert D. Leigh (Chicago: University of Chicago Press, 1940). For more recent efforts along the same lines, see the journal of the Pew Charitable Trusts. Richard Reeves, "Rends or Mends," *Trust* (Spring 1999): 8–14.
30. Reeves, "Rends or Mends," 13.
31. Adapted after the style of C. S. Lewis, *The Screwtape Letters* (New York: Macmillan), 1961.
32. I am less pessimistic than some: "Some critics argue that the seductive culture spawned by television and related communications technologies has already obliterated, beyond repair, the very premises of democratic promise." William Greider, *Who Will Tell the People: The Betrayal of American Democracy* (New York: Touchstone, 1992), 312. "If the mass-media culture has permanently robbed people of their democratic capacities, then the deeper governing problems—or their remedies—will have no meaning to ordinary citizens" (313).
33. "[T]he United States contains more citizens who value religion than other Western industrial societies." Hatch, *Democratization of American Christianity*, 210.
34. Bruce Wilkinson, *The Prayer of Jabez* (Sisters, OR: Multnomah Publishers, 2000), and Tim F. LaHaye and Jerry B. Jenkins, *Desecration: Antichrist Takes the Throne* (Carol Stream, IL: Tyndale House, 2002), ninth in the *Left Behind* series (cited in Brown, *Word in the World*, 243).
35. "By degrees religion itself took on the shape of a commodity. . . . [It] looked for ways to appeal to all consumers using the techniques of advertising and publicity employed by other merchants." R. Laurence Moore, *Selling God: American Religion in the Marketplace of Culture* (New York: Oxford University Press, 1994), 6.
36. Heather Hendershot, *Shaking the World for Jesus* (Chicago: University of Chicago Press, 2004), 20.
37. Ibid., 24.
38. Marsden, *Soul of the American University*, 4.
39. See "Introduction," ibid., 3–9; also Burtchaell, *Dying of the Light*, 819–51.
40. Stanley Fish, "All in the Game: One University under God," *The Chronicle of Higher Education*, January 7, 2005, C1. Fish wrote, "When Jacques Derrida died I was called by a reporter who wanted to know what would succeed high theory

and the triumvirate of race, gender, and class as the center of intellectual energy in the academy. I answered like a shot: religion."

41. In a news release dated September 13, 2005, CNN announced that it had designated Delia Gallagher as religion correspondent.
42. Nathan Hatch, himself a prominent academic, former provost of the University of Notre Dame, now president of Wake Forest University, wrote, "In the world of higher education, theologians and church leaders no longer operate from a position of strength. To avoid being considered second-class citizens, they are pressured to make accommodations to the secular definition of values at the core of the university" (*Democratization of American Christianity*, 119).
43. Murray Sperber, "College Sports, Inc.: How Big-Time Athletic Departments Run Interference for College, Inc.," in Donald G. Stein, *Buying In or Selling Out* (New Brunswick, NJ: Rutgers University Press, 2004), 24.
44. "Suddenly, State Universities Have More Allure," *The New York Times*, November 10, 2002. I recall an instance when a Baptist deacon who had just made a seven-figure gift to a state university gave the offertory prayer at his church, in which he prayed: "Lord, all that we have is yours. Help us to direct those resources entrusted to us to those places that most please you. . . ." How is it that Baptist people are so willing to render unto Caesar the things that are the Lord's?
45. Peter Drucker, *Managing the Nonprofit Organization* (New York: HarperCollins, 1990), 45.
46. Quoted in Marsden, *Soul of the American University*, 408.
47. Robert Wuthnow, *The Struggle for America's Soul: Evangelicals, Liberals, and Secularism* (Grand Rapids: Eerdmans, 1989), 34–35.

Chapter 14

1. I wish that I could claim that this description of the privileged place of Baptists in Southern culture was original, but I owe it to my colleague Stanley Hauerwas, who is never shy of reminding Southern Baptists the irony—and indeed the scandal—of their own Constantinianism.
2. The classic study of Southern evangelicalism as a "social process" and "religious perception" is Donald G. Mathews, *Religion in the Old South* (Chicago: University of Chicago Press, 1977), xvii. Mathews shows how Baptists and other Southern evangelicals were formally committed to the *de jure* disestablishment of the church, because the power of their *de facto* establishment rested not on law but on the social function they fulfilled to their communicants (57). This thesis has been widely demonstrated in standard texts of the field of Southern religion like Samuel S. Hill, *Southern Churches in Crisis* (New York: Holt, Rinehart & Winston, 1967) and *Southern Churches in Crisis Revisited* (Tuscaloosa: University of Alabama Press, 1999); and more recently by Christine Leigh Heyerman in *Southern Cross: The Beginnings of the Bible Belt* (Chapel Hill: University of North Carolina Press, 1997).
3. See Reinhold Niebuhr, *Beyond Tragedy: Essays on the Christian Interpretation of History* (New York: Charles Scribner's, 1937).

4. E. Brooks Holifield, *The Gentlemen Theologians: American Theology in Southern Culture, 1795–1860* (Durham, NC: Duke University Press, 1978), 5–23.
5. Ibid., 13.
6. Mathews, *Religion in the Old South*, 94.
7. Larry Lyon, "Religious Identity, Academic Reputation, and Attracting the Best Faculty and Students," ch. 7 in this book.
8. Burtchaell, *Dying of the Light*, 819–51.
9. "The Future of Baptist Higher Education," conference program, April 18–19, 2005.
10. The debate about secularization began on the first day of the conference when, in his presentation, Bill Leonard said, "If the light has gone out at Wake Forest University, then why invite me?" He continued, "If a public apology is not given, I will pack my bags and go home right now, and I'll return to Wake Forest where we are trying to keep the light burning." Donald Schmeltekopf, provost emeritus at Baylor University, stood and asked Leonard to accept his apology for any offense. Schmeltekopf later explained that the language in the program was derived from a book by James Burtchaell, *The Dying of the Light*. On the following day, Larry Lyon presented a study in which he refuted the notion that national universities with religious roots must become secularized to achieve a strong academic reputation. One subheading in his paper, which was distributed to participants, raised the question: "Will Baylor go the way of Wake Forest?" At the conclusion of Lyon's presentation, Leonard again spoke against a "regrettable generalization" of Wake Forest University. As evidence of Wake Forest's commitment to religion, Leonard cited the selection of Nathan Hatch, who is a widely respected evangelical Presbyterian and former provost at the University of Notre Dame, as the university president. Schmeltekopf was quoted as sharing Leonard's view that the selection of Hatch as Wake Forest's president is a very positive sign for the school's Christian identity. The summary of these conference discussions may be found in an article by Ken Camp, "Dissenting Voices Deserve Hearing on Campus, Historian Asserts," *Baptist Standard*, April 29, 2005, accessible online at http://www.baptiststandard.com/postnuke/index.php?module=htmlpages&func=display&pid-3253.
11. Michael S. Hamilton, "A Higher Education," *Christianity Today*, May 27, 2005, accessible online at http://www.christianitytoday.com/ct/2005/006/20.30.html. "Catholic educators lost the ability to say why there should be such a thing as a Catholic college. Unable to answer the question, nearly all of their colleges gradually slipped into secularization." Also: "Joining them at the bottom of the slope were the mainline Protestant colleges. In the 1950s and 1960s, these schools were caught in the same current that secularized Catholic colleges. Study after study showed that the mainline colleges were Christian in name only. By the 1980s scholars quit studying the phenomenon because the colleges had become so secular."

12. Thomas E. Corts, "The University, the Church, and the Culture"; see ch. 12 in this book.
13. Mathews, *Religion in the Old South*, 94.
14. Clyde Edgerton, *Killer Diller* (New York: Ballentine, 1991), 34, 92.
15. Ibid., 7.
16. Ibid., 209.
17. Ibid., 239.
18. Ibid., 155–56.
19. Jacques Barzun, *From Dawn to Decadence* (New York: HarperCollins, 2000).
20. Charles Colson, "The Wages of Secularism," *Christianity Today*, June 10, 2002.
21. Sinclair Lewis, *Elmer Gantry* (New York: Harcourt, Brace, 1927), 3.
22. George M. Marsden and Bradley J. Longfield, *The Secularization of the Academy* (New York: Oxford University Press, 1992), 5.
23. Ibid., 3.
24. The same sort of play on words might be made with the motto of Wake Forest University, *pro humanitate*, which the founders took to be a sign of their vision of a religious humanism but which contemporary critics have taken as an indication of the university's commitment to secular humanism.
25. Wolfe, *I Am Charlotte Simmons*.
26. In his review of *I Am Charlotte Simmons*, Jacob Weisberg suggests that readers will find it hard to put down Wolfe's book, but when they finish it they will wish they had. "Peeping Tom," *The New York Times*, November 28, 2004, 7, col. 1, 13. See also Michiko Kakutani, "So Where's the Zeitgeist? It Looks Just Like College," *The New York Times*, October 29, 2004, E33.
27. This point is made by William H. Willimon and Thomas H. Naylor in *The Abandoned Generation: Rethinking Higher Education* (Grand Rapids: Eerdmans, 1995).
28. Richard Franklin, "Who Will Our Students Be in a Postmodern, Postdenominational, and Materialistic Age," and Albert Reyes, "Can Baptist Institutions of Higher Education Meet the Needs of Increasingly Diverse Constituencies?"; see ch. 6 and ch. 9 respectively in this book.
29. For another view of the secularization thesis from a Baptist perspective, see William H. Brackney, "Secularization of the Academy: A Baptist Typology," *Westminster Studies in Education* 24, no. 2 (2001): 111–28; and "Secularization in the Academy: A Challenge to Baptist Historians," *Baptist History and Heritage* 39, no. 1 (2004): 59–79.
30. Harvey Cox, *The Secular City* (New York: Macmillan, 1965), 3; Dietrich Bonhoeffer, *Letters and Papers from Prison*, rev. ed. (New York: Macmillan, 1967), 279–81, 324–28, passim. Cox's endorsement of secularization should be distinguished from the celebration of secularity in "the death of God" theology as represented by Thomas J. J. Altizer and William Hamilton, *Radical Theology and the Death of God* (Indianapolis: Bobbs-Merrill, 1966).

31. Harvey Cox, *Religion in the Secular City* (New York: Simon & Schuster, 1984), 11–26.
32. Such a celebration of secularization in the university is found in William A. Clebsch, *From Sacred to Profane America: The Role of Religion in American History* (New York: Harper & Row, 1968).
33. Cuninggim, *Uneasy Partners.*
34. William E. Hull, "Building on a Shared Identity Within a Shared History"; see ch. 3 in this book. It is interesting to compare Hull's list of three Baptist principles with which he proposes to interrogate the curriculum with those that Donald E. Miller identifies for Brethren (a baptistic group) to keep central in "The Brethren Philosophy of Higher Education," *Brethren Life and Thought* 49 (2004). These principles include: (1) the priesthood of all believers; (2) a community of mutual respect and discernment; (3) religion of the heart; (4) openness to new evidence and new understanding of truth; (5) the sense of integrity; (6) production in good measure; (7) service above profit; (8) reconciliation, justice, and nonviolent resolution of conflict; and (9) responsible dedication to the well-being of the local and global communities.
35. David S. Dockery, "Blending Baptist with Orthodox in the Christian University"; see ch. 5 in this book. See my forthcoming article, "God in Three Persons: Baptist Unitarianism and the Trinity," *Perspectives in Religious Studies* (Spring 2006), in which I show that "most Baptists are Unitarians that simply have not yet gotten around to denying the Trinity."
36. Dockery, "Blending Baptist with Orthodox in the Christian University."
37. James William McClendon, *Witness: Systematic Theology* (Nashville: Abingdon, 2000), 3:399.
38. The Orthodox Creed, XXXVIII, in William L. Lumpkin, *Baptist Confessions of Faith*, rev. ed. (Valley Forge: Judson Press, 1969), 326.
39. David P. Gushee, "Integrating Faith and Learning in an Ecumenical Context," ch. 2 in this book. Gushee's recommendation of the Catholic *magisterium* as a pattern for Baptists to follow needs more clarification. As the recent implementation of *Ex Corde Ecclesiae* indicates, the application of the *mandatum*, which would roughly correspond to something like affirmation of the Apostles' Creed, applies only to teachers of theology. It respects the integrity of the range of academic disciplines outside theology. See my articles, "A Baptist Looks at '*Ex Corde*': A Lesson for Catholics?," *Commonweal*, April 5, 2002, 20–23; and "Confessing Our Faith and Practice," *Perspectives in Religious Studies* 29 (2002): 331–33; and "Confessing the Faith," coauthored with Steven R. Harmon, Elizabeth Newman, and Philip Thompson in *The Biblical Recorder*, July 8, 2004, accessible online at http://www.biblicalrecorder.org/content/opinion/2004/7_8_2004/gc080704 confessiong.shtml. My own participation in this discussion comes mostly from my experience at a small Baptist college that the president regularly described as "an evangelistic society thinly disguised as a university." I appreciate the difficulty of attempting to keep to the high road of theological discourse. I also had the privilege of teaching in a Catholic university as the religious studies department

struggled to come to terms with the implementation of *Ex Corde Ecclesia* and its dreaded *mandatum*. Quite frankly, I believe that the Catholics may have more theological resources to make sense of higher education within their mission than do most Protestants and those of the Free Church. I found the Catholic conversations about the teaching of religion in the university in relation to the ministry of the church invigorating rather than repressive. Such dialogue is crucial if we as theological educators and teachers of religion are to consider our role in shaping the discourse about religion in the university.

40. Hull, "Building on a Shared Identity within a Shared History." Smyth was initially connected with the group that became the first General Baptist congregation in England, but Williams was (briefly) associated with the Providence church that arose independently in America and which later became identified with the Six-Principle (General) Baptists. Although Leland preached an Arminianized Calvinism, he was a Regular (Particular) Baptist. Telling the Baptist story so that these names are linked in a continuous historical narrative assumes an anachronistic notion of denominationalism. One might make just as strong a historical case for the insertion of other baptists like Balthasar Hubmaier, Michael Sattler, or Menno Simons. The truth is that General Baptists and Particular Baptists in the seventeenth and eighteenth centuries viewed one another as distinctly different groups. Indeed, Particular Baptists in England often regarded themselves to be closer to the Congregationalists (Independents) than to the General Baptists.
41. Bill J. Leonard, "Fostering Dissent in the Postmodern Academy"; see ch. 4 in this book. Leonard's polygenetic account is implicit in the title of his book *Baptist Ways*, esp. 10–15. The language of "polygenesis" (versus "monogenesis") appears in the debates about Anabaptist theories of origins. See, e.g., Arnold Snyder, "Beyond Polygenesis: Recovering the Unity and Diversity of Anabaptist Theology," in *Essays in Anabaptist Theology*, ed. H. Wayne Pipkin (Elkhart, IN: Institute of Mennonite Studies, 1994), 1–33. These polygenetic accounts trace Anabaptist beginnings to various sources (e.g. Switzerland, South Germany/Austria, the Netherlands/North Germany) rather than a single *successio Anabatistica*. Leonard presupposes Martin E. Marty's characterization of this "messiness" as a distinct contribution of the Baptists to American religion, in "Baptistification Takes Over," *Christianity Today*, September 2, 1983, 33–36.
42. Leonard, "Fostering Dissent in the Postmodern Academy."
43. Gushee, "Integrating Faith and Learning in an Ecumenical Context."
44. Martin E. Marty, "The Future of Baptist Higher Education: Secular or Religious?"; see ch. 13 in this book.
45. E.g., Justin Martyr, *Dialogue with Trypho*, 80–81, in *Ante-Nicene Fathers* (Grand Rapids: Eerdmans, 1979), 1:239–40; Irenaeus, *Against Heresies* 5.33–36, in *Ante-Nicene Fathers*, 1:56–67.
46. E.g., Eusebius, *Oration in Praise of Constantine*, in *Nicene and Post-Nicene Fathers*, 2nd ser. (Grand Rapids: Eerdmans; repr. 1976), 1:481–540. The old chiliastic eschatology survived in the fourth century as a minority voice in the writings of

Lactantius, *Divine Institutes*, 7.24, *Corpus Scriptorum Ecclesiasticorum Latinorum* (Vindobonae: F. Tempsky, 1890–1897), 19:660.

47. *The Theodosian Code* 16.1.2, trans. and ed. Clyde Pharr (Princeton: Princeton University Press, 1952).
48. Jerome, *Letters* 123.17 and 126.2, in *Nicene and Post-Nicene Fathers*, 2nd ser., 6:237, 252.
49. Augustine, *City of God*, 15.20, trans. Henry Bettenson (New York: Penguin, 1984), 630.
50. Augustine, *Sermons on the Psalms*, 149.3, in *Nicene and Post-Nicene Fathers*, 1st ser. (Grand Rapids: Eerdmans; repr. 1979), 8:678.
51. John Henry Newman, *The Idea of a University* (New York: Holt, Rinehart & Winston; repr. 1960).
52. Dietrich Bonhoeffer, *Ethics*, ed. Eberhard Bethge (New York: Macmillan, 1965), 144.
53. McClendon *Witness*, 398–420.
54. Gal. 4:26 (RSV).
55. Kenneth R. Miller, *Finding Darwin's God* (New York: Cliff Street Books, 1999).
56. William H. Willimon, "Recreational Sex: Lost Souls at the University," *Christian Century*, April 19, 2005, 20–22.

Contributors

Thomas E. Corts, President, Samford University

James C. Denison, Senior Pastor, Park Cities Baptist Church, Dallas, Texas

David S. Dockery, President, Union University

Richard Franklin, Vice President and Dean of Students, Samford University

Curtis Freeman, Research Professor of Theology and Director of the Baptist House of Studies, Duke University

R. Kirby Godsey, President, Mercer University

David P. Gushee, Graves Professor of Moral Philosophy, Union University

William E. Hull, Provost Emeritus, Samford University

Bill J. Leonard, Dean and Professor of Church History, Divinity School, Wake Forest University

Denton Lotz, General Secretary, Baptist World Alliance

Larry Lyon, Dean of the Graduate School, Senior Vice Provost, and Professor of Sociology, Baylor University

Martin E. Marty, Fairfax M. Cone Distinguished Service Professor Emeritus, University of Chicago

Albert Reyes, President, Baptist University of the Americas and President, Baptist General Convention of Texas

Donald D. Schmeltekopf, Provost Emeritus and The Hazel and Harry Chavanne Professor of Christian Ethics in Business, Baylor University

Daniel Vestal, Coordinator, Cooperative Baptist Fellowship

Dianna M. Vitanza, Associate Professor of English, Baylor University

Index